WHO DECIDES SOCIAL POLICY?

WHO DECIDES SOCIAL POLICY?

Social Networks and the Political Economy of Social Policy in Latin America and the Caribbean

Alejandro Bonvecchi and Carlos Scartascini

WORLD BANK GROUP

IDB

1300 New York Avenue NW, Washington, DC 20577
Telephone: 202-623-1000; Internet: www.iadb.org; Email: res@iadb.org
1 2 3 4 23 22 21 20

A copublication of the Inter-American Development Bank and The World Bank.

ISBN (paper): 978-1-4648-1572-0
ISBN (electronic): 978-1-4648-1573-7
DOI: 10.1596/978-1-4648-1572-0

Cover illustration: © Ejti Stih. "Architects," oil on canvas. Used with permission of Ejti Stih. Further permission required for reuse.
Cover design: Bill Pragluski, Critical Stages, LLC.

Library of Congress Control Number: 2020914229

Latin American Development Forum Series

This series was created in 2003 to promote debate, disseminate information and analysis, and convey the excitement and complexity of the most topical issues in economic and social development in Latin America and the Caribbean. It is sponsored by the Inter-American Development Bank, the United Nations Economic Commission for Latin America and the Caribbean, and the World Bank, and represents the highest quality in each institution's research and activity output. Titles in the series have been selected for their relevance to the academic community, policy makers, researchers, and interested readers, and have been subjected to rigorous anonymous peer review prior to publication.

Advisory Committee Members

Titles in the Latin American Development Forum Series

Fiscal Rules and Economic Size in Latin America and the Caribbean (2020) by Fernando Blanco, Pablo Saavedra, Friederike Koehler-Geib. and Emilia Skrok

Who Decides Social Policy? Social Networks and the Political Economy of Social Policy in Latin America and the Caribbean (2020) by Alejandro Bonvecchi and Carlos Scartascini

Wage Inequality in Latin America: Understanding the Past to Prepare for the Future (2018) by Julián Messina and Joana Silva

Stop the Violence in Latin America: A Look at Prevention from Cradle to Adulthood (2017) by Laura Chioda

Innovative Experiences in Access to Finance: Market-Friendly Roles for the Visible Hand? (2017) by Augusto de la Torre, Juan Carlos Gozzi, and Sergio L. Schmukler

Beyond Commodities: The Growth Challenge of Latin America and the Caribbean (2016) by Jorge Thompson Araujo, Ekaterina Vostroknutova, Markus Brueckner, Mateo Clavijo, and Konstantin M. Wacker

Left Behind: Chronic Poverty in Latin America and the Caribbean (2016) by Renos Vakis, Jamele Rigolini, and Leonardo Lucchetti

Cashing in on Education: Women, Childcare, and Prosperity in Latin America and the Caribbean (2016) by Mercedes Mateo Díaz and Lourdes Rodriguez-Chamussy

Work and Family: Latin American and Caribbean Women in Search of a New Balance (2016) by Laura Chioda

Great Teachers: How to Raise Student Learning in Latin America and the Caribbean (2014) by Barbara Bruns and Javier Luque

Entrepreneurship in Latin America: A Step Up the Social Ladder? (2013) by Eduardo Lora and Francesca Castellani, editors

Emerging Issues in Financial Development: Lessons from Latin America (2013) by Tatiana Didier and Sergio L. Schmukler, editors

New Century, Old Disparities: Gaps in Ethnic and Gender Earnings in Latin America and the Caribbean (2012) by Hugo Ñopo

Does What You Export Matter? In Search of Empirical Guidance for Industrial Policies (2012) by Daniel Lederman and William F. Maloney

From Right to Reality: Incentives, Labor Markets, and the Challenge of Achieving Universal Social Protection in Latin America and the Caribbean (2012) by Helena Ribe, David Robalino, and Ian Walker

Breeding Latin American Tigers: Operational Principles for Rehabilitating Industrial Policies (2011) by Robert Devlin and Graciela Moguillansky

New Policies for Mandatory Defined Contribution Pensions: Industrial Organization Models and Investment Products (2010) by Gregorio Impavido, Esperanza Lasagabaster, and Manuel García-Huitrón

The Quality of Life in Latin American Cities: Markets and Perception (2010) by Eduardo Lora, Andrew Powell, Bernard M. S. van Praag, and Pablo Sanguinetti, editors

Discrimination in Latin America: An Economic Perspective (2010) by Hugo Ñopo, Alberto Chong, and Andrea Moro, editors

The Promise of Early Childhood Development in Latin America and the Caribbean (2010) by Emiliana Vegas and Lucrecia Santibáñez

Job Creation in Latin America and the Caribbean: Trends and Policy Challenges (2009) by Carmen Pagés, Gaëlle Pierre, and Stefano Scarpetta

China's and India's Challenge to Latin America: Opportunity or Threat? (2009) by Daniel Lederman, Marcelo Olarreaga, and Guillermo E. Perry, editors

Does the Investment Climate Matter? Microeconomic Foundations of Growth in Latin America (2009) by Pablo Fajnzylber, Jose Luis Guasch, and J. Humberto López, editors

Measuring Inequality of Opportunities in Latin America and the Caribbean (2009) by Ricardo Paes de Barros, Francisco H. G. Ferreira, José R. Molinas Vega, and Jaime Saavedra Chanduvi

The Impact of Private Sector Participation in Infrastructure: Lights, Shadows, and the Road Ahead (2008) by Luis Andres, Jose Luis Guasch, Thomas Haven, and Vivien Foster

Remittances and Development: Lessons from Latin America (2008) by Pablo Fajnzylber and J. Humberto López, editors

Fiscal Policy, Stabilization, and Growth: Prudence or Abstinence? (2007) by Guillermo Perry, Luis Servén, and Rodrigo Suescún, editors

Raising Student Learning in Latin America: Challenges for the 21st Century (2007) by Emiliana Vegas and Jenny Petrow

Investor Protection and Corporate Governance: Firm-Level Evidence across Latin America (2007) by Alberto Chong and Florencio López-de-Silanes, editors

Natural Resources: Neither Curse nor Destiny (2007) by Daniel Lederman and William F. Maloney, editors

The State of State Reform in Latin America (2006) by Eduardo Lora, editor

Emerging Capital Markets and Globalization: The Latin American Experience (2006) by Augusto de la Torre and Sergio L. Schmukler

Beyond Survival: Protecting Households from Health Shocks in Latin America (2006) by Cristian C. Baeza and Truman G. Packard

Beyond Reforms: Structural Dynamics and Macroeconomic Vulnerability (2005) by José Antonio Ocampo, editor

Privatization in Latin America: Myths and Reality (2005) by Alberto Chong and Florencio López-de-Silanes, editors

Keeping the Promise of Social Security in Latin America (2004) by Indermit S. Gill, Truman G. Packard, and Juan Yermo

Lessons from NAFTA for Latin America and the Caribbean (2004) by Daniel Lederman, William F. Maloney, and Luis Servén

The Limits of Stabilization: Infrastructure, Public Deficits, and Growth in Latin America (2003) by William Easterly and Luis Servén, editors

Globalization and Development: A Latin American and Caribbean Perspective (2003) by José Antonio Ocampo and Juan Martin, editors

Is Geography Destiny? Lessons from Latin America (2003) by John Luke Gallup, Alejandro Gaviria, and Eduardo Lora

All books in the Latin American Development Forum series are available for free at https://openknowledge.worldbank.org/handle/10986/2167.

Contents

Figures

Tables

Acknowledgments

First and foremost, our gratitude goes to Julia Johannsen. Julia provided the inspiration for this book several years ago when she reached out to us to write a book on social network analysis for understanding social policy in the region. That original effort led to the publication in 2015 of the book *¿Quiénes deciden la política social?* by the Inter-American Development Bank. This book uses some of the material we developed with Julia. Most important, we learned a great deal from her, which we hope shows in this book. We are also grateful to José Henríquez and Natasha Morales, who provided valuable inputs for a few chapters in that book. We build here on some of those chapters too.

We are also in great debt to Mariano Tommasi, Professor of Economics at Universidad de San Andrés, formerly at the Cabinet Chief's Office in the Government of Argentina. Mariano provided us with access to Argentine authorities and wrote chapters 4 and 7 with us. Even more important, Mariano has guided and collaborated with us for many years. We have borrowed most of our great ideas from him.

This book would not have been possible without the encouragement and support of Florencia Attademo-Hirt, former Inter-American Development Bank Representative to The Bahamas, who pushed us to write an English version of our book by including Caribbean country cases. We also benefited from the diligent disposition of the policy makers and societal actors who agreed to be interviewed and the extraordinary assistance of the staff at the Inter-American Development Bank country offices in The Bahamas, Bolivia, and Trinidad and Tobago. We are extremely grateful to Julia Johannsen and all the Social Department staff at the Bolivia country office; to Ian Ho-A-Shu, Priya Ramsumair, and Amrita Deonarine at the Trinidad and Tobago country office; to Florencia Attademo-Hirt, Alexandre Veyrat-Pontet, Natalie Bethel, Michael Nelson, Amanda Marray, and Gevon Moss at The Bahamas country office. The interest in, and practical support for, this project by all these individuals made it possible for us to interview the actors on the basis of whose testimonies this book was written.

Rita Funaro edited this book, and Tom Sarrazin has been a great ally for making sure it sees the light. Without them, it would not have been possible to bring this project to its happy conclusion.

The authors are also grateful to our colleagues who participated in formal workshops and informal debate and contributed their comments, input, and valuable interpretations about the preliminary outcomes of this research, in seminars held at Universidad de Salamanca, Universidad Torcuato Di Tella, and the Inter-American Development Bank's Research Department. We are particularly grateful to Mercedes García Montero, Stephen Kaplan, Iván Llamazares, Francisco Sánchez, and Catalina Smulovitz for their comments and suggestions. We are also thankful for the comments and contributions of two anonymous reviewers.

The opinions expressed here belong to the authors and do not necessarily reflect the viewpoints of the Inter-American Development Bank, its Executive Board, or the countries it represents.

About the Authors

Alejandro Bonvecchi is an ordinary adjunct professor at the Department of Political Science and International Studies, Torcuato Di Tella University, and independent researcher at the National Council for Scientific and Technical Research of Argentina (CONICET). He was a visiting professor at Yale University, lecturer at the University of Essex, Fulbright Fellow at George Washington University, and junior scholar in the Study of Democracy Fellowship at the Woodrow Wilson International Center for Scholars. He has published four books, and his research has appeared in *Comparative Politics*, *Legislative Studies Quarterly*, *Presidential Studies Quarterly*, *Publius*, *Latin American Politics and Society*, *Journal of Politics in Latin America*, *Problémes de l'Amerique Latine*, and several Spanish journals. He was an adviser for the ministers of economy, finance, and production of Argentina, and a consultant for the World Bank, the Inter-American Development Bank, and the Economic Commission for Latin America and the Caribbean. He holds a PhD in government from the University of Essex.

Carlos Scartascini is leader of the Behavioral Economics Group and principal technical leader at the Research Department of the Inter-American Development Bank. He currently focuses on expanding the use of behavioral economics and leading many field experiments with governments in Latin America and the Caribbean. In addition to behavioral economics, his areas of expertise include political economy and public finance. He has published seven books and more than 45 articles in edited volumes and specialized journals. He is associate editor of the academic journal *Economía*, and head and founding member of the Latin American Economic Association's (LACEA) BRAIN (Behavioral Insights Network). A native of Argentina, he holds an MA and a PhD in economics from George Mason University.

Abbreviations

IDB	Inter-American Development Bank
ILO	International Labour Organization
NGO	nongovernmental organization
OAS	Organization of American States
PMP	policy-making process
SNA	social network analysis
UN	United Nations
UNICEF	United Nations Children's Fund
VPMG	Vice-Ministry for Medium and Large Scale Industrial Production

Note: The specific country abbreviations for the different agencies, ministries, and organizations discussed in the chapters can be found in appendix A.

1

Social Policy in Latin America and the Caribbean

Progress and Persistent Challenges in the Social Sector

During 2019, Latin America was shocked by protests and social unrest. The year ended with people on the streets of Bolivia, Chile, Colombia, and Ecuador; but protests had been a regular occurrence during the year in Argentina, Guatemala, Honduras, Nicaragua, República Bolivariana de Venezuela, and many more. Some of these protests, particularly in countries like Chile, are generally surprising given that Latin America has achieved significant progress in terms of social results over the past few decades. One of the most striking facts is that poverty has fallen by almost 50 percent since the 1990s. Although in the 1990s, almost one in two Latin Americans was poor, now only one in four is poor[1]—and only one in seven if a more restrictive measure is used (poverty rate of $2.50 per day in purchasing power parity dollars). Extreme poverty is at about 4 percent. Over the same period, average life expectancy has increased substantially: the average Latin American currently lives six years more than in 1990, partly because mortality in children under five has been cut by more than half: from about 50 per 1,000 live births to fewer than 20 in 2017.[2] Today, most children attend primary school, and about three out of four start secondary education.

This remarkable progress in social indicators can be accounted for largely by two factors: fast-paced economic growth of the early 2000s fueled by the commodities boom and progress made in social policy in recent decades. Between 1990 and 2016, regional social expenditures grew more than 50 percent in terms of gross domestic product (Izquierdo, Pessino, and Vuletin 2018).

Aided by a favorable political backdrop, one of the driving mechanisms of this social progress has been conditional cash transfer programs (Mesa-Lago and Márquez 2007). Such programs began in Mexico in 1997 with Progresa (Make Progress), later known as Oportunidades (Opportunities) and currently as Prospera (Thrive). Similar initiatives ensued, including Bolsa Familia (Family Shopping Bag) in Brazil and Familias en Acción (Families in Action) in Colombia. Noncontributory pensions have also expanded substantially in the last decade, reaching almost 20 million individuals.[3] As countries struggled to reduce poverty, noncontributory pension schemes became increasingly common (Galiani, Gertler, and Bando 2016), doubling as a share of social sector spending in the last 20 years (Izquierdo, Pessino, and Vuletin 2018). Spending in other social areas grew too. For example, since 2000 public spending per student has increased in real terms by almost 80 percent (Izquierdo, Pessino, and Vuletin 2018).

The pace of improvement, however, has come to a halt in recent years in the face of the region's economic slowdown (World Bank 2017). If anything, governments are looking to revert the growing tendency of government spending and rein it in. The composition of spending has also been highly skewed against the investments that would ensure long-term growth, even though higher growth was the main engine in the reduction of poverty in the region (Izquierdo, Pessino, and Vuletin 2018).

Although higher spending and the programs it financed made inroads in reducing poverty and improving social indicators (Ibarrarán et al. 2017; Levy and Schady 2013), the implemented policies have not always been the most efficient or effective because of flaws in their technical design, execution, or operational implementation. More often than not, policies did not realize their potential in terms of positive effects, or even produced unexpected negative effects on the incentives of beneficiaries, such as disincentives to formal employment (Levy and Schady 2013). Many social programs still suffer from flaws in their technical or operational design that have already been identified and for which solutions have been proposed.

One of the most serious problems with these programs is the presence of leakages (for example, almost 50 percent of the beneficiaries of noncontributory pensions are nonpoor.) Reassigning subsidies and transfers adequately would help cover all the extreme poor without having to increase spending (Izquierdo, Pessino, and Vuletin 2018). In many countries, public moneys are spent with a pro-rich, rather than a pro-poor, bias. Tertiary education spending is the most vivid example of expenditure that favors the higher quintiles of the income distribution. This bias also happens in other sectors of the economy, such as health, even though the lower quintiles are the ones with the most urgent needs (Izquierdo, Pessino, and Vuletin 2018).

Consequently, making improvements in the social sector in the context of stagnated budgets requires more than an adequate technical design of policies; it demands coordination between those entities responsible for the delivery of the different goods and services required to ensure that a quality intervention reaches the population in an adequate and timely manner. To determine how to make and implement these inherently political choices, it is important to understand the policy-making process behind decisions that favor those who do not need help and to identify the sources of leakages and inefficiencies. Only by understanding how policies are designed and the sources of their coordination failures can we start to make inroads in understanding citizens' discontent in spite of overall improvements of social indicators.

The importance of coordination has become very salient with the recent coronavirus pandemic. A proper response requires not only international coordination but also very strong local coordination between those in charge of health ministries and those in charge of security and first responses, and between health scientists, epidemiologists, and those in charge of communication. Because the economic consequences can be severe, a proper response also requires the coordination of policy makers in the ministries of finance, those in charge of social protection, and even those who manage infrastructure. Although coordination can be dictated and written down in an organizational chart, the different responses across countries show that effective coordination requires more than that. Understanding how policy actors interact is fundamental to being able to explain policy design and implementation.

Political Economy and Social Network Analysis: A Two-Pronged Approach to Social Policy Making

Despite numerous impact evaluation studies of particular programs, few analyses focus on the decisions leading to the formulation of social policy, the development of social protection networks, the interinstitutional coordination mechanisms and processes in general, and the lessons from institutional, normative, and operational factors that improve their chances for success or lead to their failure. There is also no comprehensive, systematic study of how social programs and institutional coordination mechanisms—formal or informal—can make a difference in the operational effectiveness and impact of a social program.

This book attempts to fill that void, under the premise that exploring these issues is critical for improving the efficiency and effectiveness of state intervention in the social sector. Social policies must be endowed with an institutional and operational setting that favors their design, adoption, adequate implementation, and sustainability over time. In other words, if the process of formulating and implementing policy is not structured in a way that guarantees the existence of efficient, sustainable technical designs and operational processes—which also entails considering the relationships and networks between actors—higher public spending on health or any other social sector, for that matter, will not necessarily result in significant improvements. In the case of Peru, for instance, Carranza, Chávez, and Valderrama (2009) illustrate how a 50 percent increase in primary education expenditure between 1998 and 2004 did not enhance students' performance because the actors' incentives were not aligned at the time for public expenditure to be efficient. In more general terms, Ardanaz, Scartascini, and Tommasi (2011) have proved how a more favorable environment for policies correlates with better results in human development. In turn, Scartascini and Tommasi (2010) submit evidence on how a better trained and more professional public sector tends to generate better public policies. Izquierdo, Pessino, and Vuletin (2018) provide numerous examples of inefficient allocation of social spending.

In order to explain the characteristics of public policies, it is necessary to know the actors, their incentives, and the rules that govern their interactions. The political economy approach can help in this regard. Comparative research has shown that policies are less coherent and effective when the number of actors involved in negotiations and decisions is excessive, when actors engage in the process in a fragmented manner and with short-term goals, when policy debates are held in extremely varied settings, and when few efficient compensation mechanisms exist to reach agreements (Lora and Scartascini 2010; Scartascini et al. 2011).

When the nature of policies and programs is multisectoral and multilevel—as in the case of social protection networks and the specific social programs and policies that constitute them—their study requires customized conceptual and methodological tools to understand how institutional actors are organized and work to produce concrete social programs that provide certain services.

In light of this evidence, the authors of this book combine the two aforementioned complementary methodological lenses to produce an innovative research tool. The political economy analysis that studies the policy-making process (PMP) by which public policies are formulated and implemented makes it possible to characterize the quality of public policies and identify the conditions that define them. This approach addresses social policies in practice. Meanwhile, social network analysis (SNA) helps determine the role played by the actors that participate in public policy design and execution. Thus, this combined approach provides additional, detailed information on the how and why of the process underlying the observed results in terms of social policy formulation or execution.

The political economy approach seems appropriate to shed light on the policy framework, that is, the conditions that promote stability, adaptability, coherence, and efficiency, among others. Nevertheless, it does not necessarily account for the details that underlie the design and implementation of a specific policy, nor clarify why it is designed or implemented one way or another, or why some actors and not others benefit from intervention. The PMP analysis described in Scartascini et al. (2011) illustrates this point and helps explain why Brazil has introduced more adaptable policies than Ecuador (IDB 2005); why policy instability abounds in Argentina (Spiller and Tommasi 2011); why public employment is used as a bargaining chip in Paraguay (Molinas, Pérez-Liñán, and Hallerberg 2009); and why Uruguay is renowned for electoral cycles of spending (Moraes, Chasquetti, and Bergara 2009), among other phenomena. It does not, however, accurately explain why a specific social protection policy was not passed as it had been initially designed, or why a vaccination policy did not reach all of the intended beneficiaries, or why a hospital was finally built in a certain district and not another, among other situations.

More specifically, the general PMP analysis shows that in Argentina and Bolivia, for instance, the degree of coordination and efficiency in public policy is low, and the quality of implementation intermediate. It also helps determine which factors account for the quality of human resources, the planning process for the use of public resources, and the allocation of cabinet portfolios, as is done in more detailed studies of Bolivia's PMP (for example, Scartascini and Stein 2003).

Only SNA can elucidate which particular actors participate in social policy design and implementation. The main added value of the SNA approach is that it identifies the participants in the design or execution of policies and programs, identifies the nature of the relationships that bind them, assesses each actor's importance and role, and analyzes the network structure and its effects on its own operation. All of these tasks are crucial to specify the sectoral configuration of the public policy process, in both the formulation and the implementation stages.

Understanding Actor Networks from Policy Design through Execution

Public policies emerge from decision-making processes that involve multiple political and social actors interacting in various settings. The initial capacity of policies to produce positive results depends partially on the quality of the process in which these are defined, debated, and approved, and on the way social and institutional actors interact in it.

To improve the effectiveness, efficiency, and targeting of policies, recommendations should take into account who decides on these policies, when, and how. They should also understand who the key actors are and how they relate to each other, and how money, information, and ideas flow. In most cases, these networks of relationships are very different from the formal rules designed and enshrined in legal texts.

With these motivations, the authors of this book carried out case studies using SNA on how decisions are made regarding social policies and program design and implementation in Argentina, Bolivia, The Bahamas, and Trinidad and Tobago. Country selection for the case studies sought to expand our understanding across several dimensions. On the one hand, it took into account the differences that arise from the institutional setting. Having two presidential and two parliamentary countries serves this purpose. On the other hand, the authors looked for variation in terms of size and economic and social indicators. The Caribbean nations are much smaller in size than their South American counterparts; however, their gross domestic product per capita is more than four times that of Bolivia.

Although the case studies try to cover different realities, they do not necessarily represent regional or subregional patterns. Instead, they serve as illustrations of the use of the SNA methodology in different scenarios of social policy formulation. Thus, this book looks to exemplify the productivity of SNA for the understanding of actors, their relations, and the way they influence the failure or success of public policies and social programs. It also attempts to shed light on several aspects of the PMP in the social sector that usually remain hidden with the use of more traditional analytical tools.

Structure and Content of the Book

This volume is structured in eight chapters, including the present one. Chapter 2 presents the theoretical foundations for analyzing the political economy of public policies and establishes its usefulness for research and planning of interventions in the social sector. The chapter briefly introduces the general concepts behind the PMP model and sets the basis for the SNA of social policy. Because each sector has its own actors, the chapter argues that it is important to go beyond the general analysis and expand the study of specific social networks.

Chapter 3 proposes a basic methodological approximation to SNA that should allow the reader to follow the case studies more closely. This type of analysis has expanded significantly in the last few decades as a tool to understand the relations among actors within social structures. Despite the variable nature of such relations—emotional bonds, information flows, or exchange of resources—it is possible to systematically analyze their different contents. Certainly not every actor within a network has the same level of importance and power, which is why it is useful to understand those differences in order to identify how those actors intervene in specific ways. The chapter presents a methodological review of some of the most important attributes of SNA, giving careful attention to the so-called centrality measures and to visual network analysis.

Chapter 4 presents the case study of social policy formulation at the level of the central government in Argentina (during the Mauricio Macri administration) from the SNA perspective. The study shows that the social policy formulation process in Argentina is marked by fragmentation in the provision of ideas, information, and resources, and by limited coordination from the apex of government. These patterns are consistent with the previous literature on PMPs in Argentina.

Chapter 5 presents the SNA of social policy formulation at the central government level in Bolivia during the Evo Morales administration. The formal institutional design of this process is aimed at developing an intense coordination among social sector ministries under the political leadership of the presidency and vice presidency. Analysis of the actual networks of production and circulation of ideas and information, transfers of economic resources, and political power shows that, in practice, interministerial coordination is scarce, and the process of developing social policies is politically coordinated on a shared basis by the presidency and grassroots organizations.

Chapter 6 presents the case studies of the social policy formulation processes in The Bahamas and Trinidad and Tobago. Both countries have Westminster-type political regimes that combine parliamentary government with majoritarian electoral systems that significantly strengthen the power and policy initiative of the executive, and Whitehall-type bureaucracies that mandate interministerial coordination and stakeholder consultations for policy development. With these arrangements, the expectation is for hierarchically structured processes in which the cabinet and prime minister are the central providers of ideas and resources as well as the main sources of political power, and the social area units are the central providers of information. SNAs show that the hierarchies expected from the formal rules exist only for political power, whereas the provision and circulation of ideas, information, and resources are more horizontal.

Chapter 7 provides a comparative analysis of the four case studies that seeks to explain the patterns identified in the SNAs by looking into macro- and micro-institutional factors: political regimes, party systems, state structures, types of bureaucracy, and governance structures. Comparisons suggest that the types of political regime and bureaucracy, and to a lesser extent the governance structures, have more explanatory power than party systems and decentralization. We cannot stress enough that, whereas in some countries the outcomes of SNA tend to be time invariant, in others the outcomes appear to be highly susceptible to the particular style of the president. This is another difference between the more volatile cases of Argentina and Bolivia and the more stable cases of the parliamentary Caribbean countries.

Finally, chapter 8 draws some conclusions based on the articulation between the theory of the political economy of social policies introduced in chapter 2 and the empirical findings of SNAs reported in chapters 4 to 6. The key players—as well as the coordination patterns and challenges identified in the analyses of social policy formulation networks—are consistent with the expectations emerging from the nature of the transaction costs inherent to the organization and the provision of the type of benefits offered by social policies.

Certainly, the decision-making processes through which these policies are developed could improve their institutionalization and efficiency. Network analysis shows, however, that, where the theory of the political economy of social policies identifies inefficiencies and institutionalization problems in practice, social networks develop responses aimed at fulfilling—albeit in less than efficient ways—the functional objectives of social programs. Finally, chapter 8 reflects upon the limitations of doing SNA of social programs and proposes a research agenda designed to bridge the existing information gaps about this public policy area.

In all, this book makes two types of contributions. On the one hand, it presents theoretical and methodological tools to study the political economy of social policies from the perspective of SNA. These tools help to accurately identify actors, their resources and interaction, and the consequences they have for policy making. On the other hand, this book illustrates the utility of identifying the social networks that define the design of social programs, and the effects these networks have on the political economy and the success or failure of social policies.

These analytical and methodological contributions, combined with specific examples of policies and programs in the region, aim to enhance the efficiency, efficacy, and sustainability of public policies in the social area.

Notes

1. Data come from the World Bank's LAC Equity Lab data-sharing platform. For more information, see https://www.worldbank.org/en/topic/poverty/lac-equity-lab1/overview.
2. Data come from the World Bank's *World Development Indicators*.
3. Data come from the Inter-American Development Bank's Sociómetro dataset. For more information, see https://www.iadb.org/en/sociometro-bid/sociometro-bid.

References

Ardanaz, M., C. Scartascini, and M. Tommasi. 2011. "Political Institutions, Policymaking, and Economic Policy in Latin America." In *The Oxford Handbook of Latin American Economics*, edited by J. A. Ocampo and J. Ros. Oxford: Oxford University Press.

Carranza, I., J. Chávez, and L. Valderrama. 2009. "Success in Sustainability? The Case of Peru." In *Who Decides the Budget? A Political Economy Analysis of the Budget Process in Latin America*, edited by M. Hallerberg, C. Scartascini, and E. H. Stein. Cambridge, MA: Harvard University Press and Inter-American Development Bank.

Galiani, S., P. Gertler, and R. Bando. 2016. "Non-contributory Pensions." *Labour Economics* 38 (C): 47–58.

Ibarrarán, P., N. Medellín, F. Regalia, and M. Stampini, eds. 2017. *How Conditional Cash Transfers Work: Good Practices after 20 Years of Implementation*. Washington, DC: Inter-American Development Bank.

IDB (Inter-American Development Bank). 2005. *The Politics of Policies: Economic and Social Progress in Latin America and the Caribbean 2006 Report*. Washington, DC: Inter-American Development Bank.

Izquierdo, A., C. Pessino, and G. Vuletin, eds. 2018. *Better Spending for Better Lives*. Washington, DC: Inter-American Development Bank.

Levy, S., and N. Schady. 2013. "Latin America's Social Policy Challenge: Education, Social Insurance, Redistribution." *Journal of Economic Perspectives* 27 (2): 193–218.

Lora, E., and C. Scartascini, eds. 2010. *Consecuencias imprevistas de la Constitucion de 1991*. Bogotá: Alfaomega.

Mesa-Lago, C., and G. Márquez. 2007. "Reform of Pension and Social Assistance Systems." In *The State of State Reform in Latin* America, edited by E. Lora. Washington DC: Inter-American Development Bank.

Molinas, J. R., A. Pérez-Liñán, and M. Hallerberg. 2009. "Weakened Policymaking Process, Deteriorating Fiscal Outcomes: The Case of Paraguay." In *Who Decides the Budget? A Political Economy Analysis of the Budget Process in Latin America*, edited by M. Hallerberg, C. Scartascini, and E. H. Stein. Cambridge, MA: Harvard University Press and Inter-American Development Bank.

Moraes, J. A., D. Chasquetti, and M. Bergara. 2009. "Fiscal Rules That Fit Political Cycles: The Case of Uruguay." *In Who Decides the Budget? A Political Economy Analysis of the Budget Process in Latin America,* edited by M. Hallerberg, C. Scartascini, and E. H. Stein. Cambridge, MA: Harvard University Press and Inter-American Development Bank.

Scartascini, C., P. T. Spiller, E. Stein, and M. Tommasi. 2011. *El juego político en América Latina: ¿Cómo se deciden las políticas públicas?* Washington, DC: Inter-American Development Bank.

Scartascini, C., and E. Stein. 2003. *The Bolivian Budget (1990–2002): A Year-Long Bargaining Process*. Washington, DC: Inter-American Development Bank.

Scartascini, C., and M. Tommasi. 2010. "The Politics of Productivity." In *The Age of Productivity: Transforming Economies from the Bottom Up*, edited by C. Pagés. New York: Palgrave Macmillan.

Spiller, P. T., and M. Tommasi. 2011. "Un país sin rumbo. ¿Cómo se hacen las políticas públicas en Argentina?" In *El juego político en América Latina: ¿Cómo se deciden las políticas públicas?* edited by C. Scartascini, P. Spiller, E. H. Stein, and M. Tommasi. Washington, DC: Inter-American Development Bank.

World Bank. 2017. *World Development Indicators 2017*. Washington, DC: World Bank.

2

The Political Economy of Public Policy: From Institutions to Social Networks

Beyond the Social Planner: Determinants of Social Policy

The expansion of social programs in countries in Latin America and the Caribbean had its origin in both economic and political factors. The commodity boom provided the conditions, and certain changes in political processes facilitated it. The Caribbean, largely excluded from the commodities bonanza, experienced less dramatic increases than the rest of the region. The new economic perspectives, as well as global trends in favor of higher investment in social policies—promoted in part by the Millennium Development Goals—also created favorable conditions for Latin America and the Caribbean. Political changes provided an additional boost. These shifts were partly brought about by social discontent with the economic results of the 1990s, which favored a turn to the left, as well as by political reforms that fostered greater inclusion, as was the case with the Colombian constitutional reform of 1991. These changes have served as natural vehicles to spark renewed interest in social investment (Lora and Scartascini 2010). Particularly, the rebirth of democracy in most countries in the region, along with a strong decentralization process—as in Bolivia and Peru—has led to an increase in the funds allocated to social policies (Faguet 2008; Mesa-Lago and Márquez 2007). The region's turn to the left in the ideological spectrum would seem to account for a new distribution of expenditures (Izquierdo, Pessino, and Vuletin 2018; Machado, Scartascini, and Stein 2013).

The existing political institutions in the region significantly affect the incentives of politicians to provide increased social expenditure in the form of transfers instead of public investment. Countries with proportional representation systems are likely to have a larger public sector than those where representatives are elected in uninominal districts using majority rule. Additionally, in proportional representation systems in districts where multiple representatives are elected, the trend favors higher transfers and social expenditure (Crain and Scartascini 2002; Keefer, Scartascini, and Vlaicu 2018; Milesi-Ferretti, Perotti, and Rostagno 2002; Persson and Tabellini 2003). Movement in the region toward more fragmented electoral systems accounts for part of the change in recent decades (Lora and Scartascini 2010; Scartascini et al. 2011).

Budget institutions favoring the executive branch over the legislative and narrowing the separation of branches—a development that took place around the turn of the century—have also reduced the incentives of the president to keep a smaller public sector in presidential countries. Essentially, the increased power to control expenditure allocation from the executive creates incentives to increase such expenditure (Ardanaz and Scartascini 2014).

Another factor that may have affected the size and composition of spending is the public's waning confidence in political institutions. How much citizens trust their government affects the composition of spending. As trust goes down, so does the demand for policies that require substantial government involvement and take a long time to come to fruition (for example, investment projects). Consequently, if anything, citizens prefer transfers from the government over the provision of long-term public goods (Keefer, Scartascini, and Vlaicu 2018).

Although looking at the overall level and composition of spending and understanding some of their determinants is important, differences in the types of policies introduced (both between countries and policy areas within the same country) can be substantial and broader than institutional differences can explain. The reason for such differences across and within countries lies in the fact that public policies are not mere objects of choice for a social planner. They arise from a decision-making process involving a great variety of political actors interacting in a wide array of scenarios. Therefore, the potential for policy measures to yield positive results depends on the quality of the process in which such policies are discussed, adopted, and implemented. Even the best ideas may not bear the expected fruits if the gestation process is not suitable.

Therefore, it is important not only to determine which policies could prove effective in resolving a particular problem and assess their design and specific contents but also to analyze their subsequent implementation process. Doing so requires describing the political game or policy-making process (PMP). It means understanding the fundamental process that shapes policies, boosts them from idea to implementation, and sustains them over time. The policies that are ultimately adopted will depend precisely on these dynamics, which, in turn, endow public policies with some common characteristics and greatly determine their chances of success. For example, the political game can contribute to public policy stability or to sharp fluctuations. Whereas stability generates credibility and shapes capabilities, volatility—usually caused by changes of administration—produces the opposite effect. That is the reason why investors refrain from committing their resources in countries or sectors at risk of unexpected changes.

Likewise, the political game can facilitate—or hinder—policy adaptability when, for instance, confronted with an economic shock or evidence that certain measures are failing or generating excessive rigidity. The characteristics of these dynamics can produce policies that promote public welfare (such as vaccination campaigns or health care provision in general) or benefit private interests (pressure groups such as business associations or unions). In sum, policy-making and implementation processes can affect the nature and quality of public policies in several ways, and in turn condition the possibilities for social and economic development of countries. It is, thus, essential to understand how those processes work.

In democracies in Latin America and the Caribbean, the PMP takes place within political systems in which the variety of actors involved ranges from the president or prime minister to electors in small rural communities, through members of Congress or Parliament, judges, public opinion leaders, officials at different governmental levels, unions, business associations, nongovernmental organizations (NGOs), and social movements. The complex interaction of these actors is influenced by the institutions and political practices of each country, which affect the actors' roles and incentives, the scenarios in which they interact, and the nature of the transactions involved.

Figure 2.1 shows that countries with better PMPs—those whose public policies exhibit desirable characteristics such as stability, adaptability, coordination

FIGURE 2.1: **PMP Results and Public Policy Quality, Latin America and the Caribbean versus the Rest of the World**

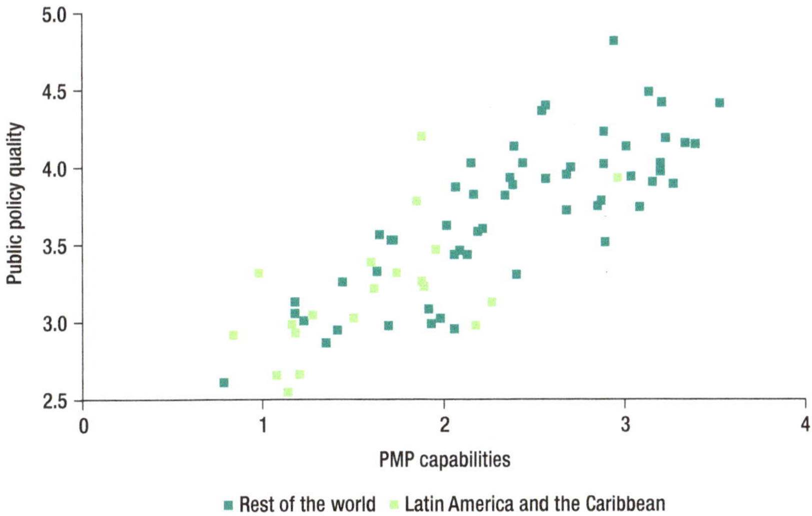

Source: Scartascini and Tommasi 2010.
Note: PMP = policy-making process.

and coherence, regulation compliance and implementation, efficiency, and correlation with public interest—achieve the best results: more access to credit, a more neutral tax system, and greater neutrality in state subsidy allocation, among others. The horizontal axis of figure 2.1 plots countries according to their capabilities, and the vertical axis assesses the desirable characteristics of their policies.

Likewise, countries that have better PMPs achieve greater impact through their social policies. For example, if the PMP is not structured so as to ensure policy sustainability over time, spending more on health does little to improve life expectancy (Scartascini, Stein, and Tommasi 2009). As shown in figure 2.1, the quality of policies varies widely among countries.

The factors influencing the PMP—such as the number of actors taking part in decision-making processes, their incentives, and the relationships shaping their interactions—define the quality of public policy. For instance, in countries where many actors participate in decision making, and where each of them has certain incentives to obtain profits and benefits in the short term, it is difficult to formulate policies whose benefits materialize in the long term.

In the case of Latin America and the Caribbean, PMPs are highly diverse and, consequently, so are their results for each country. The region displays some common characteristics, however: it shows backwardness compared to several regions of the world in terms of the six desirable policy characteristics mentioned above (stability, adaptability, coordination and coherence, regulation compliance and implementation, efficiency, and correlation with public interest) as well as in terms of the Policy Index that groups those countries and averages the six components. In this index, Latin America and the Caribbean scores only slightly above Sub-Saharan Africa and South Asia. Additionally, the index's absolute value is low, not even reaching 2 on a 0–4 scale (see table 2.1).

Considering the index's individual components, the outlook does not improve substantially. The gap is particularly striking in the area of coordination and coherence, which measures the ability of multiple actors in the same policy field to synchronize their actions and implement them coherently. This gap should come as no surprise; in Latin America and the Caribbean, government ministries and levels of government tend to have difficulty communicating with one another, and multiple government agencies often pursue the same objective simultaneously (IDB 2005; Stein and Tommasi 2007). The measurement of policy compliance and implementation as well as efficiency of policy regulation yields similar results: traditionally, the region has not complied with rules and regulations. For example, tax evasion is widespread, audits are unusual (Corbacho, Fretes, and Lora 2013), and labor regulation compliance is rarely monitored (Ronconi 2012). Public policy efficiency is also problematic. For example, marked increases in educational expenditure have not yielded better results, as shown in earlier country-specific research (Carranza, Chávez, and Valderrama 2009) as well as in comparative analyses (OECD 2009).

TABLE 2.1: **Ranking of Desirable Characteristics of Public Policies, by Region**

Region	Policy characteristics						
	Stability	Adaptability	Coordination and coherence	Regulation compliance and implementation	Efficiency	Correlation with public interest	Policy Index
OECD high-income countries	1	1	1	1	1	1	1
East Asia and Pacific	3	2	2	2	2	4	2
Europe and Central Asia	2	3	4	3	4	5	3
Middle East and North Africa	6	6	3	4	3	2	4
Latin America and the Caribbean	4	4	5	5	5	3	5
Sub-Saharan Africa	5	7	7	6	6	6	6
South Asia	7	5	6	7	7	7	7

Source: Franco Chuaire and Scartascini 2014.
Note: The Policy Index comprises the average of all the other components. For more information on the index, the components, and the sources, see Franco Chuaire and Scartascini 2014. OECD = Organisation for Economic Co-operation and Development.

Characterizing public policies may require going beyond the specifics of policies to look at the actors that develop them and the ways those actors relate to each other within the PMP.

The Role of Actors

Both the PMP and the social network analysis (SNA) frameworks require a deep understanding of the actors that participate in the process of policy design and implementation. In the case of the PMP, the key questions are the following:

- Who are the key players involved in the PMP?
- What are their powers and roles?
- What are their preferences, incentives, and capacities?
- What are their time horizons?
- In which arenas do they interact? What are the formal and informal rules under which these arenas work?
- What kinds of exchanges and transactions do they engage in?

- What types of political and economic resources exist to compensate those who may oppose?
- What mechanisms ensure the credibility of promises?

Although it is important to identify the actors that participate in policy making, it is also important to note that the main actors may change across policy areas. This book takes a broad view of social policy, but specific studies should look at the particularities of each sector. The general characteristics of public policy in a given country are affected by certain elements of that country's political and institutional structure. At the same time, each policy area may also differ because of its intrinsic traits. Therefore, after mapping the elements that distinguish each country, it is important to identify and understand the characteristics that differentiate each policy area from the others. Each area involves different actors and requires different abilities from those actors in the PMP to achieve intertemporal cooperation. This area specificity is especially true in policy areas that are decided on and paid for today but have economic and social implications for the next generation. Early childhood development programs and the pension system, in which coordination between actors to ensure intertemporal cooperation is of the utmost importance, are cases in point.

In contrast, other policy areas may require only short-term agreements that are easier to implement. An example would be a vaccination campaign due to the outbreak of a disease that was thought to be eradicated, or emergency action in response to an unexpected natural disaster.

Some policy areas may differ less in terms of the need to enter into long-term agreements, but differ more in the composition of the actors that participate in the decision-making process. For instance, in education policy, teachers' unions are usually central actors in the provision of education services. Not surprisingly then, their role as a pressure group is to ensure that the results of policy debates usually tend to promote their interests. Thus, differences among countries are often explained by distinctive features such as the power of the teachers' union, the way it is organized relative to other political actors with whom it transacts, and the general structure of the political system that enables or prevents the union's participation in programmatic debates. In this respect, Chile's education sector sets a remarkable example. Reforms therein tend to be more difficult to implement than in any other policy area because the way in which several interests (students', unions', businesses') are aligned within the PMP does not allow party coalitions to reach agreements on how to reform the sector (Aninat et al. 2010). In the health sector, the key may not reside in the power of a particular union but instead in the number of unions and, more generally, of actors involved, because the provision of health care services is usually more complex than that of education services. The situation is even more complex in decentralized contexts like Bolivia's.

Differences may also arise from whether the formulation and implementation of policies in a certain area can be delegated to the bureaucracy or decentralized to lower levels of government. Certainly, some policies call for political actors to agree every time a new modification is introduced. In some cases, however, delegating policies to a specialized bureaucracy takes those policies out of the bargaining process, especially when it is not always feasible to reach long-term agreements. Consider, for instance, monetary policy, which is delegated to an independent central bank guided by inflation targets. As a result, the quantity of money the central bank decides to issue depends on predetermined rules and the decision of independent authorities, instead of being a recurring bargaining issue among political actors. This lack of bargaining can also occur in other areas such as unemployment benefits, among others. In all cases, the individual characteristics of each policy distinctively shape the process by which it is defined and formulated, and, given the political context in which the policies are decided, make it easier for some of them to be modified—if necessary—or maintained over the years.

Consequently, studies on sectoral PMPs and SNA should always include a comprehensive description of the actors and their incentives, as well as the benefits, duration, and characteristics of public policies. The next section provides a general description of the actors that intervene in social policy making.

The Actors in the Social Policy–Making Process

The PMP analysis (IDB 2005) and the literature on the political economy of social policy suggest that some actors participate in the PMPs of all social sector areas: the national government, the national legislature, local governments, unions, businesses, and international financial institutions. The three governmental actors are subdivided into political actors (that is, parties and political authorities) and bureaucratic actors (that is, technical and permanent officials). Political actors typically seek to develop policies that represent their support coalitions, whereas bureaucratic actors prefer those that increase their power within public administration. Bureaucratic actors, in turn, have different incentives according to their position: politically appointed managers and rank-and-file employees are typically interested in maximizing their budget and their capacity to spend it at their discretion, whereas permanent government officials in ministries or sector-specific agencies generally seek to increase their regulatory power over the entire sector (Dunleavy 1991).

The national government and the legislature aim to develop general policies, such as those related to regulatory frameworks, levels or sources of funding, benefit provision, quality standards, and so on. In turn, local governments are usually interested in increasing their power to manage those financial resources linked to policy implementation. Notably, in federal or highly decentralized countries, and under conditions of high political competitiveness and availability of funding at the subnational level, local governments may focus on developing their own policies, different from those set by the national government (Bonvecchi 2008). Consequently, political actors would typically intervene in policy-making processes by providing power and policy ideas to get the bureaucracy running, whereas bureaucratic actors would typically provide information and resources to make policies happen.

Unions participate in social policy making differently across areas. In health care, they typically intervene as providers, in competition with private organizations, seeking to influence regulatory frameworks and minimize operational costs. In education, they participate as budget maximizers, pressing for higher wages, but also as managers seeking to increase their autonomy within schools. In social security, they intervene as stakeholders purporting to expand benefits—though in some cases they may also play the part of pension fund managers looking to increase profits. In social assistance and labor policies, they participate as budget maximizers, but in the latter case also as providers of training courses—and hence as interested parties in the definition of contents and regulation of provision. In all, then, unions bring to social policy making their power, ideas, information, and resources.

In contrast, businesses intervene in social policy making mainly as providers of ideas and information. In health policy, they operate as stakeholders in the regulation of health insurance for workers; in education, either as providers or as interested parties in the definition of contents and links between schools and labor markets; in social security, as stakeholders in the definition of the tax burden on employment and the management of pension funds; and, in social assistance and labor policy, as interested parties in the definition of skills and training policies for the labor market.

International financial institutions—including multilaterals and international cooperation agencies—typically intervene in social policy making through the provision of ideas, resources, and information about policies. As argued previously, they face competition in each of their contributions.

In addition, some policy areas feature sector-specific actors. In health, professional associations of doctors and nurses, as well as NGOs, provide ideas and information on regulatory rules and standards. In education policy, religious orders, NGOs, and families intervene with ideas and information about performance. In social assistance and labor policies, NGOs and grassroots organizations provide ideas, information, and resources for targeting and allocation of benefits.

Whereas PMP analysis is certainly useful in identifying the general incentives of actors and accounting for the differences between, for example, educational reforms in Argentina and Mexico in terms of decentralization processes and teachers' incentives and evaluations (IDB 2005), SNA offers a useful theoretical and methodological complement to understand and predict the decision-making dynamics of policy change. Whether social networks are regarded as independent or dependent variables in the analysis, this approach shows how the ways actors and organizations relate, and the resources exchanged in such relationships, contribute to generating or processing the transaction costs of policy making and implementation.

The Role of Social Networks

Why are social networks so important to the political economy of social policy? First, the PMP is developed by way of relations among groups of actors, which constitute the foundation of any social network. Second, the production and allocation of public goods in certain policy areas requires establishing and managing social networks.

Why is it so important to understand the workings of such networks? The way networks work helps determine which actors actually participate in the design and execution of public policies. This information can be extremely valuable when it comes to implementing a program. For instance, if a health policy results from negotiations between the PTE and subnational governments, or between the PTE and grassroots organizations, and its design assumes the leadership of the ministry of health, the policy may not be effective if that ministry did not participate in the process.

Each social policy area produces or distributes goods and services of a different nature; thus, the conditions and transaction costs inherent to decision-making processes are also different in each area. According to the theory of networks, differences revolve around four dimensions: (1) certainty about the conditions for the supply and demand of goods or services; (2) the degree of specificity of the goods or services provided; (3) the complexity of the tasks and the time it takes to provide them; and (4) the frequency of exchanges among the actors in each area (Jones, Hesterly, and Borgatti 1997). The actual conditions occasioned by these dimensions in each area determine the organizational format of the decision-making process: a hierarchical structure, a market mechanism, or a network scheme.

Economic transactions are carried out as exchanges among social network actors if they meet four conditions: (1) uncertainty about the stability of the demand for goods and services; (2) high degree of specificity of the exchanges inherent to the provision of such goods and services; (3) high complexity and tight time restrictions for the tasks involved in the provision of such goods and services; and (4) high frequency of exchange among the actors (Jones, Hesterly, and Borgatti 1997). This argument can also be applied to the analysis of the conditions and transaction costs inherent to the political economy of different social policies.

When demand is uncertain, hierarchies and market mechanisms are inefficient for organizing and sustaining transactions: neither format manages to acquire or process enough information to reduce uncertainty and allow actors to make properly informed decisions (Jones, Hesterly, and Borgatti 1997). This uncertainty usually occurs in the areas of health and social assistance. In both cases, epidemics, natural disasters, and significant transformations in economic and social policies, among others, can suddenly modify service demand in the short and medium term. In education policy, instead, technological advances can affect the conditions for students to develop and use cognitive abilities, but the process is relatively slower. The same does not apply for social security, where service demand can be calculated reasonably accurately with actuarial methods. As for employment policy, technological advances that lead to dramatic increases in productivity can affect the demand for skills from the workforce as well as the kind of training or retraining required; however, such changes tend to become relatively predictable. Demand shocks arising from economic policy changes are not necessarily predictable, particularly when they are brought about by variations in external conditions (for example, a global financial crisis).

When exchanges are highly specific, coordination among the parties becomes necessary to carry out the promised transactions, which are particularly vulnerable to changes in the supply and demand of the resources needed to complete them (Jones, Hesterly, and Borgatti 1997). Here, however, neither hierarchies nor market mechanisms can ensure transactions, given that neither guarantees the required cooperation, proximity, or frequency.

This situation is also found in the areas of health, education, social assistance, and employment. The supply of health services should be adjusted to each individual's diagnoses and the epidemiological profile for each country's climatic region. Education services should be adjusted to the students' cognitive skills and cultural and physical limitations. Social assistance should respond to the needs and emergencies of individuals and families (or types of beneficiaries). Training and retraining should meet the demands of the labor market and match workers' skill stocks and deficits. As in the previous case, the same does not apply to social security, where exchanges consist of impersonal payments to individuals.

When tasks are complex and time constraints are high, coordination among actors with different skills must be ensured. If demand is uncertain and highly specific, neither hierarchies nor market mechanisms could respond appropriately (Jones, Hesterly, and Borgatti 1997). Such is the case in the areas of health, social assistance, and employment. In terms of health and social assistance, an appropriate response to epidemics, natural disasters, and other contingencies generally entails the immediate mobilization of doctors, nurses, laboratories, private companies, administrative staff, and eventually the armed forces. In the employment area, adapting training and retraining programs involves mobilizing teachers, companies, workers, and public servants fast enough to provide qualified labor in a timely manner, in order to seize the productivity potential of emerging new technologies. Again, this would not apply to the case of social security, where the tasks are simple and regular, or to education, where tasks, although complex, are not subject to tight deadlines.

When the frequency of exchanges among actors is high, their specificity tends to increase, together with the need to coordinate transactions. When demand is uncertain, however, it may not be satisfied by means of market mechanisms or hierarchies (Jones, Hesterly, and Borgatti 1997). As noted earlier, this uncertainty may occur in the areas of health, social assistance, and education. In the health sector, the interaction among doctors and medical staff, patients, and administrative employees and instances of social accountability are constant and repeated, and they may take place within a complex context of joint funding and coordination among administrative levels in decentralized countries. In education policy, the same interaction occurs among teachers, students, families, and school managers. In noncontributory social assistance, an equivalent dynamic plays out among individuals or families from vulnerable sectors and party leaders, social movements, NGOs, or unions that provide assistance. Once again, social security, which has practically no interaction between beneficiaries and administrative staff, and employment, in which the interaction between workers and trainers is merely contingent, are the exceptions.

Thus, in the areas of noncontributory health and social assistance, and to a lesser extent in education and employment, a decision-making process for public policy formulation and implementation must be organized to meet three paramount needs: those related to adapting to environmental changes resulting from demand uncertainty; coordination needs that arise from the complexity of tasks and time constraints for implementation; and those needs related to protecting the exchanges arising from the parties' interest in safeguarding the specificity of their transactions.

Social networks, hence, become the appropriate organizational model to fulfill such requirements, because they promote highly complex and specific exchanges while coordinating the contributions of different actors that frequently interact with one another. The frequency of these exchanges allows for more specific demands, fosters their articulation within a complex set of benefits, and makes it possible to coordinate efforts, find enough information on environmental changes, and adapt tasks to such changes in order to protect the specificity of their transactions (Jones, Hesterly, and Borgatti 1997).

In these social policy areas, therefore, decisions arise through negotiations that involve relatively stable networks of political, business, and union leaders; social organizations; and administrative staff. Thus, the tools of SNA are useful for studying the political economy of social policies in these areas.

The Value of SNA for the Political Economy Analysis of Social Policy Making

The preceding pages suggest that SNA adds value to the political economy analysis of social policy making in at least three ways: description of the actors, identification of coordination issues, and operational predictions about processes. SNA describes the actors involved in social policy making, both by identifying their participation in networks and by establishing how they relate to each other—that is, their connections, which in turn define their place in the networks. It complements political economy analysis by providing a wealth of information about actors that cannot be obtained or inferred using other qualitative or quantitative collection techniques.

SNA identifies the existence of coordination issues among actors in the networks by mapping their location therein, the distance between actors formally or operationally required for coordination of decision-making processes, and the nature—political, bureaucratic, or societal—of the actors to whom any actor must relate. This mapping complements political economy analysis by providing information on coordination issues that is independent from, and unbiased by, qualitative accounts of decision-making processes.

SNA can therefore make predictions about the operation of PMPs that complement political economy analysis by being grounded in data—that are systematic, exhaustive, and reliable—about actors and the contents of their relations. Having identified the actors, their role in the networks, and the nature and extent of the coordination issues that may arise therein, SNA can predict biases in the provision of ideas, information, and resources, as well as competition and conflict among actors with different levels and sources of power.

SNA can add this value by performing four tasks: (1) specifying the boundaries of the network of participants in the decision-making process of design or execution, and identifying its members; (2) determining the nature of the relations that bind them together; (3) weighing in the function and importance of each actor; and (4) defining the general structure of the network and its effects on its operation. All of these tasks are crucial to specifying the sectoral configuration of the policy formulation and implementation process for the following reasons:

- By specifying the network and identifying its members, SNA goes beyond institutional characterization and avoids restricting participants in decision-making processes to institutional actors such as political leaders or the board of directors of social and economic associations.
- By determining the nature of the relationships among actors, SNA shows the ways in which actual relations resemble or diverge from those that are institutionally prescribed. The case studies in this volume analyze this point in detail. The same exercise allows for the specification of the level of complexity of ties and helps estimate the transaction costs among certain actors.
- By assessing the role and importance of each actor within a network, SNA helps determine which actors are key to the structure, the current configuration of decision-making processes, and how actors influence processes and results.

These aspects are analyzed in detail in the case studies in chapters 4 through 6 of this book.

References

Aninat, C., J. M. Benavente, I. Briones, N. Eyzaguirre, P. Navia, and J. Olivari. 2010. "The Political Economy of Productivity: The Case of Chile." Working Paper No. 105, Inter-American Development Bank, Washington, DC.

Ardanaz, M., and C. Scartascini. 2014. "The Economic Effects of Constitutions: Do Budget Institutions Make Forms of Government More Alike?" *Constitutional Political Economy* 25 (3): 301–29.

Bonvecchi, A. 2008. "Políticas sociales subnacionales en países federales. Argentina en perspectiva comparada." *Desarrollo Económico* 48 (190/191): 307–39.

Carranza, I., J. Chávez, and L. Valderrama. 2009. "Success in Sustainability? The Case of Peru." In *Who Decides the Budget? A Political Economy Analysis of the Budget Process in Latin America,* edited by M. Hallerberg, C. Scartascini, and E. H. Stein. Cambridge, MA: Harvard University Press and Inter-American Development Bank.

Corbacho, A., V. Fretes, and E. Lora, eds. 2013. *More than Revenue: Taxation as a Development Tool.* New York: Palgrave McMillan.

Crain, W. M., and C. Scartascini. 2002. "The Size and Composition of Government Spending in Multi-Party Systems." Working paper 02-23, George Mason University, Fairfax, VA.

Dunleavy P. 1991. *Democracy, Bureaucracy, and Public Choice: Economic Explanations in Political Science.* London: Prentice-Hall.

Faguet, J. P. 2008. "Decentralization's Effects on Public Investment: Evidence and Policy Lessons from Bolivia and Colombia." *Journal of Development Studies* 44 (8): 1100–21.

Franco Chuaire, M., and C. Scartascini. 2014. "The Politics of Policies: Revisiting the Quality of Public Policies and Government Capabilities in Latin America and the Caribbean." Policy Brief No. 220, Inter-American Development Bank, Washington, DC.

IDB (Inter-American Development Bank). 2005. *The Politics of Policies: Economic and Social Progress in Latin America and the Caribbean 2006 Report.* Washington, DC: Inter-American Development Bank.

Izquierdo, A., C. Pessino, and G. Vuletin, eds. 2018. *Better Spending for Better Lives.* Washington, DC: Inter-American Development Bank.

Jones, C., W.S. Hesterly, and S. Borgatti. 1997. "A General Theory of Network Governance: Exchange Conditions and Social Mechanisms." *The Academy of Management Review* 22 (4): 911–45.

Keefer, P., C. Scartascini, and R. Vlaicu. 2018. "Shortchanging the Future: The Short-Term Bias of Politics." In *Better Spending for Better Lives*, edited by A. Izquierdo, C. Pessino, and G. Vuletin. Washington, DC: Inter-American Development Bank.

Lora, E., and C. Scartascini, eds. 2010. *Consecuencias imprevistas de la Constitucion de 1991.* Bogotá: Alfaomega.

Machado, F., C. Scartascini, and E. Stein. 2013. "The Politics of Taxation." In *More than Revenue*, edited by A. Corbacho, V. Fretes, and E. Lora. New York: Palgrave Macmillan.

Mesa-Lago, C., and G. Márquez. 2007. "Reform of Pension and Social Assistance Systems." In *The State of State Reform in Latin America,* edited by E. Lora. Washington DC: Inter-American Development Bank.

Milesi-Ferretti, G. M., R. Perotti, and M. Rostagno. 2002. "Electoral Systems and Public Spending." *Quarterly Journal of Economics* 117 (2): 609–57.

OECD (Organisation for Economic Co-operation and Development). 2009. *Perspectivas económicas de América Latina 2009.* Paris: OECD.

Persson, T., and G. Tabellini. 2003. *The Economic Effects of Constitutions.* Cambridge, MA: The MIT Press.

Ronconi, L. 2012. "Globalization, Domestic Institutions and Enforcement of Labor Law: Evidence from Latin America." *Industrial Relations* 51 (1): 89–105.

Scartascini, C., P. T. Spiller, E. Stein, and M. Tommasi. 2011. *El juego político en América Latina: ¿Cómo se deciden las políticas públicas?* Washington, DC: Inter-American Development Bank.

Scartascini, C., E. Stein, and M. Tommasi. 2009. "Political Institutions, Intertemporal Cooperation, and the Quality of Policies." Working paper No. 676, Inter-American Development Bank, Washington, DC.

Scartascini, C., and M. Tommasi. 2010. "The Politics of Productivity." In *The Age of Productivity: Transforming Economies from the Bottom Up*, edited by C. Pagés. New York: Palgrave Macmillan.

Stein, E., and M. Tommasi. 2007. "The Institutional Determinants of State Capabilities in Latin America." In *Conferencia anual de sobre economía del desarrollo del Banco Mundial: Más allá de la transición*, edited by F. Bourguignon and B. Pleskovic. Washington, DC: World Bank.

3

Social Network Analysis: Basic Toolkit and Research Design

This chapter describes the research design employed in the case studies of social policy making in Argentina, The Bahamas, Bolivia, and Trinidad and Tobago. To this aim, it first introduces the main concepts and methodological tools of social network analysis (SNA), as well as the measures used in the case studies to map the social networks. Subsequently, it presents the design followed for the collection and processing of network data that constitute the theoretical and methodological bases for the case studies included in this book. An introduction to their nature, characteristics, and heuristic uses is necessary to understand the logic of the empirical research compiled here, as well as to assess the relevance of its results. This chapter presents the foundations, basic concepts, and potential empirical uses of SNA, and discusses the main methodological problems that any research using SNA must resolve: the selection and sampling of the target population, the levels of analysis of the information, and the use of visual network analysis.

Basic Concepts of SNA

SNA studies the relations among actors. These can be individuals, groups, corporations, or social collectives—any form of social grouping. SNA does not assume their agency and is concerned only with links among them (Wasserman and Faust 1994). In social network graphs, the actors are represented by nodes, and their relations are represented by lines called ties.

Ties are the links by which actors connect in a network. They represent various types of specific relational contents (Knoke and Kuklinski 1982)—which are the substance of the relations among actors. These contents can range from those by which one person evaluates or perceives another (such as expressions of friendship, appreciation, or respect), to those by which material or nonmaterial resources (such as money or information) are transferred, and to those that represent association and affiliation to a group or situation or that formally institutionalize that condition (such as authority, coordination, dependency, and kinship).

Ties can be graphically represented as lines with distinct characteristics: directed, nondirected or binary, valued, and nonvalued. Directed lines denote the orientation of ties; nondirected or binary lines, in turn, show that ties have a reciprocal nature. Valued lines denote positivity or negativity in the link between one node and others; nonvalued lines, in turn, suggest the absence of mutual evaluation among the nodes they connect.

SNA measures relations among actors on five levels: dyads, triads, subgroups, groups, and networks. At the most fundamental level, a relation is established between two actors; the unit of analysis is the dyad, which can be defined as a pair of actors and the ties between them. A triad is a set of three actors and the ties among them. In triad-based studies, the object of research is generally the transitivity or the balance among relations. A group is a finite set of actors—theoretically defined by each researcher—whose ties are the object of analysis. The specification of its boundaries constitutes the central methodological question in SNA and involves solving at least three issues: the definition of the group itself, the specification of the network's boundaries, and the sampling of its components (Scott 2000). The networks SNA investigates are constituted, partially or completely, by the groups each researcher theoretically defines as relevant, which are in turn represented by network graphs. The section below describes the procedure used to specify network boundaries for the case studies in this book.

An important property of groups is their cohesion, that is, the reciprocity, closeness, and frequency of the links between network members. A network, or a group of actors within it, displays a higher level of cohesion the higher the reciprocity, closeness, and frequency of links among its members. Cohesion matters for the operation of networks: the higher the cohesion, the more likely that relational contents and coordination among network members will flow smoothly.

A clique is a highly cohesive subgroup structured by relational patterns that differ from those of their network. Identifying cliques is important for understanding not only their position in the network and the behavior of their actors but also their effects on the performance of the general network. Figure 3.1 illustrates dyads, triads, and, in an extremely simplified version, a clique.

The line that connects the clique to the rest of the network in figure 3.1 is called a bridge. Bridges are intermediate ties that link two groups in a network without specifically belonging to either of them (Everett 1982). In turn, the node in the clique that connects it with the rest of the network by way of the bridge is a cutpoint, because its removal would increase the number of components in the figure (Hage and Harary 1983): instead of a figure with three dyads and a clique, two subfigures would each have three dyads. Bridges and cutpoints are important for identifying the nodes and

FIGURE 3.1: **Graph Representation of a Dyad, Triad, and Clique**

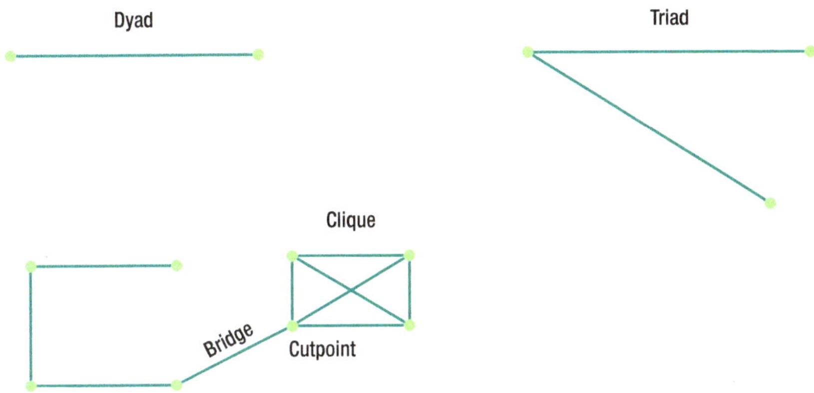

Source: Original figure for this publication.

ties whose removal or positional change would alter the structure of the network and, thus, both its general operation and the relations among its actors. Cutpoints, in particular, are actors whose absence from a network would break up or fragment the network structure. This concept helps identify which actors are essential to maintain or modify the network structure. The more cutpoints a network displays, the easier it is to divide it and the greater the influence of actors that are not necessarily central.

Of the many properties of networks on which SNA can shed light, the case studies in this book analyze the following: cohesion, distance, density, fragmentation, form, and centrality. Cohesion, as noted above, refers to the network's connectedness—that is, the degree to which its nodes are interconnected. At this level of analysis, researchers measure properties such as the distance between nodes, network density, and the degree of centrality and fragmentation.

Figure 3.2 illustrates some of these measures. The distance (also known as geodesic distance) between two points is the number of lines that make up the shortest path connecting them. This measure enables researchers to establish the number of nodes through which an actor, a resource, and an order or a message must pass in order to reach its potential destination. A path is a sequence of lines or walks that connects different points and lines without repeating any. In figure 3.2, points A and C are directly connected by the AC path and indirectly connected by paths ABC and ADC.

Density is the number of lines in a figure, measured as the share of the highest possible number of lines. This measure enables researchers to estimate how close or how far a network is from the complete interconnection of its nodes (Scott 2000). Figure 3.2 has five lines, but it could have six if a line directly connected D to B. Consequently, the figure's density is 0.83, equivalent to 5/6.

FIGURE 3.2: **Density and Distance of a Network**

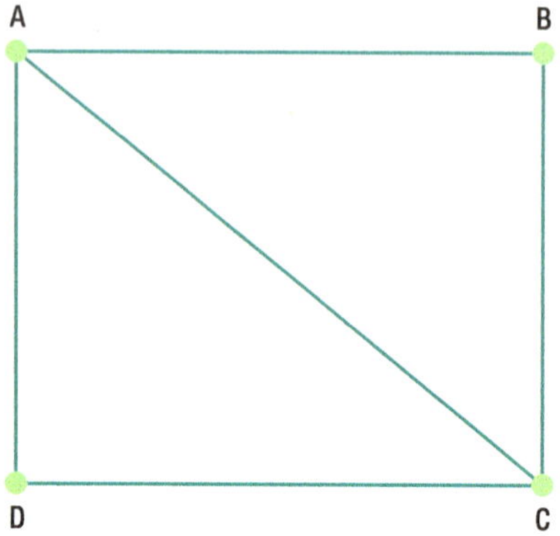

Source: Original figure for this publication.

The fragmentation of a network, in turn, is the share of pairs of nodes that are not tied to each other or through others. In figure 3.2, if D and C were not tied to B and A, then the network would be fragmented.

The study of distance is crucial for the analytical contribution of SNA. Members of weakly connected networks—because of the number or intensity of ties or the distance among those ties—are less likely to act in solidarity with other actors in the network, or will react more slowly to outside stimuli, than members of densely connected networks. Distance is also a key to evaluate the effects of exchanges within networks: short paths allow for quicker, more effective exchanges.

In turn, the study of network forms deals with the distribution of ties within the network, and it measures aspects such as cores and peripheries, or the presence of significant subgroups. In the visual analysis of networks, the identification of cores and peripheries is essential. Graph theory conceives of networks as structures in which two classes of nodes can be distinguished: (1) the core, made up of actors that form a cohesive group and are densely tied to each other, and (2) the periphery, made up of actors not densely tied to the cohesive group (Borgatti and Everett 1999). Whatever the relational content linking the actors in the networks, it flows more intensely within the core, and only reaches the periphery through nodes and bridges—probably cutpoints—that may connect peripheral actors by way of cliques. Consequently, it is also important to identify cliques and determine their size and location. Networks with small cores would operate in a hierarchical way, whereas those without cores would operate in a decentralized and possibly fragmented way. Networks with a large number of cliques—particularly if the cliques are small—would limit and encapsulate the flow of relational contents, thus generating low connectedness and contributing to hierarchical coordination. The empirical studies in this book locate cores, peripheries, and cliques in all the networks under study, and show how these structures condition the circulation of ideas, information, resources, and power among members.

The concept of centrality identifies the most important actors in a network. The notion of importance naturally varies across research topics and, hence, across the web of social relations that constitute the relevant networks. As a rule, however, centrality is structurally defined as the position of an actor within a network and can be determined using four measures: degree, betweenness, closeness, and eigenvector centrality.

In general, for undirected graphs, the degree centrality of a node or actor is defined by the number of ties. A node is central if it is tied to a high number of nodes within the network. In directed graphs, however, a distinction is made between the nodes to which the higher number of ties is directed (in-degree) and the nodes from which the higher number of ties emerge (out-degree), which makes it possible to measure two types of centrality: inward and outward centrality. Degree centrality allows for the comparison of nodes within and across networks—the latter by normalizing centrality as the share of nodes that are adjacent to a given node.

An actor's degree centrality is considered an indicator of its connectedness, and therefore of its influence on other actors and the opportunities to be influenced by them. In practice, an actor's centrality can be useful for determining its importance for the diffusion of relational contents within an organization, or for pondering the effect of its absence on institutional or organizational stability.

Betweenness centrality measures the degree to which a node is located between the other nodes in a network graph—that is, the degree to which a node plays the part of a broker or a gatekeeper in the network's operation. Betweenness centrality is defined as the ratio between the number of geodesic distances that pass through a given node and the total number of geodesic distances that actually exist within the network. For comparative purposes, it is rendered through an index, whose maximum value is 1. Betweenness can also serve to identify cutpoints. Consequently, this measure can be interpreted as an indicator not only of the level of interpersonal relations of any actor but also of that actor's power, particularly if research focuses on the flow of authority or resources.

Closeness centrality measures how close an actor is to the other actors within a network. Actors are central if they are close to the others, because they can quickly interact with them. Closeness centrality is defined as the average distance of all geodesic distances from one node to the rest. For comparative purposes, it is also standardized through an index that takes the value of 1 when the actor is adjacent to all the other actors. This value can also be calculated for subgroups or groups of actors. Closeness centrality helps to determine which nodes have easier access to the rest of the actors within a network. This knowledge is particularly useful when the topics of research are the diffusion of innovation, the access and dissemination of information, or, in the health policy area, the transmission of infectious diseases (Wasserman and Faust 1994).

Eigenvector centrality measures the influence of a node over the other nodes in a network. Each node can be a vector of influence insofar as it transmits information, resources, orders, diseases, and so on to other nodes. A node has eigenvector centrality when it operates as the origin of a chain of influences that circulates within a network. The eigenvector centrality of a node is proportional to the sum of the eigenvector centralities of all the nodes directly connected to it. A node with high eigenvector centrality is tied to other nodes with similar centrality. In practice, this measure may indicate the popularity rank of an actor on the basis of the number of relations established within a network, as well as the actor's risk position and the subsequent risk for the actor's contacts. Its visual representation requires the use of directed lines.

The case studies in this book use the different centrality measures to establish which actors are central to social policy making and in what ways. Given that these measures capture different aspects of centrality, scores may differ across measures for any given actor. Consistent scores across measures indicate that nodes are central to the network for connectedness, distance, and influence; different scores, in contrast, indicate that nodes are more central in one or another of those dimensions. These scores may also matter when comparing networks concerned with different relational contents: the same actor may be central in many networks but in different dimensions of centrality across networks.

Research Design

The aim of our SNAs of social policy making in this book is twofold. On the one hand, we intend to describe the networks of actors involved in social policy-making processes. On the other hand, we purport to use the network data to shed light on the workings and political economy of those processes. For these purposes, our research design must solve in the clearest and most consistent way possible two fundamental methodological issues: the selection of the population to be investigated and the sampling of that population. Selecting the population requires solving the boundary problem. Sampling the population requires solving endogeneity problems in the construction of the sample and the selection of collection techniques.

Marsden (2005) identifies three strategies for establishing social network boundaries: positional, event-based, and relational. The positional strategy resorts to actors' formal characteristics and membership criteria, such as employment in specific organizations; the event-based strategy uses the active presence of actors in events, such as board meetings, parties, or clubs; and the relational strategy is based upon the connections that actors themselves declare to have with each other. Each boundary specification strategy focuses on a different dimension of social network membership: formal participation, actual presence, and interpersonal recognition of the latter.

The social networks we study involve all these dimensions. Because they emerge within and around public policy-making processes, they inevitably include actors formally mandated to participate—that is, public officials and even societal actors in countries where stakeholder consultation is mandatory. The nature of the policies formulated within these processes involves societal actors, so many of these actors may not be formally mandated but contingent—albeit regular—participants. Because these processes occur regularly and require frequent contact among actors, consistent relations among them may emerge.

The previous discussion suggests that the issue of selecting the population for our case studies should be solved by combining all boundary specification strategies. That combination is more feasible for smaller networks such as ours may turn out to be. In large networks, it is extremely costly—in both time and resources—to interview all the potentially relevant actors in order to determine whether they must be included or excluded from the network. Consequently, we decided to combine boundary specification strategies in order to construct a sample of the population.

To this end, we employed a variant of the snowball sampling procedures that allowed for characterizing and carving out a representative set of the population without incurring endogeneity problems that might invalidate the use of relational data to make inferences about the case. Following Marsden (2005), we began by building an initial list of informants to interview inspired by our own research question—that is, who decides on social policy? Three criteria were combined to define this list: the selection of the ministries in charge of social policies; the inclusion of all the actors indicated as participants in the process according to the formal institutional design of the social policy formulation process as described above; and the inclusion of all permanent secretaries, directors, and other senior officials in charge of supporting policy formulation. The choice of these criteria was motivated by their objectivity: the ministries in charge of social policies were selected following the standards of the academic literature; the formal institutional design is the one by which the countries under study organize their social policy-making process; and the formal organization of the ministries, also defined by governments, identifies the units with the mandate to support policy formulation.

Per the first criterion, the sample included the ministries of health, education, social development, and labor because these areas are regularly considered in the literature as social policy areas (Esping-Andersen 1990; Mares 2003) and enjoy ministerial status in Argentina, The Bahamas, Bolivia, and Trinidad and Tobago. Per the second criterion, the sample included two other types of agencies: the ministry of finance and the center of government—that is, the offices tasked with directly assisting the head of government: the cabinet chief's office in Argentina; the Vice Presidency and the Ministry of the Presidency in Bolivia; and the prime minister's and cabinet offices in the Caribbean countries. Per the third criterion, the sample included the legal counsel services, secretaries, and undersecretaries at all the aforementioned ministries. This sample was subsequently increased following the snowballing technique until it reached the whole networks specified in the next chapters. This list constituted the basis for both sampling and identifying relevant information. To the actors in this list, we administered a questionnaire (see appendix B) that includes both name-generator questions, which enable researchers to identify the actors to which interviewees are tied, and name-interpreter questions, which help researchers gain information about the relations among those actors (Burt 1984).

Name-generator questions help researchers find out with whom the actors maintain specific types of relations: with whom they discuss important matters, whom they feel close to, with whom they are friends, and so on. These questions make it possible to preliminarily specify the boundaries of the population, which would be constituted by the nodes identified by the actors themselves.

Name-interpreter questions, in turn, serve to find out the specific nature of the relations that bind actors: their intensity, frequency, and hierarchy. These questions allow for cross-checking the information from the name-generator questions—for example, to discard certain nodes from a network because of the low intensity of their interactions with interviewees. This information provides foundations for constructing population samples focused on the presence or absence of specific types of relations—such as a sample of all the most proximate associates of each actor, or of all the actors with whom a person discusses important matters.

The answers to the name-generator questions were used to map the whole network of the social policy formulation process, and the answers to the name-interpreter questions to map the specific networks for four relational contents: ideas, information, resources, and power. Ideas refer to any concept or design of any social policy initiative. Information is defined as any data about the population, its living conditions, demands, or aspirations, and about the activities carried out by state units or nonstate actors. Resources are defined as money and any other form of material aid, such as the provision of logistics, tools, and human resources for targeting policies. Power is conceived as a social relation characterized by the probability of a person imposing his or her will against the resistance of others; therefore, a political relationship exists when certain actors recognize the legitimacy of others to impose their will upon them (Weber 1992).

The network maps were then analyzed using the VisuaLyzer software to determine their density, cohesion, distance, fragmentation, and centrality measures; establish their cores and peripheries; and identify their cutpoints, clusters, and cliques. These measures were subsequently employed to compare the actual networks to the formal structure of the policy-making process.

The case studies presented in the subsequent chapters provide examples of both the potential and the limitations of SNA as a methodological tool for understanding social policy making and its political economy. The case studies were not designed as parts of a regional study, nor do they strive to represent regional or subregional tendencies. Their aim is specifically to illustrate the workings of this methodology and its usefulness for studying the formulation of social policies at the central government level. Chapters 7 and 8 return to the findings of the case studies in order to reflect on the possibilities and limitations of SNA for the study and practice of the political economy of social policy.

References

Borgatti, S. P., and M. G. Everett. 1999. "Models of Core/Periphery Structures." *Social Networks* 21 (4): 375–95.

Burt, R. S. 1984. "Network Items and the General Social Survey." *Social Networks* 6 (4): 293–339.

Esping-Andersen, G. 1990. *The Three Worlds of Welfare Capitalism*. Princeton: Princeton University Press.

Everett, M. G. 1982. "A Graph Theoretic Blocking Procedure for Social Networks." *Social Networks* 4 (2): 147–67.

Hage, P., and F. Harary. 1983. *Structural Models in Anthropology*. Cambridge: Cambridge University Press.

Knoke, D., and J.H. Kuklinski. 1982. *Network Analysis*. Beverly Hills: SAGE.

Mares, I. 2003. *The Politics of Social Risk: Business and Welfare State Development*. New York: Cambridge University Press.

Marsden, P. 2005. "Recent Developments in Network Measurement." In *Models and Methods in Social Network Analysis*, edited by P. Carrington, J. Scott, and S. Wasserman. Cambridge: Cambridge University Press.

Scott, J. C. 2000. *Social Network Analysis: A Handbook* (Second Edition). London: SAGE.

Wasserman, S., and K. Faust. 1994. *Social Network Analysis: Methods and Applications*. Cambridge: Cambridge University Press.

Weber, M. 1992. *Economía y Sociedad*. México: Fondo de Cultura Económica.

4

Who Decides Social Policy in Argentina? A Social Network Analysis

Between June 18 and August 23, 2018, during the interviews with policy makers and societal actors that constituted the main input for this case study, Argentina entered yet another macroeconomic crisis triggered by negative external shocks on its exports and the cost of refinancing its foreign debt. While senior policy makers in the Ministry of Education (MINED), Ministry of Health (MINSAL), Ministry of Labor (MINTRAB), and Ministry of Social Development (MDS), struggled to carry on with their jobs, and kindly found time for interviews, the government was preparing a fiscal adjustment package to tackle the crisis. A week after we finished our interviews, the package was launched. It included the elimination of MINSAL, which was downgraded to State Secretary, and of several secretary and undersecretary positions throughout the government, and a cabinet reshuffling that ended the term in office of many of our previous interviewees—who had held their positions for over two and a half years. This was hardly the first time the Argentine national bureaucracy underwent such an adjustment: the same measures had been adopted by President Carlos Menem in 1990 and 1996, and by President Fernando de la Rúa in 2001. Those earlier measures had led, as did the September 2018 package, not only to the forced resignation of officials who had acquired significant job experience but also to the interruption of policy programs.

Using a social network analysis of how ideas, information, resources, and power circulate in the social policy formulation process, this chapter explores who decides on social policy formulation in Argentina during the presidency of Mauricio Macri. Argentina was an early developer of welfare policies in the region and is considered a high-welfare-effort country in terms of the share of its gross domestic product allocated

This chapter is coauthored with Mariano Tommasi.

to welfare policies (Segura-Ubiergo 2007). Given this trajectory, and several features of the formal structure of the country's policy-making environment, social policy formulation could be expected to develop as a hierarchical process, politically coordinated by the PTE and technically informed and advised by the social area ministries. But the instability of both political regimes and governments and the volatility of public policies previously identified in the literature on Argentine policy making could indicate a more decentralized and poorly coordinated process in which the input of more stable societal actors may be as influential as, if not more influential than, those of unstable public bureaucracies. The findings of our study suggest the latter to be the case.

The Formal Social Policy Formulation Process

The institutional setting of policy-making processes in Argentina is characterized by three main features: a presidential regime of government, a federal structure of the state, and a fragmented bureaucracy.[1] Argentina's National Constitution establishes a presidential regime in which both legislative initiative and lawmaking are shared between the executive and Congress. Congress, made up of a Chamber of Deputies elected by proportional representation and a Senate elected by majority-minority first-past-the-post, may initiate legislation on any topic except the budget. The executive, directly elected in single-district contests with runoff, has not only unrestricted legislative initiative but also total and partial veto of any bill passed by Congress, and discretional legislative decree power on any topic except tax, penal, electoral, and political party legislation (National Constitution, Articles 75 and 99). Thus, both the president and legislators may initiate policy, but legislators cannot enact policy without executive consent unless they can muster a two-thirds majority in both chambers of Congress to override a presidential veto (National Constitution, Article 83).

The Constitution defines the state as a federal republic and grants provincial governments all powers not explicitly conferred to the federal government (National Constitution, Articles 121, 126, and 127). The provinces have their own constitutions and elect their own governments in separate elections. Provincial governments are free to exercise their competences as defined previously, as well as to run any service or function decentralized to them by federal law. Per constitutional mandate, the federal government must assign the financial resources for provincial governments to provide whatever service or function is decentralized (National Constitution, Article 75, Clause 2). Therefore, provincial governments have both legislative initiative and ultimate authority over those policy areas that constitutional mandates or decentralization laws have placed under their jurisdiction. Neither the president nor Congress can unilaterally make policy in those areas.

Beyond the formal constitutional rules, previous scholarship has identified a number of operating features of the Argentine policy-making process.[2] Provincial governors are influential actors not only in provincial but also in national politics and policy making (Ardanaz, Leiras, and Tommasi 2014). Governors are often considered undisputed bosses of provincial-level party branches. In a decentralized party system, this influence makes them crucial actors in national politics because of, among other factors, the power that some governors have over the legislative contingent of their provinces in Congress, which rests on electoral control of legislators' political careers (Jones and Hwang 2005; Jones et al. 2002). Provinces are politically strong but fiscally weak (Ardanaz, Leiras, and Tommasi 2014; Benton 2009). Congress, however, is often considered a relatively weak link in the policy-making process (Jones et al. 2002; Jones et al. 2007).[3] National executives tend to have some discretion in intergovernmental fiscal affairs (Bonvecchi and Lodola 2011), but they need votes in a Congress partly dominated by provincial cliques; this situation often leads to an exchange of federal monies to the provinces for votes in Congress (Bonvecchi and Zelaznik 2012; Gibson and Calvo 2000). The party system has experienced significant change in recent decades, as punctuated by the implosion of the two-party system in 2001, the transformation of the Peronist party into a clientelistic organization, and its recurrent division since the mid-2000s. To complete the picture, the Argentine judiciary has usually been considered a weak enforcer, lacking independence relative to the executive, at least when the latter was electorally strong (Bill Chavez, Ferejohn, and Weingast 2011; Helmke 2002, 2005; Iaryczower, Spiller, and Tommasi 2002).

In addition, studies on public administration have usually underlined the weakness, lack of autonomy, high politicization, and low performance of Argentine state bureaucracies (Iacoviello, Zuvanic, and Tommasi 2003; Oszlak 1999; Scherlis 2009; Spiller and Tommasi 2007).[4] Argentina lacks a professional civil service. The federal bureaucracy is divided between permanent officials—typically leftovers from previous administrations, who populate low to senior nonpolitical positions and who got those positions through political loyalty—and political appointees of incumbent governments—who typically fill both top management positions and lower posts, and may be key to obtaining information or supervising the workings of agencies (Spiller and Tommasi 2007). This fault line generally results in conflicts between political appointees eager to design and promote their government's initiatives and permanent officials either discouraging those initiatives or becoming distrusted and excluded from policy-making processes if they do not collaborate with appointees. The federal bureaucracy typically clashes with provincial bureaucracies, where the previously described fault line is generally more acute. Consequently, appointees at the federal or provincial levels are typically the sources of policy initiatives, permanent officials at both levels produce and (decide how to) circulate information, and intergovernmental policy processes are conflictive.

The formal social policy formulation process in Argentina partially varies from these patterns depending on whether the social policy function is under federal government jurisdiction or has been decentralized to provincial governments. Of the four social policy areas analyzed in this book, labor and social assistance policies are mostly under federal jurisdiction, whereas health and education policies are decentralized to provincial governments.

Social policy formulation processes share four sources of initiatives regardless of their jurisdiction: the area ministries, the president, the office of the Chief of Cabinet (Jefatura de Gabinete de Ministros [JGM]), and Congress. The area ministries are typically the main source, because they are empowered as either policy makers—for the centralized functions—or regulators—for the decentralized ones. Secretaries and undersecretaries in the area ministries draft bills and decrees, which are then reviewed by the legal services within their ministries and eventually sanctioned by ministers, who in turn send them to the presidency's legal secretary, the JGM, and the president for approval. The president's office may also initiate policy by proposing ideas for the area ministries to develop. The JGM may proceed the same way as the president or, alternatively, set up interministerial committees—which have typically been labeled social cabinets[5]—for area ministries to come up with policies on issues that cut across their respective jurisdictions. Upon receiving any initiative from any of these sources, the president has full discretion either to approve it—and send it to Congress as a bill or legislative decree, or publish it in the Official Bulletin as a regulatory decree or resolution—or to refer it back to the drafting ministries or the Social Cabinet for further discussion and amendment. The only requirement, apart from review by the legal secretary, when expenditure is involved, is clearance by the MINH/Treasury Ministry particularly by the treasury secretary, who manages the federal government's budgetary and financial system (National Constitution, Articles 75 to 83 and 99; Law 19,549 of Administrative Procedure; Law 24,156 of Financial Administration).

Congress may also initiate policy, either by drafting bills and discussing their contents with area ministries, the JGM, or the president, or by proposing and passing bills that would subsequently be sent to the executive for ratification and implementation. In turn, the executive may totally or partially veto any bill and set policy by decree on any social policy issue. Policy making in Congress typically involves the area committees' chairpersons, who set the agenda for committee work and operate as gatekeepers for the floor agenda insofar as they can be overruled only by discharge motions from the floor, which require a qualified majority for approval (Calvo 2014). Both the Senate and the Chamber have committees specialized in each of the four social policy areas: labor, health, education, and social assistance. Once bills have been reported from committee, they are placed on the agenda only if approved by the Parliamentary Labor Commission, the floor's agenda setter, which is made up of all parliamentary group leaders including the leader of the majority party/coalition or, if no majority exists, the first two or three plurality parties (Calvo 2014).

For decentralized social policy functions, provincial governments may also be policy initiators, and their opinion and agreement must be obtained for any decision. They participate in the process through two intergovernmental bodies—the Federal Health Council (COFESA) and the Federal Education Council (CFED)—whose membership consists of the respective area ministers from each of the provinces. Consultation and consensus in COFESA is required for general regulations concerning the nature of health care programs, the extent of their coverage, the monitoring of performance, and the specifics of any type of federal financing. CFED must set national mandatory curricula, performance evaluation criteria, wage bargaining guidelines, and conditions for any type of intergovernmental transfer specifically assigned to provincial education systems. Consequently, initiatives on any of these matters may originate in either provincial governments or the federal government, but regardless of their origin must be debated and approved by provincial governments through the federal councils (see Laws 22,047; 24,195; and 26,206 for CFED and Law 22,373 and Resolution 269/2003 for COFESA).

Formal rules only partially regulate how the actors participate in policy-making processes. For centralized policy functions, the Law of Administrative Procedure (Law 19,549), which specifies how the federal government works, merely states concerning decision-making procedures that the president will settle jurisdictional disputes among ministers (Article 4), and that the administration's legal counsel must be consulted when decisions may affect the rights or interests of third parties (Article 7). This law's regulatory decree (Decree 1883/1991) adds that any issue requiring the participation of more than one administrative unit must be dealt with simultaneously by all units involved (Article 18). No rules specify, however, how this simultaneous involvement in policy making should proceed, how the cabinet operates as a collective body, or how the president is to settle disputes among ministers. For decentralized policy functions, the laws that regulate how CFED works (Laws 22,047; 24,195; and 26,206) stipulate only that decisions are made by plurality in sessions with a quorum consisting of a majority of members; Law 22,373, which created COFESA, makes no mention of decision-making rules at all.

The formal structure of the social policy formulation process in Argentina leads to several expectations about its actual operation. First, it suggests that the main sources of policy ideas would be the area ministers and top political appointees (secretaries and undersecretaries) and the provincial governments, particularly for decentralized functions. Second, it suggests that the main sources of information for policy formulation would be the permanent officials from lower-level intraministerial units of the federal and provincial governments, the legal counsel offices at the area ministries, the social area ministers, and the provincial authorities that make up COFESA and CFED. The MINH/Treasury Ministry and the JGM would be the main providers of resources, whereas the other actors would be merely recipients. Finally, the president, the JGM, and the provincial governments would be the most powerful actors in the network, likely followed by the area ministries, and—last—congressional leaders.

In addition to these expectations emerging from the formal rules, the scarce literature on the actual operation of social policy making in Argentina suggests the following: uneven organizational and technical capabilities within the federal government, particularly benefiting the expertise of the National Social Security Administration (ANSES) and the labor ministry compared to the other social area ministries; absence of a coordination entity with an integral approach to social policy to ensure a strategic orientation and management; preeminence of the federal executive over subnational levels of government; and changing roles for the private sector, unions, nongovernmental organizations (NGOs), and international organizations, contingent upon the political orientation of the federal government (Repetto 2014).

All in all, then, the formal rules suggest that the core actors in the social policy formulation networks would be the social area ministries and secretaries for ideas and information, the MINH/Treasury Ministry and the JGM for economic resources, and the president, the JGM, and the provincial governments for political power. These core actors should be in hierarchically superior positions as measured by network centrality indicators. In contrast, extragovernmental actors would be in the networks' peripheries. The networks should be denser for the decentralized than for the centralized functions, because decentralized functions involve more actors at the subnational level.

Figure 4.1 depicts the network of social policy formulation processes as emergent from the above description. The lines represent the relational contents of the links among the actors: red lines represent political power; orange lines, ideas and information; and green lines, economic resources. The absence of links between the extragovernmental actors—that is, the private sector, unions, NGOs, and international organizations—is not intended to convey the absence of relational contents, but merely shows their indeterminacy as emergent from the formal structure of the policy-making process. Because the involvement of legislators,

FIGURE 4.1: **The Formal Network of Social Policy Formulation, Argentina**

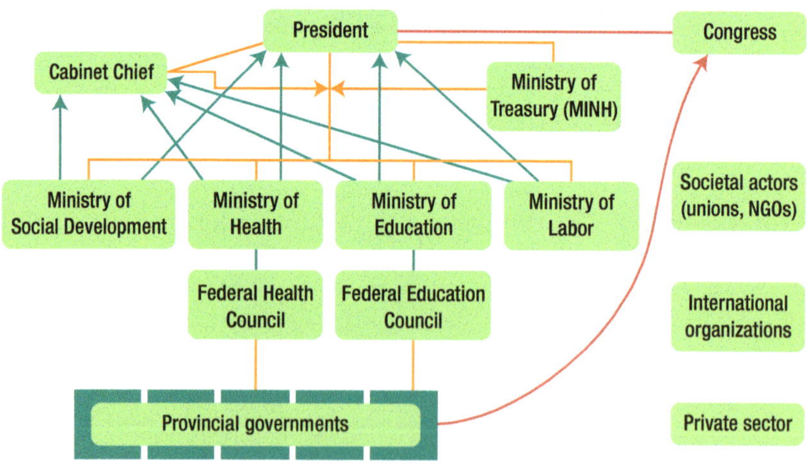

Sources: National Constitution of Argentina, Laws of Administrative Procedure and Financial Administration, and organic legislation for the Federal Health Council and the Federal Education Council.
Note: Red lines represent political power, orange lines represent ideas and information, and green lines represent economic resources. NGOs = nongovernmental organizations.

secretaries, and undersecretaries is contingent to the issue at hand, and that of provincial authorities would be typically restricted to the decentralized functions, the number of actors in the social policy formulation network would range between 8 and 91: 8 if only one minister and secretary are involved, including the ministerial legal counsel, the finance minister, the treasury secretary and legal counsel, the presidency's legal secretary, and the president; and 91 if the issue involves all area ministries, COFESA and CFED, all relevant congressional committee chairpersons, the parliamentary leaders of three plurality parties per chamber, the JGM, and the president's office.

Social network analyses were performed to determine the extent to which the actual social policy formulation process conforms to the formal structure of the policy-making process. Following the research design outlined in the previous chapter, snowball sampling was used to specify the network boundaries: the initial sample of policy makers included the top-tier officials in the social area ministries (MDS, MINED, MINSAL, and MINTRAB) who were interviewed between May and June 2018 using a questionnaire that contained name-generator questions aimed at identifying the actors and administrative units with which the interviewees typically interact in the social policy formulation process (see appendix B). Then, using the same questionnaire, those actors absent from the initial sample but mentioned by at least 75 percent of the initial interviewees were interviewed until no new actors were mentioned. The complete list of identified actors and their acronyms is included in appendix A.[6]

In total, 69 percent of the initial sample was available for interview, and their responses yielded a network of 130 members. The average tenure of the social area officials interviewed was two and a half years; only 33 percent of them had previous experience in public service, and only 15 percent had more than 10 years' experience. These data are consistent with the turnover patterns of the Argentine bureaucracy and indicate that most of these officials were political appointees.

The interviews also included name-interpreter questions to determine the content of the relations that each interviewee had with the actors he or she mentioned in response to the name-generator questions. Therefore, the answers to the name-generator questions were used to map the network of the social policy formulation process and the answers to the name-interpreter questions to map the networks specific to the four relational contents of interest for our research: ideas, information, resources, and power.

The network maps were then analyzed using the VisuaLyzer software to determine their density, cohesion, and centrality measures; establish their cores and peripheries; and identify their cutpoints, clusters, and cliques. These measures were subsequently employed to compare the actual networks to the formal structure of the policy-making process. The following sections present and discuss the network maps, focusing on each specific relational content.

The Whole Network of Social Policy Formulation in Argentina

This section presents the map of the whole network of actors that, according to interviewees, participate in social policy formulation processes in Argentina. This map includes all connections among all the actors named by the interviewees, regardless of the relational contents of those connections. The graph is undirected, which means it does not depict any particular node (actor) as the source or the recipient of any particular relational content. The size and color of the nodes are uniform, again, in order to avoid depicting any type of hierarchy among actors. Consequently, the map constitutes a neutral depiction of the network of actors involved in social policy formulation.

Figure 4.2 shows that the whole network of social policy formulation in Argentina is a connected network, with no isolated components. It is also, however, a low-density

FIGURE 4.2: **Whole Network of Social Policy Formulation, Argentina**

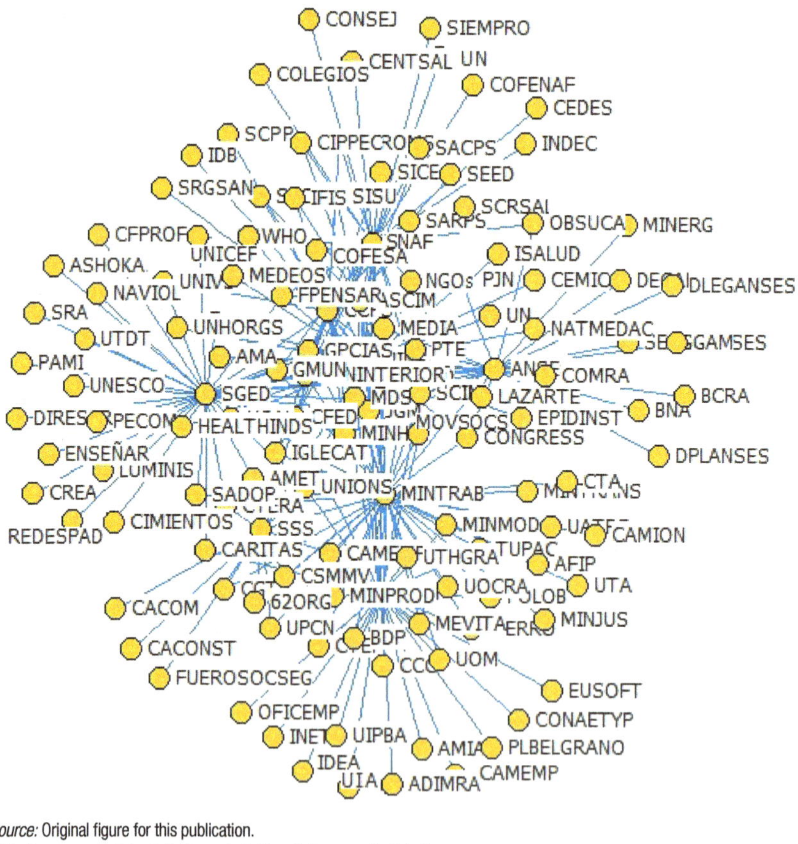

Source: Original figure for this publication.
Note: See appendix A for definitions of all abbreviations used in this figure.

network, with a 0.0302 value, which indicates that only a few of the possible links among its nodes have actually emerged. Consistent with this low density, nodes and ties in this network are located at an average geodesic distance of 2.6, which indicates that, on average, any given actor must go through more than two and a half other actors to contact any other actor in the network. These traits suggest that some of the relational contents linking the actors in this network may be creating either a hierarchical or a fragmented structure that prevents the emergence of other theoretically possible ties. In the same vein, they also suggest the policies generated by this network may not be coherent and coordinated, stable, or adaptable: low density and connectedness would typically preclude the fluidity and frequency of links that facilitate coordination, stability, and adaptability of policies.

The whole network of social policy formulation in Argentina presents two main features that distinguish it from the formal policy-making network. The first is the number of network actors: 130, compared to a minimum of 8 and a theoretical maximum of 91. The difference in the number of network members is explained by the presence of (1) societal stakeholders such as unions, business associations, NGOs, and social movements; (2) multilateral actors, such as the United Nations (UN), the Inter-American Development Bank (IDB), and the United Nations Children's Fund (UNICEF); and (3) other government agencies with information or resources that social area ministries require to formulate and implement their policies, such as the Ministry of the Interior (MININTERIOR) and the National Institute of Statistics and Census (INDEC).

The second difference between the whole network of social policy formulation and the formal policy-making network is the absence of a core. Although the formal structure of the policy-making network suggested the president and the JGM would be central actors because of their political power, the MINH/Treasury Ministry because of its control over resources, and the social area ministries because of their technical capacity, the actual network has no core; therefore, none of these actors is at its heart. The absence of a core may be explained by the relatively low centrality scores of the aforementioned actors. Even though all of them have degree and closeness centrality scores higher than the network averages, the scores are below 41 percent for degree centrality and below 61 percent for closeness centrality.

In turn, the relatively low centrality scores of the theoretically more central actors may be explained by the fragmentation of hierarchy that is typical of administrative delegation: when government or agency leaders delegate to others below their hierarchical status, they effectively reduce their interaction with the rest of the network and may eventually limit it to the top managers; these managers increase their interaction only with the actors located within their designated area. In this network of fragmented hierarchies, some ministers and secretaries are more central than the president and the JGM, some secretaries are more central than ministers, and none is central enough to structure the whole network around it.

In addition, this network displays two notable traits. First, all the cutpoints in the network are government actors: MINTRAB and MINSAL; the Secretary for Education Management (SGED), the Secretary for Employment (SEMP), the Secretary for Social Security (SSS) and the Secretary for Childhood, Adolescence, and Family (SNAF); and the president of the National Council for Social Policy Coordination (CNCPS). Considering the formal network structure, it is unlikely that the actual network would become disconnected by the severance of any of these points. Second, the number of cliques within the network is relatively high: 75 of 235 links. Thus, 29 percent of the actors in the network are highly connected and cohesively linked in ways that are distinct from those that connect the rest of the network participants. To determine how these distinct links affect the social policy formulation process, it is necessary to disaggregate the whole network according to the different relational contents reported by the actors.

The Network of Ideas

This section presents and discusses the network map for the circulation of ideas in the social policy formulation process of Argentina. The green nodes in figure 4.3 indicate that those actors are net producers of ideas within the network, that is, they provide more ideas to more actors than they receive. The red nodes, on the contrary, indicate that the actors are net recipients of ideas; they receive more ideas from actors than they provide. The yellow nodes indicate that the actors in question provide and receive ideas from the same number of actors. The size of the nodes conveys the extent of their provision or reception of ideas: the higher the number of links that provide or receive ideas, the larger the node.

The ideas network in Argentina is a connected, low-density network with a 0.0486 value and only 236 ties among 99 nodes. Consistent with the structure of the whole network, the average geodesic distance in the ideas network is 2.7914. Contrary to the expectations from both the formal structure of the policy-making process and the structure of the whole network, the ideas network in Argentina is open, fragmented, and not particularly hierarchical.

The network is considered open because government actors are neither the only nor the main participants in the network. Federal, provincial, and municipal government actors, including the federal councils for decentralized social policy functions, the judiciary, and Congress, account for only 43 percent of the network membership whereas the rest are private sector or multilateral actors. In addition, 46 percent of the government actors that participate in the network are either net recipients of ideas or as much recipients as providers, because they receive ideas from extragovernmental actors. Thus, although government actors are net recipients of ideas, the extragovernmental actors are both more numerous in the network and constitute most of the net providers of ideas. This finding suggests that, in contrast with a simplistic reading of the formal policy-making structure, social policies in Argentina are nurtured by extragovernmental as much as by governmental actors.

The ideas network in the social policy formulation process is fragmented both across and within policy areas. Both patterns can be appreciated through the network's cutpoints. On the one hand, the eight cutpoints themselves cut across and within social policy areas: SSS and SEMP fall within MINTRAB's jurisdiction; ANSES is located between MINTRAB and MDS; MINSAL itself is another cutpoint; SNAF is placed under MDS; SGED is within MINED; and the Adviser to the Secretary for Interministerial Coordination (ASCIM) and CNCPS are located within the JGM's office. On the other hand, these cutpoints are the nodes by which 63 of the 99 network members are connected to the network structure: MINSAL connects 14 actors, SEMP 21, ANSES 7, SSS and CNCPS 6 each, SGED 5, SNAF 3, and ASCIM 1. Moreover, as figure 4.3 shows, the connections between these cutpoints and the actors they bring into the network are dyadic. Consequently, none of the actors connected via these cutpoints is directly linked to those connected via the other cutpoints, and the network itself is fragmented into eight parts. This fragmentation implies

FIGURE 4.3: **Network of Ideas in the Social Policy Formulation Process, Argentina**

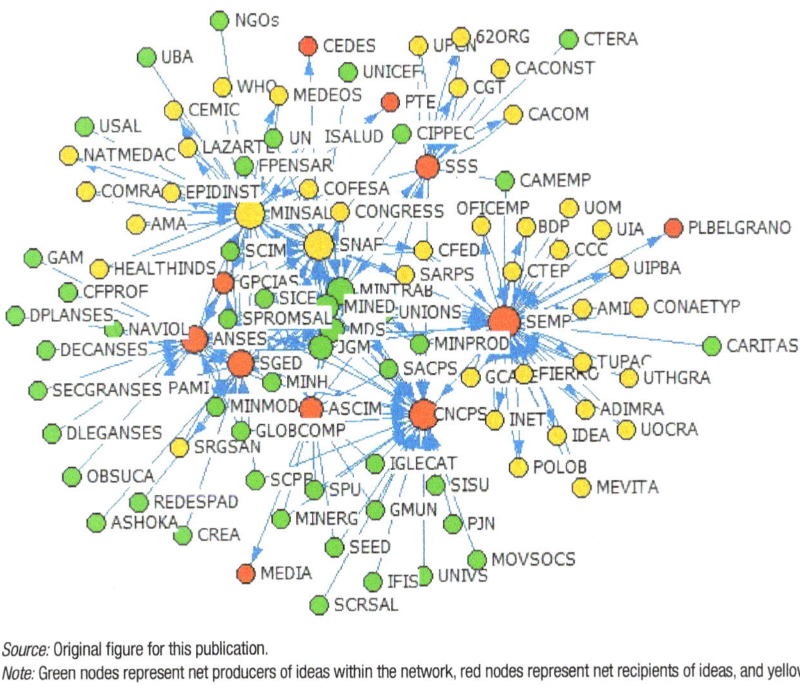

Source: Original figure for this publication.

Note: Green nodes represent net producers of ideas within the network, red nodes represent net recipients of ideas, and yellow nodes represent actors that both provide and receive ideas from the same number of actors. The size of the nodes conveys the extent of their provision or reception of ideas: the higher the number of links that provide or receive ideas, the larger the node. See appendix A for definitions of all abbreviations used in this figure.

that ideas circulate mainly in dyads within each of the network fragments and are communicated to the remaining 33 network members only indirectly through the cutpoints. The circulation of ideas is thus fragmented within and across policy areas.

The network of ideas in the Argentine social policy formulation process is not particularly hierarchical for two reasons. First, consistent with the whole network's structure, the network of ideas lacks a core: no network member is central enough, either as a provider or a recipient of ideas, to organize the network around it. The highest network degree centrality score is 56.1 percent for SEMP, but this actor is linked to only 21 of 98 remaining nodes, so it is neither close to nor between enough actors to make it the core of the network. In addition, only 16 of 99 members have scores above average. The combination of an empty core and a majority of nodes with below average centrality means that no actor attains hierarchy.

The other reason this network is not particularly hierarchical is that the actors with highest centrality scores are either net recipients of ideas or mostly connected among themselves rather than to the rest of the network's members. The former is the case with ANSES, ASCIM, CNCPS, SEMP, SGED, SSS, and the provincial governments (GPCIAS). The latter is the case with the JGM, MDS, MINED, MINH, the Ministry of Production (MINPROD), and MINTRAB. By operating as net recipients of ideas, or by linking dominantly with actors of their own formal hierarchical status, these agencies effectively do not act as vectors for the circulation of ideas within the network.

All in all, then, contrary to expectations, ideas in the Argentine social policy formulation process do not seem to come either from the second and third lines of technical agencies within social policy areas or from the top political authorities. Instead, ideas come from the societal actors to which social policy area units are directly linked. The circulation of ideas is encapsulated within the network's fragments and not prompted by any actor in a formal or informal hierarchical position to coordinate it. Ideas thus seem to flow within policy (sub)areas, but only in a limited fashion across areas by way of the cutpoints or the social area ministers. This network structure diminishes the likelihood that the social policy–making process will generate adaptable, coherent, and coordinated policies.

The Network of Information

This section presents and discusses the network map for the circulation of information in the social policy formulation process in Argentina. In figure 4.4, the green nodes represent actors who are net producers of information within the network; the number of actors to whom they provide information is greater than that from whom they receive information. The red nodes, on the contrary, indicate actors who are net recipients of information; more actors provide them with information than receive it. The yellow nodes indicate actors who provide to and receive information from the same number of actors. The size of the nodes conveys the extent of their provision or

FIGURE 4.4: **Information Network in the Argentine Social Policy Formulation Process**

Source: Original figure for this publication.
Note: Green nodes represent net producers of information within the network, red nodes represent net recipients of information, and yellow nodes represent actors that provide and receive information from the same number of actors. The size of the nodes conveys the extent of their provision or reception of information: the higher the number of links that provide or receive information, the larger the node. The light purple lines that encircle the graph indicate the clusters of nodes into which it can be divided. See appendix A for definitions of all abbreviations used in this figure.

reception of information: the higher the number of links that provide or receive information, the larger the node. The light purple lines that encircle the graph indicate the clusters of nodes into which it can be divided.

The information network in Argentina is a connected, low-density network with a 0.0299 value and only 196 ties among 115 nodes. The average geodesic distance—3.0371—is even larger than that of the whole network. Like the ideas network, however, this network is fragmented across and within policy areas, it is not particularly hierarchical, and the positions of the government actors are significantly different than those expected from the formal structure of the policy-making process.

The network's fragmentation can be observed through the cutpoints and clusters shown in figure 4.4. Almost the same cutpoints that divide the ideas network also fragment the information network: ANSES, CNCPS, MINSAL, SEMP, SGED, SNAF, SSS, and MINTRAB instead of ASCIM. As in the ideas network, these cutpoints cut across and within policy areas; in all they connect 61 percent of the actors to the network by way of dyadic links (compared to 63 percent in the ideas network). This means that information, as ideas, is mostly encapsulated within dyads and circulates to the remaining 36 network members only through the cutpoints.

The clusters in figure 4.4 show the information network is fragmented in halves; one half groups the actors connected to labor policy and the other brings together those connected to health, education, and social assistance policies. The labor policy cluster is structured around ANSES, MINTRAB, SEMP, and SSS; and it connects 57 actors that are typically main stakeholders in this policy area. These stakeholders are mostly unions such as the General Confederation of Workers (CGT) and the Metal Workers Union (UOM); the Union of Hotel and Restaurant Workers of the Argentine Republic (UTHGRA); the Association of Technical School Teachers (AMET), the Confederation of Education Workers of the Argentine Republic (CTERA), and the Union of Private Teachers (SADOP); social movements such as the Confederation of Popular Economy Workers (CTEP), the Evita Movement (MEVITA), and the Tupac Amaru Movement (TUPAC); and business associations such as the Association of Metal Industries of the Argentine Republic (ADIMRA) and the Argentine Industrial Union (UIA). The other multiarea cluster is structured around MINSAL, SNAF, and SNED. It links 58 highly diverse actors such as NGOs (the Association of Argentine Israelite Mutual Organizations [AMIA], the Ashoka Foundation [ASHOKA], and Caritas Argentina [CARITAS]); multilaterals (international finance institutions, the UN, and UNICEF), professional associations (the Argentine Medical Association [AMA], the Centre for Medical Research and Clinical Education [CEMIC], and the Institute for Epidemiology [EPIDINST]); and area-related governmental actors such as COFESA, MINED, MDS, the Secretary for Promotion of Health (SPROMSAL), and the Secretary for University Policy (SPU). The links within these clusters are, again, mostly dyadic, which helps explain both the low density and the fragmentation of the network.

Like the ideas network, the information network is not particularly hierarchical for two reasons: the absence of a core and the low centrality scores of network actors. The highest degree centrality score is 39.74 percent for MINTRAB, but that ministry is connected to only 45 actors, or 39 percent of the network. In addition, only 18 of 115 actors have centrality scores above average. Consequently, no actor is connected enough, and no group of actors is central enough, to hierarchically structure the network.

The positions of the government actors in this network differ from those expected from the formal policy-making structure. Whereas the formal process suggests that information comes mainly from secretaries and undersecretaries in the relevant area ministries, the actual network shows that only 42.8 percent (15 of 35) of the government actors in the network are subministerial units that operate as net providers of information. The rest of the government actors are, contrary to expectations, either net recipients of information or as much recipients as providers. In addition, and also contrary to expectations, 54.7 percent of the net providers of information in the network are nongovernmental actors.

These patterns suggest that information in the Argentine social policy formulation process, like ideas, comes from extragovernmental, rather than governmental, sources; is mostly encapsulated in dyadic links; and does not circulate hierarchically. Information seems to flow largely within policy-related clusters and to circulate across areas by way of actors with ministerial rank but who are not central enough to hierarchically organize information flows. Again, these structural characteristics of the information network reduce the likelihood that the social policy–making process will generate adaptable, coherent, and coordinated policies.

The Network of Resources

This section describes and compares the network maps for the circulation of resources in the social policy formulation processes of Argentina. The resources in question are monies, logistical assistance (for example, mobilization of an agency's human and budgetary resources to identify target beneficiaries of a program run by another agency), and nonmonetary forms of aid (for example, food, clothing, and so on). The green nodes in figure 4.5 indicate that the actors represented by them are net providers of resources within the network; red nodes indicate that the actors are net recipients of resources. The yellow nodes indicate that the actors provide to and receive resources from the same number of actors. The size of the nodes conveys the extent of their provision or reception of resources: the higher the number of links that provide or receive resources, the larger the node. The nodes inserted into squares constitute the core of the network, and the remaining nodes constitute its periphery.

The network of resources in the social policy formulation process in Argentina is a connected, low-density network with a 0.0773 value and only 80 ties among 46 nodes. The average geodesic distance—3.2019—is even higher than in the whole network. Its structure is partly consistent with theoretical expectations from the formal policy-making process: as expected, JGM and MINH are the most important net providers of resources, and most social area units are net recipients, but the network is, again, not hierarchical.

Consistent with the formal competences assigned to them by the Constitution and the Financial Administration Law, JGM and MINH are the most important net providers of resources in the network. The difference between their in- and out-degree centrality scores indicates the net number of ties that flow into or out of each node. These two actors have the highest net out-degree scores in the network; they provide

FIGURE 4.5: **Resources Network in the Argentine Social Policy Formulation Process**

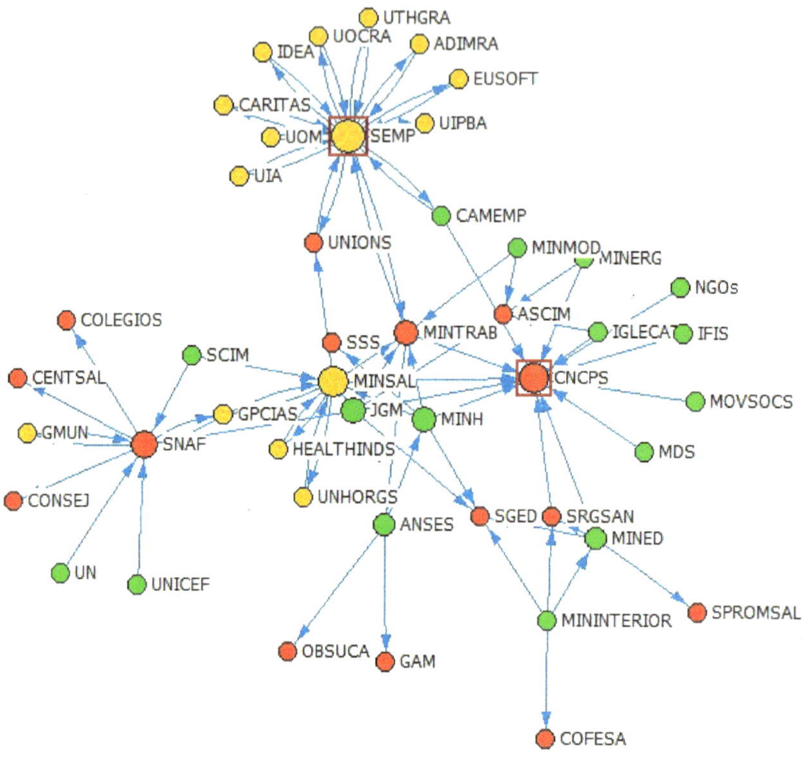

Source: Original figure for this publication.

Note: Green nodes represent net providers of resources within the network, red nodes indicate net recipients of resources, and yellow nodes indicate actors that provide to and receive resources from the same number of actors. The size of the nodes conveys the extent of their provision or reception of resources: the higher the number of links that provide or receive resources, the larger the node. The nodes in squares constitute the core of the network, and the remaining nodes constitute its periphery. See appendix A for definitions of all abbreviations used in this figure.

resources to six and five times more actors, respectively, than they receive resources from. As demonstrated in figure 4.5, however, neither JGM nor MINH has a hierarchical position in the network, which can be explained by three factors.

First, the most central actors in the network, including the core nodes, are either net recipients of resources, or as much recipients as providers, rather than net providers. The two core actors, SEMP and CNCPS, are also the most central in the network with 53.3 percent and 28.8 percent degree centrality scores, respectively. As figure 4.5 shows, however, SEMP is as much a recipient as a provider of resources, and CNCPS is a net recipient.[7] The third most central actor, MINSAL, with 26.6 percent degree centrality, is as much a recipient as provider; the fourth most central node, MINTRAB, is a net recipient, as are the remaining nodes with above average centrality scores (ASCIM and SGED). Only ANSES, JGM, MDS, MINED, MINH, MININTERIOR, and SCIM are net providers of resources; among these, only ANSES, JGM, MINED, MINH, and MININTERIOR have centrality scores above average. Other social area units are net recipients.

Second, the network includes other net providers of resources, both from within and outside government, apart from JGM and MINH. Within government, ANSES is an important provider, as the payer of pensions and conditional cash transfer programs; MDS manages funds for workfare and food programs; MINED transfers funds to prop up provincial education wage bills and finance the entire expenditure of public universities; and the Ministry of Energy (MINERG) pays household subsidies for utility prices. Outside government, multilateral actors such as international financial institutions, the UN, and UNICEF are also net providers. Even though none of these actors is as central to the network as JGM and MINH, some—like ANSES and MINED—have only slightly lower centrality scores. All told, the whole set indicates that social area units may obtain resources from several providers.

Finally, many social policy units exchange resources with a number of nongovernmental actors. This is particularly the case within the labor policy area, where both MINTRAB and SEMP, according to interviewees, exchange resources with unions (UOM, UTHGRA, and the Construction Workers' Union of the Argentine Republic [UOCRA]) and business associations (ADIMRA, UIA, and the Industrial Union of the Buenos Aires Province [UIPBA]). Within the social assistance policy area, SNAF exchanges resources with NGOs such as CARITAS. Within the education policy area, SGED exchanges resources with schools (COLEGIOS); within the health policy area, MINSAL exchanges resources with the union-run health care providers (UNHORGS) and the health industries (HEALTHINDS).

These patterns explain both findings contrary to expectations: why the resources network is not hierarchical, and why not all social area units are net recipients of resources. Although the main providers in the network are those expected from the formal structure of the policy-making process, the higher centrality scores of net providers or recipients/providers, the presence of other governmental and nongovernmental net providers, and the relations between social area units and nongovernmental actors prevent the hierarchical control of resources intended by institutional design. Consequently, this network structure suggests that the distribution of resources cannot be effectively used to increase the adaptability, coherence, and coordination of social policies.

The Network of Power

This section presents and discusses the network map of power in the social policy formulation processes of Argentina. In figure 4.6, the origin of the arrows indicates the

FIGURE 4.6: **Network of Power in the Social Policy Formulation Process, Argentina**

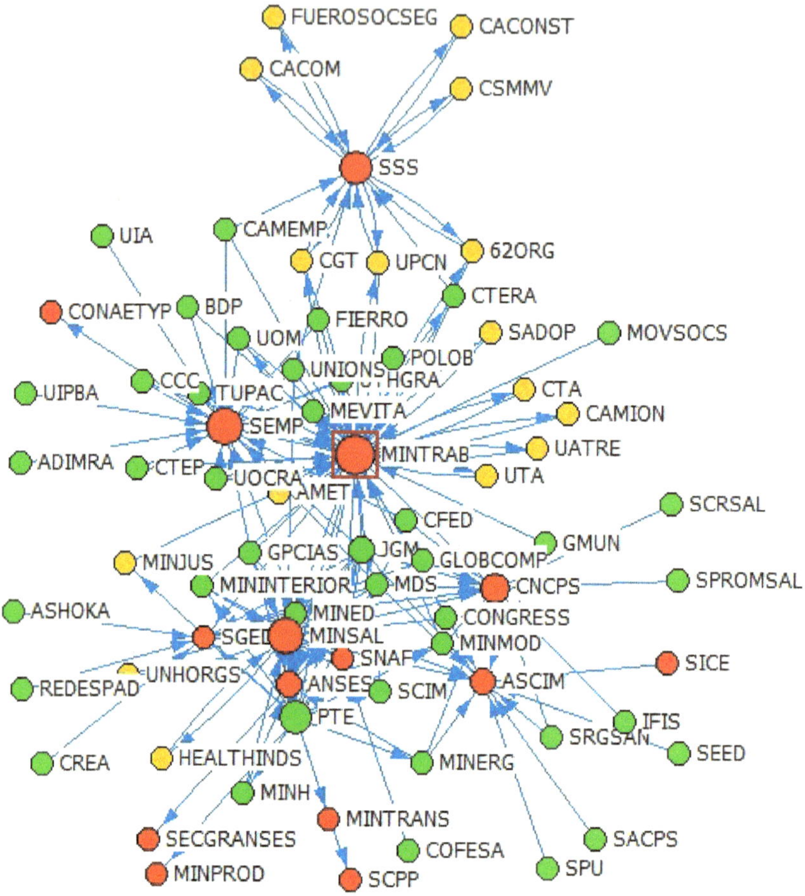

Source: Original figure for this publication.
Note: Origin of the arrows indicates source of power; destination points to the node over which that power is exercised. Green nodes are net sources of power, red nodes are net subjects of power, and yellow nodes indicate that the actors recognize and are recognized as sources of power by the same number of actors. The size of the nodes conveys their centrality to the network of power: the higher the number of actors they subject or are subjected by, the larger the node. Nodes in squares constitute the core of the network; remaining nodes constitute its periphery. See appendix A for definitions of all abbreviations used in this figure.

source of power, and their destination points to the node over which that power is exercised. The green nodes identify actors who are net sources of power; they are recognized as sources of power by more actors than they recognize as sources of power. The red nodes indicate actors who are net subjects of power; they recognize more actors as sources of political power than others recognize them as such. The yellow nodes indicate that the actors recognize and are recognized as sources of power by the same number of actors. The size of the nodes conveys their centrality to the network of power: the higher the number of actors they subject or are subjected by, the larger the node. The nodes inserted into squares constitute the core of the network, and the remaining nodes constitute its periphery.

The power network in Argentina is, like all the previous networks, a connected, low-density network with a value of 0.0658, only 173 ties among 73 nodes, and an average geodesic distance of 2.6556, which is also in line with the value for the whole network. Despite these similarities, however, the network of power has a hierarchical structure consistent with theoretical expectations from the formal design of the policy-making process. Still, this hierarchical structure is not particularly strong, because several net sources of power—within and outside government—and a number of net subjects of power fragment the network.

The network of power in the Argentine social policy formulation process displays a hierarchical structure consistent with theoretical expectations for two reasons. First, as expected, the president (represented by PTE in the figure), JGM, GPCIAS, and (some of) the social area ministries (MDS and MINED) are the most important net sources of power: as measured by their net out-degree centrality scores, these actors are recognized as sources of power by more actors than they recognize as such. The positions of the PTE and JGM are consistent with their senior constitutional roles as chief executive and chief administrator of the federal government; the position of the provincial governments is consistent with their roles as policy makers in the decentralized social policy areas; and the positions of MDS and MINED are consistent with their roles as providers of resources.

The other reason for the network's hierarchical structure is that these actors are the only net sources of power with degree centrality scores above average. Although other actors are more central to the network, they are net subjects of power, precisely of the aforementioned net sources of power. The president is the fifth most central actor, with 23.6 percent degree centrality, but the first most central net source of power. JGM is the seventh most central actor, with 15.2 percent degree centrality, but the second most central net source of power. GCPIAS represents the tenth most central actor, with 6.9 percent degree centrality, but the third most central net source of power. In contrast, MINTRAB is both the core of the network and its most central actor, with 75 percent degree centrality, but it is a net subject of power. The same is the case for SEMP, the second most central actor, with 30.5 percent degree centrality, and MINSAL, the third most central actor, with 27.7 percent degree centrality. SGED, SNAF, and SSS, as well as ANSES, ASCIM, and CNCPS, constitute the rest of the nodes with degree centrality scores above average, but they are all net subjects of power.

Three factors, however, make the power network's hierarchical structure not particularly strong. The first factor is the proliferation of net sources of power both within and outside government. The network includes 43 net sources of power

(58.9 percent of the nodes), of which 16 (21.9 percent of the network members, and 37.2 percent of the net sources) are governmental units and 27 (36.9 percent of the network membership, and 62.7 percent of the net sources of power) are extragovernmental actors. Over two-thirds of the governmental net sources of power (11 of 16, or 68.7 percent) have below-average degree centrality scores. As figure 4.6 shows, their low scores indicate that those governmental actors have so few ties that they are not only located in the network's periphery but also tend to fragment the network into dyads. This is, for example, the case with most secretaries under MDS, MINED, and MINSAL (the Secretary for Social Assistance and Protection [SACPS], the Secretary for Health [SCRSAL], the Secretary for Evaluation in Education [SEED], the Secretary for Innovation and Quality in Education [SICE], SPROMSAL, and SPU), COFESA, and the main business associations (represented by ADIMRA, UIA, UIPBA in the figure).

The second factor behind the weak hierarchical structure is the centrality of net subjects of power. Some 60 percent of the actors with above-average degree centrality scores are net subjects of power. This set of actors includes the core node (MINTRAB) and the eight nodes with highest degree centrality (MINTRAB, SEMP, MINSAL, SSS, CNCPS, ASCIM, ANSES, and SNAF). The ties coming into these nodes amount to 76.8 percent of all links of reported exercises of power of some actors over others in the network. Moreover, regardless of their directionality, the ties linking these actors to the rest of the network account for 98.8 percent of all the network's links. The higher degree centrality of net subjects of power counterbalances the proliferation of net sources of power; through dyadic links, these numerous net sources from within and outside government reduce the importance of the formal net sources of power in the network's structure.

The third factor that explains the relative weakness of the network's hierarchical structure is the encapsulated structure of its cliques. The power network includes 44 cliques, of which 30 are structured around MINTRAB, 11 around MINSAL, two around the JGM, and one around ANSES. None of these cliques links units from all social policy areas, and only eight cliques connect three social policy areas. Therefore, even though net sources of power participate in 42 of these 44 cliques, the scope of their power is encapsulated in links that do not typically reach more than two social areas, indicating that net sources of power in this network tend not to spread their power across policy areas, administrative layers, or levels of government, but rather in dyadic, area-specific links.

Consequently, as expected from the formal structure of the policy-making process, the president, the JGM, the provincial governments, and two of the social area ministries are the main actors in the power network; however, their power is limited by the proliferation of net sources of power, the higher centrality of net subjects of power, and the encapsulation of power relations to comparatively few social policy areas. This network structure therefore suggests that power would have only a limited effect as a tool for increasing the adaptability, coherence, and coordination of social policies.

Summary and Conclusions

The network of social policy formulation in Argentina during the Macri administration is a connected network with no isolate components. It is, however, a low-density network, in which many theoretically possible links do not materialize. Hence, actors tend to be geodesically distant from most of the other nodes, which creates a network structure that is more fragmented than hierarchical. Two main features distinguish the actual network from the network one would expect from the formal rules. One is the presence of many nongovernmental stakeholders; the other is the absence of a core. The presence of many nongovernmental stakeholders in some cases relates to the weak institutional capacity of some social area ministries such as health; in other cases, such as with MINTRAB, it might reflect the nature of the job that leads to frequent interactions with trade unions and business actors. The absence of a core seems to be explained by the fragmentation of hierarchy that is typical of administrative delegation. The network displays two additional noteworthy traits. First, all cutpoints are government actors; second, the network includes a large number of cliques that, when focus is placed on specific relational contents, affect the operation of the networks.

The circulation of ideas is fragmented within and across policy areas. Ideas in the Argentine social policy formulation process do not seem to come from either the second or third lines of technical agencies or from the top political authorities; instead, they seem to come from the societal actors to which social policy area units are directly linked. These findings are consistent with previous characterizations of the Argentine state as one that has systematically underinvested in the technical capabilities of its agencies and resorted instead to political appointments in public administration. Ideas seem to flow more from stable actors outside government than from unstable public bureaucracies.

The information network is also a connected low-density network that, like the ideas network, is not particularly hierarchical. Information, as ideas, is mostly encapsulated within dyads. Additionally, the positions of network actors differ from those expected from the formal policy-making rules. The information network is fragmented in halves—one group of actors connected to labor policy and the other linked to health, education, and social assistance—which is consistent with the nature of policies and actors in these different sectors. Labor policy is centralized at the national level of government, involving more regulation than physical services. Its relevant extragovernmental counterparts are actors such as unions and business associations, which are—particularly on the union side—typically encompassing organizations. The other three social sectors are largely decentralized policy areas of a deeply territorial nature, which leads to interactions with many other local players.

The network of resources is a connected, low-density one. Its structure is partly consistent with theoretical expectations from the formal policy-making process: as expected, the JGM and MINH are the most important net providers of resources, and most social area units are net recipients; however, the network is, again, not hierarchical. Consistent with the formal competences assigned to them by the Constitution and the

Financial Administration Law, the JGM and MINH are the most important net providers of resources in the network. Neither of them, however, has a hierarchical position in the network. This can be explained by three factors. First, the most central actors in the network, including the core nodes, are net recipients of resources, or as much recipients as providers, rather than net providers. Second, the network includes other net providers of resources, both from within and outside government, such as ANSES, MDS, MINED, and MINERG. Outside government, multilateral actors such as international finance institutions, the UN, and UNICEF are also net providers. Finally, many social policy units exchange resources with a number of nongovernmental actors. These patterns explain why the resources network is not hierarchical and why not all social area units are net recipients of resources.

The power network is also connected and low density. Unlike the other networks, it has a hierarchical structure, consistent with expectations. Still, this hierarchical structure is not particularly strong. The main sources of power—the president, the JGM, the provincial governments, and (some of) the social area ministries—conform to expectations. But three factors weaken this hierarchy: the proliferation of power sources within and outside government, the centrality of net subjects of power (such as ANSES, MINSAL, and MINTRAB), and the encapsulated structure of its cliques.

All in all, because of both its consistencies and its inconsistencies with the formal structure of the policy-making process, the picture of the Argentine social policy formulation process that emerges from this social network analysis appears to corroborate the general patterns of policy making in Argentina identified in previous literature.

The country's federal organization has an important effect on policy making. This effect is evident in the clustering of information flows within the information network, and in the position of provincial governments within the hierarchy of the power network. Although Congress is mentioned by interviewees as a member of the ideas, information, and power networks, its position is always peripheral. Although inconsistent with expectations from the formal structure of the policy-making process, that peripheral position is consistent with the literature on the Argentine Congress and its weak policy-making role. Political parties are completely absent from these networks, which is somewhat consistent with the absence of Congress and generally consistent with the transformation of Argentine political parties into clientelistic or personalistic parties.

The effect of the bureaucratic system can be appreciated in the scant mention, and correspondingly low centrality scores, of second- and third-line government agencies (secretaries, undersecretaries, and directors). This finding is consistent with the literature's distinction between permanent and parallel bureaucracies: the parallel bureaucracy of ministers and their immediate teams of politically appointed advisers typically do not interact with the permanent bureaucrats during the policy formulation process.

Finally, the ideas and information networks do not suggest the existence of any actor or agency in charge of technical coordination of the social policy formulation process. Although the resources and power networks suggest political coordination by the PTE and JGM, that coordination seems to be contested by both intra- and extra-governmental competitors. This combination suggests that social policy areas tend to operate on their own, with low technical interaction, and that the center of government operates more as a problem solver of economic or jurisdictional conflicts than as a broker of policy debate and consensus. This characterization echoes the literature, which has classified Argentine policies as poorly coordinated (Levitsky and Murillo 2005; Spiller and Tommasi 2003, 2007). Within the logic of this policy-making process, the emergence of technical coordination structures for social policy would only be the outcome of a political coordination decision that, in itself, would only be as stable as the government that may take it.

Notes

1. The description of the formal aspect of social policy making in Argentina draws from Martínez Nogueira (2007) and Repetto (2014).
2. Spiller and Tommasi (2007) provide a good, albeit dated, source on how these interlocking pieces of the Argentine policy-making process interact in a way that leads to low-quality policies. Spiller and Tommasi (2008) summarize that argument.
3. In the words of Scherlis (2009): "Congress is not an important policymaking actor in Argentina. The National Congress is not an attractive place for top level politicians, who do not only prioritize executive positions at national and provincial governments, but also legislative positions and the provinces. . . . A Congressional Capability Index which measures technical expertise, committee strength and the professionalization of legislators considers the Argentine Congress to have low capabilities, in contrast to countries like Brazil, Chile and Uruguay (high) or Mexico (medium)." Because presidents have enjoyed majority control of Congress in only 4 of the past 35 years of democratic rule, legislators have influenced the policy-making process not only by blocking the executive's agenda but also by modifying its contents (Calvo 2014).
4. The personalization of public administration in Argentina—through favors and political patronage—has been widely investigated, particularly at the subnational level (Calvo and Murillo 2004 2013; Oliveros 2016; Zarazaga 2014).
5. The Social Cabinet has had a fluid history, in terms of both its institutional format and procedures and its influence. Its inception dates back to the 1990s during Menem's administration. It received a boost during the 2002 crisis under the Duhalde administration, with the creation of the Consejo Nacional de Coordinación de Políticas Sociales (National Council for Social Policy Coordination, CNCPS) under the president's office, whose honorary chair was the president's wife. In the following administration, President Kirchner named his sister, who was the Minister of Social Development (MDS), as chair. Under the Macri administration, the MDS retained the honorary chair; however, in practice, the high-level coordination of social policies was in the hands of the Human Development Cabinet, a group made up of MDS, MINED, MINSAL, and MINTRAB that met periodically with the Director of the National Social Security Administration (ANSES) and the Integral Medical Attention

Program (PAMI), and was coordinated by the Secretary for Interministerial Coordination (SCIM) and his staff (Stein 2017).

6. The consistency of responses to the name-generator questions across interviewees from the same policy areas was 0.74; thus, following standard procedure about intercoder reliability, the network boundaries were considered to be adequately established.
7. Even though some of these findings seem to conform to formal definitions of roles, in practice the CNCPS seems to undertake more perfunctory than substantive functions in the social policy-making process (Stein 2017).

References

Ardanaz, M., M. Leiras, and M. Tommasi. 2014. "The Politics of Federalism in Argentina and Its Implications for Governance and Accountability." *World Development* 53 (1): 26–45.

Benton, A. 2009. "What Makes Strong Federalism Seem Weak? Fiscal Resources and Presidential-Provincial Relations in Argentina." *Publius: The Journal of Federalism* 39 (4): 651–76.

Bill Chavez, R., J. Ferejohn, and B. Weingast. 2011. "A Theory of the Politically Independent Judiciary: A Comparative Study of the United States and Argentina." In *Courts in Latin America*, edited by G. Helmke and J. Ríos-Figueroa. Cambridge: Cambridge University Press.

Bonvecchi, A., and G. Lodola. 2011. "The Dual Logic of Intergovernmental Transfers: Presidents, Governors, and the Politics of Coalition-Building in Argentina." *Publius: The Journal of Federalism* 41 (2): 179–206.

Bonvecchi, A., and J. Zelaznik. 2012. "Recursos de Gobierno y Funcionamiento del Presidencialismo en Argentina." In *Presidencialismo y Parlamentarismo Cara a Cara. Estudios sobre presidencialismo, semi-presidencialismo y parlamentarismo en América Latina y Europa Meridional*, edited by J. Lanzaro, 139–70. Madrid: Centro de Estudios Políticos y Constitucionales.

Calvo, E. 2014. *Legislative Success in Fragmented Congresses in Argentina: Plurality Cartels, Minority Presidents, and Lawmaking*. Cambridge: Cambridge University Press.

Calvo, E., and M. V. Murillo. 2004. "Who Delivers? Partisan Clients in the Argentine Electoral Market." *American Journal of Political Science* 48 (4): 742–57.

Calvo, E., and M. V. Murillo. 2013. "When Parties Meet Voters: Assessing Political Linkages Through Partisan Networks and Distributive Expectations in Argentina and Chile." *Comparative Political Studies* 46 (7): 851–82.

Gibson, E. L., and E. Calvo. 2000. "Federalism and Low-Maintenance Constituencies: Territorial Dimensions of Economic Reform in Argentina." *Studies in Comparative International Development* 35 (5): 32–55.

Helmke, G. 2002. "The Logic of Strategic Defection: Court-Executive Relations in Argentina under Dictatorship and Democracy." *American Political Science Review* 96 (2): 291–303.

Helmke, G. 2005. *Courts under Constraints: Judges, Generals, and Presidents in Argentina*. Cambridge: Cambridge University Press.

Iacoviello, M., L. Zuvanic, and M. Tommasi. 2003. "Politización, estrategia y cultura burocrática: áreas de abordaje para la reforma del servicio civil en Argentina." *VIII Congreso Internacional del CLAD*, Panamá, October 28–31.

Iaryczower, M., P. Spiller, and M. Tommasi. 2002. "Judicial Independence in Unstable Environments, Argentina, 1935–98." *American Journal of Political Science* 46 (4): 699–719.

Jones, M., and W. Hwang. 2005. "Party Government in Presidential Democracies: Extending Cartel Theory Beyond the U.S. Congress." *American Journal of Political Science* 49 (2): 267–82.

Jones, M., S. Saiegh, P. Spiller, and M. Tommasi. 2002. "Amateur Legislators—Professional Politicians: The Consequences of Party-Centered Electoral Rules in a Federal System." *American Journal of Political Science* 46 (3): 656–69.
Jones, M., S. Saiegh, P. Spiller, and M. Tommasi. 2007. "Congress, Political Careers, and the Provincial Connection." Chapter 3 in *The Institutional Foundations of Public Policy in Argentina*, edited by P. Spiller and M. Tommasi. Cambridge: Cambridge University Press.
Levitsky, S., and M. V. Murillo. 2005. "Building Castles in the Sand." In *Argentine Democracy: The Politics of Institutional Weakness*, edited by S. Levitsky and M. V. Murillo, 21–45. University Park: Penn State University Press.
Martínez Nogueira, R. 2007. "Integración de Servicios Sociales." Working Paper, United Nations Development Programme, New York.
Oliveros, V. 2016. "Making it Personal: Clientelism, Favors, and the Personalization of Public Administration in Argentina." *Comparative Politics* 48 (3): 373–91.
Oszlak, O. 1999. "The Argentine Civil Service: An Unfinished Search for Identity." *Research in Public Administration* 5: 267–326.
Repetto, F. 2014. "Políticas sociales. Una mirada político-institucional a sus reformas, desafíos e impacto." In *El Estado en acción. Fortalezas y debilidades de las políticas sociales en Argentina*, edited by C. Acuña. OSDE, Siglo Vientiuno Editores.
Scherlis, G. 2009. "Neopatrimonialism in Argentina: Persistence and Change." Working Paper, Instituto Gioja, Facultad de Derecho, Universidad de Buenos Aires.
Segura-Ubiergo, A. 2007. *The Political Economy of the Welfare State in Latin America*. Cambridge: Cambridge University Press.
Spiller, P., and M. Tommasi. 2003. "The Institutional Foundations of Public Policy: A Transactions Approach with Application to Argentina." *Journal of Law, Economics, and Organization* 19 (2): 281–306.
Spiller, P., and M. Tommasi. 2007. *The Institutional Foundations of Public Policy: A Transactions Cost Approach*. Cambridge: Cambridge University Press.
Spiller, P., and M. Tommasi. 2008. "Political Institutions, Policymaking Processes, and Policy Outcomes in Argentina." In *Policymaking in Latin America: How Politics Shapes Policies*, edited by E. Stein, M. Tommasi, C. Scartascini, and P. Spiller. Cambridge, MA: David Rockefeller Center for Latin American Studies, Harvard University.
Stein, E. 2017. "Coordinación de políticas sociales en Argentina." Working Paper, Inter-American Development Bank, Washington, DC.
Zarazaga, R. 2014. "Brokers Beyond Clientelism: A New Perspective Through the Argentine Case." *Latin American Politics and Society* 56 (3): 23–45.

5

Social Policy Formulation at the Central Level of Government: The Case of Bolivia

In September 2010, when the interviews for this case study were conducted, the government of President Evo Morales was approaching its seventh year. President Morales's reelection in 2009 made his administration's tenure the longest since the country's democratization in 1982; however, the highest ranking officials at the Ministry of Education (MINED), Ministry of Health (MINSAL), Ministry of Labor (MINTRAB), and Ministry of Social Development (MDS)—most recruited either from the government party or from the grassroots organizations (OBs) that constituted the administration's political base—had been in office, on average, for just over one year. The longest-serving policy makers had been in government for less than half of its term. But this was no garden variety cabinet instability; it was, as the interviewees explained, the outcome of a deliberate rotation promoted by the grassroots organizations with the aim of expanding their presence in, and information on, the operation of the central government. This situation, as this chapter shows, constitutes a powerful illustration of the patterns uncovered in this case study.

This chapter presents results from a social network analysis (SNA) of the social policy-making process at the central government level in Bolivia and its comparison to the process prescribed by the government's formal rules during the Morales administration. The analysis of formal institutions and actual social networks yielded contrasting results. Although the formal structure of decision-making processes aims at generating an intense coordination among the ministries in the social policy area under the political leadership of the presidency and vice presidency, analysis of the actual networks involved in producing and circulating ideas and information, transferring economic resources, and exercising political power showed that interministerial coordination is rare and that the social policy formulation process is politically coordinated on a shared basis by the president and the grassroots organizations. These findings suggest that the formulation and adoption of social policy at the central level of government in Bolivia occurs through a decision-making process in which horizontal coordination among units in the social policy area is lower than predicted or prescribed by formal rules; that the organization of decision making does not necessarily stimulate the use of technical inputs generated by actors with specific capacities and long-term horizons; and that social policy–making networks may weaken the production of social policies adaptable both to conditions of uncertainty about the demand for social services and to high degrees of output specificity.

The Social Policy–Making Process in Bolivia: What the Formal Structure Shows

The social policy–making process at the central level of government in Bolivia is formally structured to generate interministerial coordination in policy formulation and implementation. Its institutional design involves the participation of both the social area ministries and the rest of the cabinet portfolios in collective debate and decision. Intervention by the government's political apex is limited to breaking the tie in case of a draw or deadlock among ministries. The formal rules of the social policy–making process would therefore instigate horizontal coordination among ministries, rather than vertical coordination through the presidency (PTE). This section describes the formal social policy–making process in Bolivia in order to illustrate these patterns, with particular emphasis on the participating actors and the sequence of their intervention.

The Actors

The actors in the formal social policy–making process in Bolivia, as defined by the current legal framework, are the social area ministries (MINSAL, MINED, MINTRAB, and MDS) and the coordination ministries (the Ministry of Development Planning [MPD] as the technical coordinator and the Ministry for the Presidency (MP) as the political coordinator). Within the ministries, the deputies perform important roles, and the president and vice president hover above the cabinet.

The MP, the VPTE, and the ministries of the Plurinational State of Bolivia are in charge of the central administration (Political Constitution of the State, articles 172, 174, 175; Supreme Decree 29894, article 7). To fulfill this role, the PTE has the following functions that are relevant for the social policy–making process:

> Proposing and directing the state and government policies; running the public administration and coordinating the state ministries' action; enacting the laws passed by the Plurinational Legislative Assembly; dictating supreme decrees and resolutions; presenting the economic and social development plan to the Plurinational Legislative Assembly; appointing the ministers of state; and submitting urgent

> economic bills, for their consideration by the Plurinational Legislative Assembly, which would debate them as a matter of priority. (CPE, article 172)

The VPTE contributes to the public policy process by fulfilling three of its constitutional functions: "coordinating the relations between the Executive Branch, the Plurinational Legislative Assembly and the autonomous governments; participating in the meetings of the Council of Ministers; and collaborating with the President of the State in the direction of the government's general policy" (CPE, article 174). The ministers of state are specifically tasked with

> proposing and collaborating in the formulation of the government's general policy; proposing and directing the government's policy in their area; managing the public administration in their corresponding area; dictating administrative rules in their jurisdiction; proposing drafts for supreme decrees and co-signing them with the President of the State; and coordinating with other Ministries in the planning and execution of government policy. (CPE, article 175)

This legal framework also defines the roles of the ministries in the social area. The Ministry of Health and Sports (MSD) has the following responsibilities: develop, enact, and evaluate health programs; regulate, plan, oversee, and direct the National Health Service made up of the public, private, and social security sectors; promote traditional medicine and integrate it with Western medicine; develop nutrition and food security programs; and draft rules and regulations for the training and performance of human resources (Supreme Decree 29894, article 90). To fulfill these tasks, the MSD is supported by three deputy ministries: the Deputy Ministry for Health and Promotion (VSP), the Vice Ministry for Traditional Medicine and Intercultural Relations (VMTI), and the Vice Ministry for Sports (VD).

The Ministry of Education (ME) is tasked with developing intracultural, intercultural, and plurilingual education policies and strategies; managing the education system; and developing educational programs and policies for scientific, technical, technological, and productive education (Supreme Decree, article 104). To fulfill these aims, it is organized into three vice ministries: the Vice Ministry for Regular Education (VER), the Vice Ministry for Alternative and Special Education (VEAyE), and the Vice Ministry for Higher Education and Professional Training (VESFP).

The Ministry of Labor, Employment, and Social Security (MTEPS) is in charge of designing, proposing, coordinating, and implementing labor, employment, and social security policies; developing wage and productivity policies; promoting the cooperative sector; producing social security policies aimed at building "a universal, supportive, and equitable social insurance"; and formulating policies related to the civil service (Supreme Decree, article 86). To fulfill these aims, it is supported by two vice ministries: the Vice Ministry of Labor and Social Security (VTPS) and the Vice Ministry for Employment, Civil Service and Cooperative Units (VESCC).

The same legal framework specifies the functions of the cabinet's coordination ministries. The Ministry for Development Planning (MPD) is tasked with planning and coordinating the country's integral development by formulating, overseeing, and evaluating the Social and Economic Development Plan; coordinating the formulation of productive, social, cultural, and political development policies and strategies; and carrying out the oversight and evaluation of the plans and programs included in the System for State Integral Development Planning (Supreme Decree, article 46). To fulfill these aims, it is organized into four vice ministries: the Vice Ministry for Planning and Coordination (VPC), the Vice Ministry for Public Investment and External Finance (VIPFE), the Vice Ministry for Strategic Pluriannual Planning (VPEP), and the Vice Ministry of Science and Technology (VCyT). It is also supported by a unit that is key for the public policy process in general, and the social policy process in particular: the Unit for Social and Economic Policy Analysis (UDAPE).

Last, the MP is charged with coordinating the PTE's political and administrative actions, the Council of Ministers, and other councils and coordinating bodies; supervising the ministries' actions; coordinating the relation between the PTE and social movements, nations, indigenous peoples, peasants, and civil society; and coordinating the political and administrative relations with the decentralized and autonomous territorial units (Supreme Decree, article 22). To carry out these tasks, it is supported by two deputy ministries: the Deputy Ministry for Coordination of Government and Territorial Management (VCGGT) and the Deputy Ministry for Coordination with Social Movements and Civil Society (VCMSSC).

The social ministries and the coordination ministries meet to discuss the former's initiatives at the National Council of Economic and Social Policy (CONAPES). CONAPES includes all state ministries plus UDAPE, which operates as its technical secretary; VIPFE from the MPD; VCGGT from the MP; and the Vice Ministry for Economic Relations and Foreign Trade from the Ministry of Foreign Affairs. The function of CONAPES is to coordinate national social and economic development policies by analyzing and making recommendations about the "viability and consistency" of the drafts of Supreme Decrees and bills proposed by the area ministries (CONAPES Internal Regulations, article 1). CONAPES submits decisions to the Council of Ministers, where all state ministries discuss the decisions with the president and vice president, who have the final say on any matter under consideration.

This constitutional and legal framework thus organizes the public policy–making process as a coordinated effort run by the ministries under the ultimate supervision of the PTE and VPTE. The technical ministries have jurisdiction and legislative initiative in their specific areas, as well as constitutionally sanctioned say in the debate about the initiatives from other areas. The coordination ministries direct and organize the work of the technical ministries and the discussion of initiatives within the Council of Ministers. And the PTE and VPTE propose, supervise, and decide in the last resort.

The Process

In its formal structure, the social policy-making process in Bolivia hardly differs from the public policy process in general. As with any executive initiative, the drafts of Supreme Decrees and bills related to health, education, employment, and social security policies are generated by the area ministries, usually through interministerial consultation processes. Also like any other executive initiative, social policy initiatives are submitted to the Council of Ministers for consideration. If approved by the Council of Ministers, the drafts for Supreme Decrees on social policy issues are subsequently countersigned by the president, whereas draft bills are submitted to the Plurinational Assembly for its consideration and approval. The only difference between the social policy process and the public policy process in general is the intervention of CONAPES before the debate in the Council of Ministers.

The formal policy-making process begins with an initiative from the social area ministries, which may be processed in the regular way—that is, through discussion in the Council of Ministers with previous consideration by CONAPES—or in the expedited way, which by presidential order avoids the intervention of CONAPES and allows the draft decrees or bills to be submitted directly for debate in the Council of Ministers, and for final decision by the president or vice president.

The regular and the expedited ways of processing ministerial initiatives have the same first stage. In both processes the drafting ministry must fulfill three presentation requirements: submit the draft in both printed and magnetic versions signed by the minister; support the initiatives with technical and legal reports that adequately justify their consideration, pertinence, and viability; and propose an implementation scheme that specifies the steps to be followed in order to realize the initiative (CONAPES Internal Regulations, article 5.II). If more than one ministry has authored the draft, all ministers involved must sign it; if the draft requires additional budgetary resources or tax exemptions, the Ministry of Economy and Public Finance (MEFP) must submit a previous report; if it involves resources from international institutions, the VIPFE must also prepare a report; and, if it requires changes to the executive branch's institutional structure, the MP must prepare a legal report (CONAPES Internal Regulations, article 5.II). The initiative must be submitted to the MP, which checks that the aforementioned requirements have been fulfilled: if they have not, it sends the initiative back to the drafting ministries for correction; if they have, it sends the initiative to CONAPES, where its technical secretary—UDAPE—reviews it. If the president decides to pursue the expedited way, the initiative skips CONAPES and goes straight to the Council of Ministers.

In the second stage of the regular process of social policy initiatives, UDAPE analyzes the ministerial drafts and reports on their implications, their compatibility with the drafting ministries' functions, and their consistency with the National Development Plan and the government's fiscal policy (CONAPES Internal Regulations, article 5.IV). If the initiative goes beyond the scope of CONAPES's jurisdiction, UDAPE must return it to the MP and recommend an alternative decision-making process. If the topic falls within CONAPES's mission but the initiative lacks enough information or background material for UDAPE to justify a report, the initiative reverts to the drafting ministries with a request for supplementary information. Once enough background material has been gathered, UDAPE files its report and the draft enters the CONAPES agenda.

In the third stage of the regular process, CONAPES debates and decides on each social policy initiative. According to its regulations, CONAPES can make four types of decision: approval, in which case the draft is submitted to the MP for its subsequent discussion at the Council of Ministers; approval with comments, which returns the initiative to the drafting ministries so they can reply to the comments; postponement, which postpones debate on the initiative and enables its reconsideration at the request of the drafting ministry; or rejection, in which case the initiative is sent back to the drafting ministry, which may subsequently reactivate it if that ministry can resolve the problems invoked by CONAPES as grounds for rejection (CONAPES Internal Regulations, article 6). CONAPES can use UDAPE's report as grounds for its decision, but that report is not binding because CONAPES must also take into account the compatibility of each initiative with the National Development Plan and the government's fiscal policy.

The fourth stage in the regular process is equivalent to the second stage in the expedited process: debating the initiative in the Council of Ministers. This debate, chaired by the president—or the vice president in the president's absence—studies the consistency of initiatives with existing legislation and the National Development Plan, and may result in the decision to approve, reject, or cite observations to any draft. When dealing with drafts for Supreme Decrees, approval by the Council of Ministers leads to publication in Bolivia's Official Gazette; when dealing with draft bills, approval leads to their submission to the Plurinational Legislative Assembly for discussion and approval. Rejected or commented drafts are returned to the drafting ministries for correction or shelving (CONAPES Internal Regulations, article 7). Decisions in the Council of Ministers are made by consensus or, in its absence, by ultimate choice of the chair—that is, the president or the vice president.

The regular process for policy initiatives finishes with financial administration procedures. The Orders for Planning and Budgetary Policy, updated by each administration, establish the guidelines for planning, formulating, executing, overseeing, and evaluating the Strategic Institutional Plan, Annual Operational Plans, and Institutional Budgets. All public sector units prioritize their institutional short-, medium-, and long-term aims and objectives through their POAs, following the guidelines of the General Social and Economic Development Plan and the Sectoral Plans, which are coordinated by the MPD. Once the institutional aims and objectives are set, they are articulated with the expenditure budget by determining their cost and source of funding. Each year, in order to develop the General State Budget, all public sector units must upload their POAs to the official fiscal information system, together with their

Institutional Budgets, and submit them to the MEFP and the MDP via the VIPFE, which consolidates them to build the PGE. The aggregate and consolidated PGE is subsequently submitted to the Plurinational Legislative Assembly for its consideration. Once the PGE law is approved, public sector units schedule their quarterly budgetary execution plans. Figure 5.1 depicts the regular process of initiatives. The expedited process, as previously noted, bypasses CONAPES and submits drafts directly to the Council of Ministers.

The design of the formal social policy-making process in Bolivia therefore assigns specific roles to the actors, and establishes a unified flow for authority, information, policy ideas, and financial resources. The social area ministries must coordinate with each other to develop and implement social policy under the guidance and supervision of the MPD through its deputy ministries and UDAPE. The MP, and the PTE itself above it, coordinate the technical activities of the ministries. Political authority, therefore, flows only from top to bottom: from the PTE and VPTE to the cabinet through CONAPES and the Council of Ministers. Policy ideas and information, in contrast, flow from the bottom to top: from the social area ministries to the PTE and VPTE through UDAPE, CONAPES, and the Council of Ministers. In turn, UDAPE may take part in the flow of policy ideas and information in a reactive way only, by reporting on the ministerial drafts. Finally, economic resources seem to flow only from the MEFP and MPD: from the former through its control over tax revenues and from the latter through its control over international cooperation funding.

We performed SNA of social policy-making processes to compare them with the previous description of its formal aspects. Following the research design outlined in chapter 3, we employed snowball sampling to specify the network boundaries. In October 2010,[1] we interviewed an initial sample of policy makers that included the top-tier officials in the social area ministries (that is, ME, MSD, and MTEPS) and the coordinating ministries (that is, MP and MPD) using a questionnaire that contained name-generator questions aimed at identifying the actors and administrative units with which the interviewees typically interact in the social policy formulation process (see appendix B). Using the same questionnaire, we subsequently interviewed the actors absent from the initial sample but who were mentioned by at least 75 percent of the initial interviewees, until no new actors were mentioned. The complete list of identified actors and their acronyms is included in appendix A.

Some 77 percent of the actors in the initial sample were interviewed, which increased the network size by three and a half times—from 18 to 65 members. Only 23 percent of the increased network could be interviewed. It was not possible to interview the leaders of grassroots organizations; however, the interviews with government officials showed, as indicated by the literature (Madrid 2011, 2012; Van Cott 2008), that many of them held leadership positions in grassroots organizations, or had held those positions until they took office. This finding led to the inference that the influence attributed by these interviewees to grassroots

FIGURE 5.1: **Regular Process of Social Policy Initiatives, Bolivia**

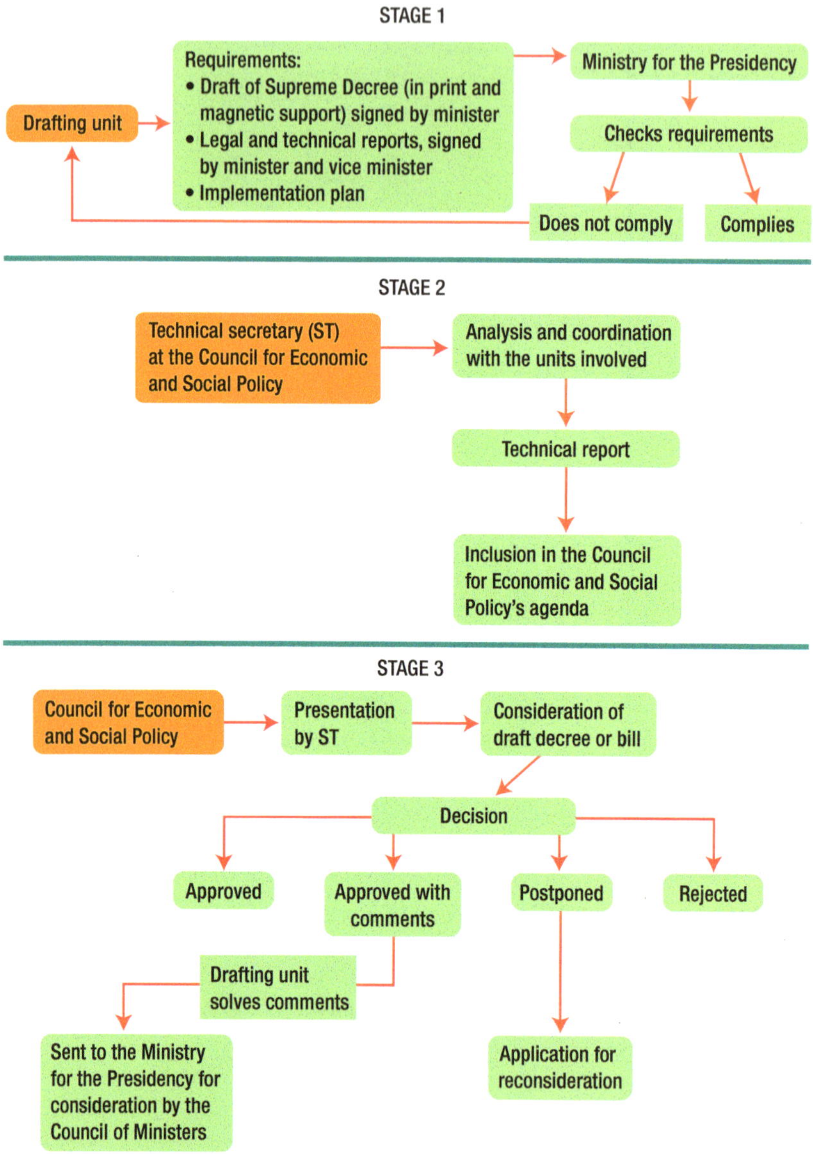

Source: National Council for Economic and Social Policy Internal Regulations, Bolivia, 2006.

organizations is, to some degree, endogenous. Unfortunately, it was not possible to interview a representative sample of all national administration officials in order to determine the effective weight and rotation rate of those officials coming from grassroots organizations.

Certain aspects of the sample must be underscored. The average tenure of interviewed officials was 14.4 months. At the time of the interview, 60 percent had been in office for less than that average time. Of those interviewees for whom complete data were available, 22.2 percent lacked experience in any social policy area before their current position; of the 77.8 percent with previous experience, 33 percent had spent 12 months in their previous position, 33 percent had 36 months experience, and only 33 percent had been in office for more than 36 months. This finding begs the inference that tenures had been relatively short and staff rotation high in the social policy area. These tendencies are consistent with previous findings about the stability and technical capacity of the national administration in Bolivia (IDB 2005; Zuvanic, Iacovello, and Rodríguez-Gusta 2010).

Finally, the networks were analyzed in terms of their density and centrality measures, the specification of cores and peripheries, and the identification of cliques and cutpoints. The maps in the next section depict the results of our analysis.

The Social Policy–Making Process: What Social Network Analysis Shows

This section presents the evidence from the SNA of interministerial coordination for social policy formulation in Bolivia using a neutral, panoramic representation of the actual network of interaction. The representation is panoramic because it comprises the whole network as identified in the interviews; it is neutral insofar as it shows only connections among the actors, without specifying their relational contents or directionality.

This map shows that the actual network through which the social policy-making process takes place in Bolivia has a higher number of members than the formal network, incorporates new actors as central, turns peripheral actors in the formal network into central actors, and exhibits fewer connections between the ministries and deputy ministries of the social area than expected from the formal network. This map suggests that horizontal coordination among the social area units is lower than expected and lower than prescribed by formal rules. In the following sections, the actual network is deconstructed according to the different relational contents of the links among actors.

Figure 5.2 displays the panoramic, neutral representation of the actual network of the social policy-making process at the central government level in Bolivia. It depicts the network in a radial way to facilitate the identification of the network's most relevant traits, such as the centrality positions of some actors. In order to visually underscore the neutrality of this representation, the nodes (that is, the actors who

FIGURE 5.2: **The Actual Network of Social Policy Making at the Central Level of Government, Bolivia**

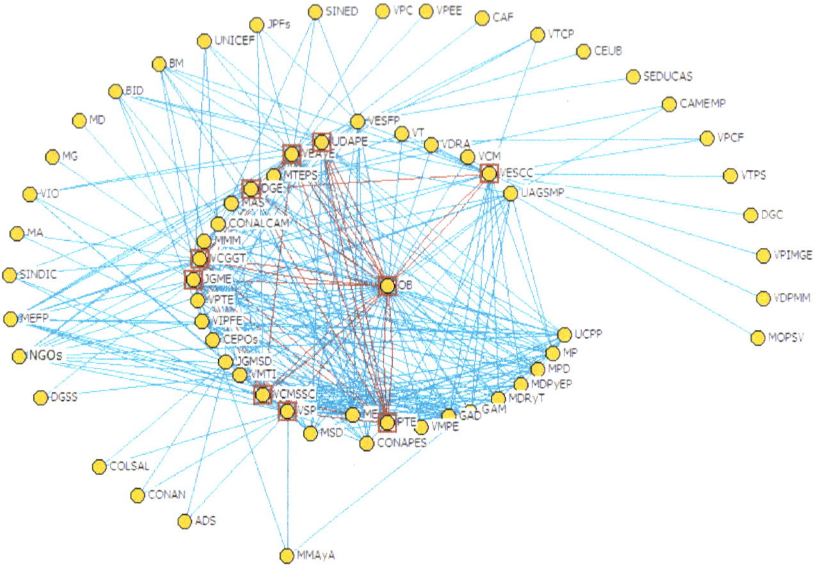

Source: Original figure for this publication.
Note: Nodes in red squares represent the network's core; nodes without red squares represent the periphery. See appendix A for definitions of all abbreviations used in this figure.

make up the network), are depicted with the same size, the ties without directionality, and the nodes with the same width and color. The nodes in red squares constitute the network's core; the nodes without red squares represent the periphery. This is a highly connected network: most of its nodes and ties are located at one geodesic distance; however, it is also a low-density network (with value 0.1380) in which only a small number of all possible ties has actually emerged.

The first notable difference between the formal and the actual network is the size of the membership: the actual network includes 65 members (nodes), whereas the formal network has only 22. This difference reflects the added presence, in the actual network, of second-tier government actors (deputy ministries, cabinet chief offices, and general directorates), subnational government actors (autonomous and municipal governments), grassroots organizations (represented by OB in figure 5.2) and their coordination bodies (National Coordination for Change [CONALCAM] and the Education Councils of Aboriginal Peoples [CEPOs]), corporate actors (unions, business associations, and professional health colleges), local actors (parents' councils and departmental health assemblies), and international organizations (Andean Development Corporation [CAF], Inter-American Development Bank [IDB],

United Nations Children's Fund [UNICEF], and World Bank). The actual network is thus made up not only of central government actors but also of local government, nongovernmental, and international actors.

The second notable difference between the actual and the formal networks is that the central actors in the actual network are not the same as in the formal network. In the formal network the central actors are the ministries and UDAPE, but in the actual network the central actors are the grassroots organizations, the president, and some deputy ministries from the social area. Grassroots organizations have the highest values in all centrality scores (62.5 percent in degree centrality, 17.1 percent in betweenness centrality, and 68 percent in closeness centrality). The president, in turn, comes in second in degree centrality (48.4 percent) and closeness centrality (60.9 percent). VEAyE holds the third position in all three measures (48.4 percent in degree centrality, 14 percent in betweenness centrality, and 60.3 percent in closeness centrality), and VESCC holds the second position in betweenness centrality (16.4 percent). These values suggest that the actual social policy–making process in Bolivia is coordinated by these actors, not by the ministries. Still, the nature of the relations among the actors must be studied in order to determine their specific influence on the policy-making process.

The third notable difference between the actual and the formal networks is that the central actors in the formal social policy formulation process appear as peripheral in the actual network. The sole exception to this pattern is UDAPE, which is not only central in the actual network but also a cutpoint within it. This position may be explained partly by its centrality scores: its degree centrality value is more than twice the average, its betweenness centrality is three times higher than the average, and its closeness centrality value is eight percentage points over the average. The role of UDAPE in the formal social policy–making process also makes it a cutpoint, insofar as it is by way of its intervention that bills and drafts of supreme decrees are circulated to the rest of the executive branch.

The fourth notable difference between the formal and the actual networks is that the formal network has fewer, and less direct, connections than the actual network. The ministries from the social area (ME, MSD, and MTEPS) are not directly connected to each other in the actual network, or to their formal coordination body (CONAPES), or to their technical coordinator (MPD), even though they do retain from the formal network their ties to UDAPE, CONAPES's technical secretariat. In contrast, these ministries are directly tied to the president, grassroots organizations, and the VCGGT at the MP, which operates as a political coordinator. In turn, the president has direct ties to some deputy ministries in the social area (VEAyE and VSP), but the ministries are scarcely linked to deputy ministries not immediately under their jurisdiction: only the ME is tied to the VSP, and only the MSD to the VESFP. This finding suggests that horizontal interministerial coordination does not exist in the actual network of social policy formulation in the central government in Bolivia; instead, coordination is vertical and indirect, because the president, rather than the ministries or deputy ministries from the social area, establishes the links between social policy units.

Figure 5.2 depicts a few traits from the actual network that are absent from the formal network because of the nature of the latter's membership. The first is that the ties between the most highly connected governmental actors after the president (deputy ministries, cabinet chief offices, and general directorates from the social area) are not reciprocal. With the exception of the ties among VESFP and VESCC, no deputy ministry from the social area reported any ties to deputy ministries from other ministries in the social area.

A second characteristic of the actual network is the difference in the positions of the grassroots organizations and the other nongovernmental actors. On the one hand, only grassroots organizations are at the core of the network. On the other hand, the other nongovernmental actors have low connectedness: they are all located more than two geodesic distances from the core and, except for nongovernmental organizations (NGOs) and multilateral banks, none of them has more than three ties with the rest of the network.

A third trait of the actual network is that all its cutpoints are second-tier central government actors: UDAPE, VCGGT, VEAyE, VESFP, VESCC, and the Social Management Support Unit at the Ministry for the Presidency (UAGSMP). This trait suggests that ministerial positions in the social area may not have a major influence on policy-making processes because they lack specific relational ties that may affect the network's connectedness and, thus, the circulation of information, ideas, resources, authority, and power among its members. The role of UDAPE as a key player is again noteworthy because of its central position both in the formal and the actual social policy-making networks.

Finally, a notable characteristic of this neutral representation of the actual network is the high number of cliques: 111 of 285 reported ties. This prevalence of cliques implies that 38.9 percent of ties are highly connected and distinct from the rest of the network by virtue of their own relational contents. To investigate the nature of these cliques, as well as their effects on the social policy-making process in the central government, it is necessary to deconstruct the network according to its different relational contents.

These structural characteristics of the social policy-making network suggest that the social policies generated therein would be adaptable, coordinated, and coherent only if political authorities and actors intervene in the process to attain those aims—because technical actors seem to be linked significantly less than expected or prescribed by the formal rules.

The Network of Ideas

The SNA of the network of social policy ideas pinpoints one of the reasons for low interministerial horizontal coordination in the social policy-making process at the central government in Bolivia: ideas do not circulate among the ministries. This deficiency can be explained by four factors: (1) social policy ideas originate largely from the apex of the government, nongovernmental actors, or subnational governments; (2) technical social policy units are net consumers, not producers, of ideas; (3) the ties among social area units are scarce; and (4) the flow of ideas is encapsulated by cliques based upon vertical relations of coordination.

Figure 5.3 depicts the network of social policy ideas at the central level of government in Bolivia. The network is presented in a hierarchical way according to each node's degree centrality, and the ties appear with directionality in order to show the hierarchies acknowledged by the actors and the extension of the ties. The ties represent ideas, and the arrows indicate the direction of their circulation. Thus, incoming arrows indicate a node is a recipient of ideas, whereas outgoing arrows indicate it provides ideas to other nodes. The green nodes are net producers of social policy ideas: those actors produce more ideas than they receive from others. In turn, the red nodes are net consumers of ideas: they receive more ideas than they produce. Last, the

FIGURE 5.3: **Social Policy Ideas Network at the Central Level of Government, Bolivia**

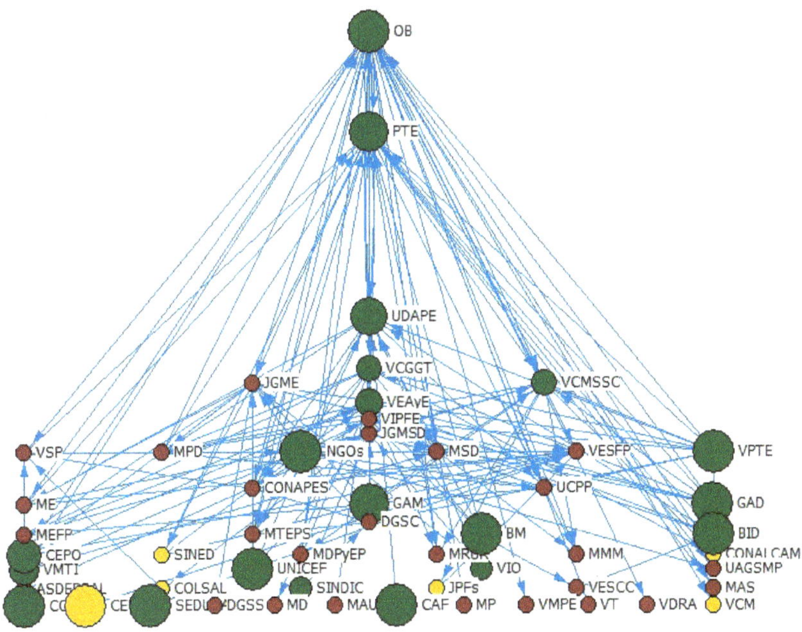

Source: Original figure for this publication.

Note: Ties represent ideas; arrows indicate direction of circulation. Green nodes are net producers of social policy ideas; red nodes are net consumers of ideas; yellow nodes are actors that both produce and consume social policy ideas. Sizes of nodes indicate the importance of the actors as producers of ideas, as perceived by those tied to them in the network. See appendix A for definitions of all abbreviations used in this figure.

yellow nodes correspond to actors who both produce and consume social policy ideas. The different sizes of the nodes indicate the importance of the actors as producers of ideas, as perceived by those tied to them in the network.

Figure 5.3 reveals that the central actors in the production of social policy ideas are OBs and the PTE: both act as net producers of ideas, and they hold the first and second positions in all centrality measures. A technical actor from the central level of government (UDAPE) comes in only third in centrality, but UDAPE specializes not in formulating policy but in analyzing its viability. Right below UDAPE in centrality scores, and certainly in a more central position than the ministries and deputy ministries from the social area, come the MP's deputy ministries, which contribute to the political coordination of the social policy network. With lower centrality scores but wider recognition from the network membership, the next level of important producers of social policy ideas includes the VPTE, multilateral institutions (CAF, IDB, UNICEF, and World Bank), the Autonomous Departmental Governments (GAD), the Autonomous Municipal Governments (GAM) with their Departmental Education Services (SEDUCAS), and other nonstate actors such as CEPOs, NGOs, and unions. Only three technical actors from the social area are net producers of ideas: VEAyE, VMTI, and the National Council for Food and Nutrition (CONAN). The central producers of ideas are, therefore, nonstate actors (OBs, multilateral institutions, and NGOs), the government's political apex (the PTE, the VPTE, and the deputy ministries for the MP), and local actors (such as GAD, GAM, and SEDUCAS).

The technical actors from the social area are net consumers of ideas. Eleven of the 14 technical actors from the social area in this network have that status: all the social area ministries, all the deputy ministries of MTEPS, all the cabinet chief offices and general directorates, one of the deputy ministries (VESFP) of the ME, and the Deputy Ministry of Health and Promotion (VSP) of the MSD. Their position as net consumers of ideas would not necessarily block the flow of ideas among the technical units in the social area if they were tied to each other, but such is not the case.

Connection among units in the social area is rare. Of the 172 ties that make up the network of social policy ideas, none strictly links ministries or deputy ministries to each other. Three ties between ministries and interministerial councils (to CONAN from the ME, MPD, and MSD) convey interministerial connections, but no direct tie between ministries was reported. Three ties between councils and deputy ministries (CONAN-VSP, CONAPES-VESFP, and CONAPES-VSP) may entail ties between ministries and deputy ministries from other jurisdictions; however, only five explicitly reported ties of this kind exist: ME-VSP, MPD-VEAyE, MPD-VSP, MSD-VESFP, and MSD-VIPFE. Only two ties exist between ministries and cabinet chief offices from other ministries: ME-JGMSD (Cabinet Chief Office at the Ministry of Health and Sports) and MPD-JGME (Cabinet Chief Office at the Ministry of Education). And only two ties were reported between ministries and units from other ministries: the ties of both the MPD and the MSD with the Management Unit for Programs and Projects (UCPP) at the MEFP. No deputy ministry from the social area reported any tie to any unit from another ministry. This finding supports the inferences that the MTEPS and its deputy ministries are disconnected from the network of social policy ideas and that the connections enabling the flow of ideas between the ME and MSD rely on the personal relationships among people in the offices rather than the hierarchical links among the offices or the ties among officials in equivalent positions. Hence, the flow of ideas among ministries is both incomplete and not institutionalized. Consequently, it cannot be counted as a regular input of the social policy process that may facilitate the production of adaptable, coherent, and coordinated policies.

The information about cliques shown in figure 5.3 corroborates these inferences: the flow of ideas is virtually encapsulated within cliques that do not include units from different social area ministries. Of the 61 cliques identified in this network, none includes more than one ministry from the social area. Only three cliques involve one area ministry and second-tier units from other ministries: the ME–VSP–OB–PTE clique, the ME–JGMSD–OB clique, and the MSD–VESFP–OB clique. In 10 intra-area cliques, units from the health and education areas are tied only to subnational and nonstate actors of their own jurisdiction. And the overwhelming majority of cliques (40 out of 61) connects, in a segmented way, units from each of the three social areas to the apex of the government (the PTE and VPTE), to the coordination ministries or deputy ministries, or to OBs. This information is consistent with the centrality of these actors in the production of social policy ideas. It is, therefore, possible that political, rather than technical, actors are the ones coordinating the social policy ideas that nurture the activities of the area units.

The examination of the ties between the government's apex and OBs suggests that the president would be the only actor able to coordinate the flow of social policy ideas. OBs receive ideas from numerous sources; however, because these organizations are not themselves a unified actor, they lack the ability to channel their own production and circulation of ideas toward the central government. The vice president is a net producer of ideas who does not receive inputs from any other actor in the network, so his ability to coordinate ideas for the social policy units relies exclusively on his personal ability to understand and generate policy proposals for the different social policy areas. In contrast, the president receives ideas from various sources, provides ideas to various sources, and, by virtue of the nature of his office, does not need to coordinate with other actors in order to make ideas flow. It is, therefore, plausible to infer that social policy ideas circulate within the central government in Bolivia vertically through the president.

The patterns identified in the network of social policy ideas are consistent with those of the network of information flows presented in figure 5.4. Clearly, the government's apex and OBs are the main recipients of information in this network. OBs have the pole positions for all three centrality measures; the president holds the second position in degree and closeness centrality; and the deputy ministries for the PTE come in third and fourth in those same indicators. No ministry, cabinet chief office, or general directorate from the social area is a net recipient of information; only VEAyE is

FIGURE 5.4: **Social Policy Information Network at the Central Level of Government, Bolivia**

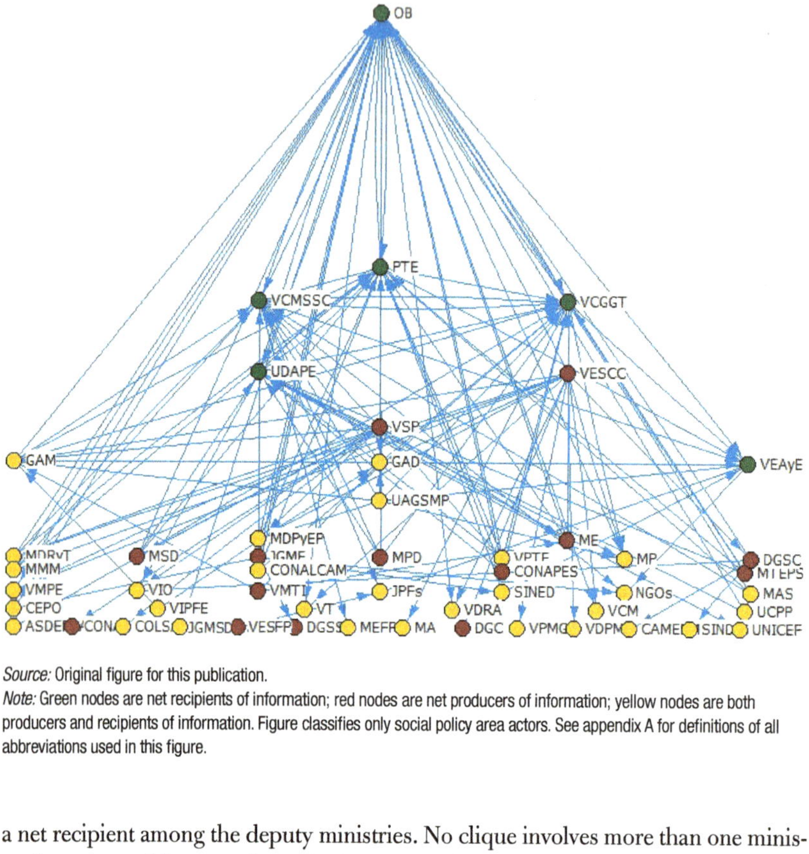

Source: Original figure for this publication.

Note: Green nodes are net recipients of information; red nodes are net producers of information; yellow nodes are both producers and recipients of information. Figure classifies only social policy area actors. See appendix A for definitions of all abbreviations used in this figure.

a net recipient among the deputy ministries. No clique involves more than one ministry from the social area, and no cliques connect deputy ministries, cabinet chief offices, or general directorates from different ministries. Only one clique crosses jurisdictional boundaries: the one tying the ME to the VSP and OBs.

These information asymmetries crystallize the vertical flow of information in the social policy network by which the president, his immediate collaborators, and OBs concentrate the reception of information. Social policy units generate information but receive virtually none from any other actors, and no registered flow of information exists among them.

The patterns identified in these two networks point to a central problem in the political economy of the formulation of social policy at the central level of government in Bolivia, and to the way the structure and operation of these social networks are set up to resolve it: the transaction costs for policy formulation that emerge from the low connectedness of social policy units and the encapsulation of ideas and information flows. Under these conditions, the high cost of accessing the ideas and information required to complete their task makes it unlikely that the actors formally in charge of developing social policies can actually develop adaptable, coherent, and coordinated policies. The solution provided by these social networks is coordination from above, by way of the PTE and OBs, who operate as producers and providers of the inputs that social policy units need to formulate policy.

The Network of Economic Resources

The analysis of the network of economic resources in the social policy formulation process at the central level of government in Bolivia reveals another factor underlying the scarce interministerial coordination that characterizes this process: the distribution of resources is not centralized. Social policy units are net recipients of resources, but no actor appears to be dominant in distributing those resources. The participation of ministries and deputy ministries as resource providers for social policy units is important, but none of them performs as the main provider. Meanwhile, social policy units receive resources from various providers and contribute only in small measure to other units. The relative weight of each provider is best appreciated when the data from the network of economic resources are combined with those from the network of ideas.

Figure 5.5 depicts the network of economic resources in the social policy formulation process at the central level of government in Bolivia. The ties are directed in order to indicate the flow of resources: incoming arrows denote the reception of resources, whereas outgoing arrows indicate provision of resources. The green nodes correspond to net providers, and their size varies according to the importance attached by the actors to each provider. The red nodes correspond to net recipients. The yellow nodes correspond to those actors that strike a balance between provision and reception of resources. This is a disconnected network because it presents two nodes that are separate from the rest; it also has low density (0.0828), which indicates high internal fragmentation.

No actor dominates the distribution of resources in this network. The centrality scores of the net providers of resources indicate that multilateral institutions, the MEFP, and NGOs are the main providers; but none of their scores indicates predominance. The MEFP's degree centrality score is barely 27.2 percent, and its closeness centrality score 57.8 percent; the respective scores for the World Bank are 15.9 percent and 43.1 percent; for the IDB, 13.6 percent and 44.8 percent; for the Programs and Projects Coordination Unit at the Ministry of Economy and Public Finance (UCCP) at the MEFP, 15.9 percent and 43.5 percent; and for NGOs, 9.09 percent and 41.5 percent. Taken together, the multilateral institutions occupy a predominant position but even so do not come close to concentrating resource flows. Something similar happens with the MEFP: it provides resources to all social policy areas but is not the predominant provider.

A possible explanation for these patterns may be found in two pieces of data that emerge from figure 5.5. First, the ministries and deputy ministries in the central government act as the main providers of resources to social policy units. For 7 of 12 social area units identified in the network of economic resources, the share of governmental units in the whole set of providers ranges from 80 percent to 100 percent: General Directorate for Employment at the Ministry of Labor, Employment and Social Security (DGE) (83 percent), JGME (83 percent), VSP (83 percent), VESCC (85 percent), ME (100 percent), MSD (100 percent), and MTEPS (100 percent). For four units, this share of government providers is 50 percent: JGMSD, UAGSMP,

FIGURE 5.5: **Network of Economic Resources in the Social Policy Formulation Process at the Central Level of Government, Bolivia**

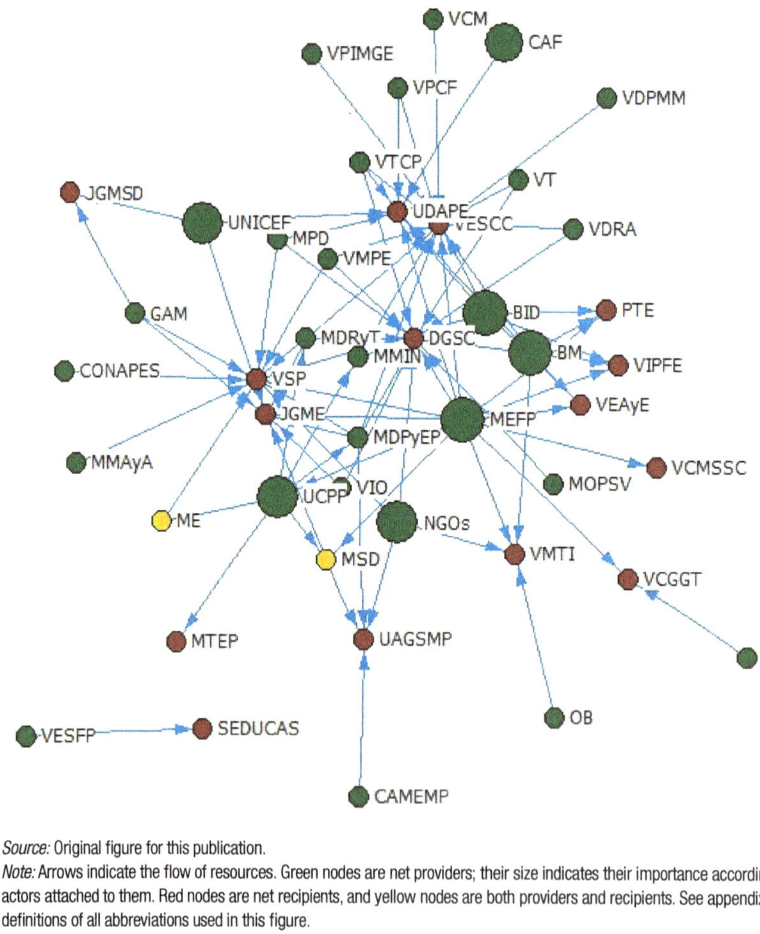

Source: Original figure for this publication.
Note: Arrows indicate the flow of resources. Green nodes are net providers; their size indicates their importance according to actors attached to them. Red nodes are net recipients, and yellow nodes are both providers and recipients. See appendix A for definitions of all abbreviations used in this figure.

UDAPE, and VMTI. Only for VEAyE do ministries account for 33 percent of all resource providers.

Second, social policy units receive resources from diverse providers. VSP obtains resources from a multilateral institution (IDB), three social policy units (CONAPES, ME, and MPD), nongovernmental actors (represented by NGOs in the figure), and seven governmental units from other policy areas. JGME has a similar set of resource providers: a multilateral institution (UNICEF), a social area ministry (MSD), and four governmental units from other policy areas. DGE obtains resources from the World Bank, NGOs, and 10 governmental units from other policy areas. VESCC captures resources from two multilateral banks (IDB and World Bank) and 12 government units from different areas. UAGSMP obtains resources from a social area ministry (MSD), an economic area ministry (MDPyEP), and two nonstate actors (NGOs and business associations, represented by CAMEMP in the figure). This dispersion in the flow of economic resources makes interministerial coordination for social policy more difficult because in practice no central government unit has the economic tools to condition the use of those resources.

The patterns shown in figure 5.5 do not prevent other actors in the social policy network from assuming a dominant position in providing economic resources and controlling other relational content, which may be inferred by comparing the network of economic resources to the network of ideas. Two types of providers in the network of economic resources hold central positions in the network of ideas: multilateral institutions and NGOs. This overlap suggests that these actors hold a dominant position in the social policy network because they contribute to the policy-making process not only ideas but also resources with which to finance their implementation.

The Network of Political Power

The SNA of the network of political power at the central level of government in Bolivia points to another important factor underlying the problems of interministerial coordination in the social policy formulation process: the existence of multiple sources of power. In this network, power is fragmented among OBs and their coordination bodies, the central government's apex, the coordination ministries, and the social area ministries. OBs and the governmental apex share the central positions, but other actors do not recognize them as the exclusive sources of power. The ministries from the social area exercise power over their subordinate units, but these units also recognize other actors as sources of power. Interministerial ties are fragmented and encapsulated under the power of the government's political coordinators. Under these conditions, direct coordination among social area ministries is unlikely, and indirect coordination through the governmental apex takes place in a compartmentalized way.

Figure 5.6 depicts the network of political power in a radial display using directed links. The radial representation helps identify the multiple sources of power and their diverse positions in the network. The green nodes correspond to the net sources of

FIGURE 5.6: **Network of Political Power over the Social Policy Formulation Process at the Central Level of Government, Bolivia**

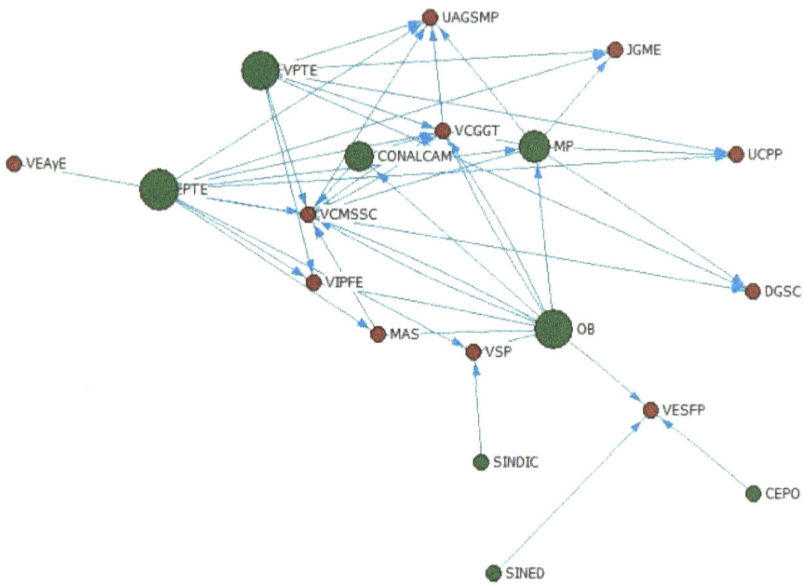

Source: Original figure for this publication.
Note: Green nodes are sources of political power; red nodes are subjects of political power. Arrows denote direction of power. Size of nodes indicates their importance. See appendix A for definitions of all abbreviations used in this figure.

political power. The red nodes correspond to the actors subjected to the political power of other actors.

The first notable trait of this network is the existence of multiple sources of political power: the PTE, the VPTE, OB, their coordination bodies, and the unions. OBs and the governmental apex constitute the core of the network: the PTE and OBs hold the pole positions in degree, closeness, and betweenness centrality, followed by the MP in the third or fourth position, depending on the indicator.

Social policy units recognize multiple sources of political power: VSP, for example, recognizes the PTE, OBs, and the unions; VESFP, in turn, recognizes OBs, the teachers' unions, and CEPOs. Thus, in the network of political power, social policy units have multiple principals and low connectedness with each other, which complicates the chances for horizontal coordination and, in contrast, facilitates those for vertical coordination.

One noteworthy characteristic of the network of political power requires further discussion: the absence of the social area ministries. Both OBs and the government's political apex prioritize appointing their members to technical and operational units within these ministries rather than to ministerial positions. These appointments enable them, at least in theory (Lewis 2008; Moe 1993), to maximize their political control over the bureaucracy. The price for maximizing political control, however, seems to be the loss of technical coordination among social policy units in the social policy-making process—hence the importance of vertical political coordination as a device to reduce the transaction costs generated by the multiplicity of principals.

Summary and Conclusions

Our study of the actual social networks in the process of social policy formulation at the central level of government in Bolivia shows that the process works in the opposite way as predicted by its formal institutional design:

- Whereas the formal design prescribes horizontal, frequent, intense interministerial coordination, the actual networks—as perceived by interviewees—show little horizontal coordination and, instead, display profuse vertical indirect coordination through the PTE and MP.
- Whereas the formal design predicts a bottom-up flow of ideas from deputy ministries and ministries toward the political apex of the government, the actual network of ideas shows a fragmented flow, torn between the vertical influence of the president and the vice president on the one hand and the extragovernmental influence of OBs and multilateral institutions on the other.
- Whereas the formal design predicts a flow of economic resources concentrated and channeled by the Ministry of Economy and Public Finance (MEFP) and the Ministry of Development Planning (MPD), the network of economic resources perceived by the actors shows a decentralized flow from various ministries, multilateral institutions, and NGOs.
- Whereas the formal design predicts a vertical flow of power from the MP and the VPTE toward the social area ministries and deputy ministries, the network of political power indicates the existence of multiple sources of power, as well as an encapsulated political coordination of social policy units.

Under these conditions, the actual social policy-making process in the central government in Bolivia does not generate a pattern of horizontal interministerial coordination, but rather exhibits a vertical coordination from the MP which is forced to share political and technical control with various actors. Many factors contribute to this outcome. First, the networks analyzed here reveal little connection among social policy units. The network of ideas displays barely 10 of 172 established ties. The network of economic resources shows a multiplicity of providers without centralization or reciprocal ties. In the network of political power, social policy units recognize various sources of power that are not necessarily tied to each other or subordinated to a common leadership. For these reasons, social policy units do not tend to generate or circulate social policy ideas to each other, to control economic resources, to operate under a centralized control of those resources, or to recognize subjection to any clearly dominant political authority.

Second, most of the social networks analyzed here place the political apex of the government and OBs in similar centrality positions. In the network of ideas, the president and OBs act as the main net producers of social policy ideas. In the network of information, they hold equivalent positions, together with the MP. In the network of political power, they have similar ranks, together with the vice president. Thus, the president and OBs can influence both the technical orientation and the political management of the social policy formulation process.

Finally, the networks analyzed here show consistently higher connectedness between the political apex of the government, OBs, and the social policy units than among social policy units themselves. Consequently, these units are tied to one another more indirectly through the president, the vice president, and OBs than directly to each other. Because social policy units have more political than technical coordination links, it can be argued that political coordination operates as the engine of the social policy formulation process.

The shared political coordination between the governmental apex and OBs in the actual operational pattern of the social policy–making process explains not only the scarce horizontal interministerial coordination identified in the course of this investigation but also the low stability and high rotation in public office in the social area identified in the interviews that served as its empirical basis. Low interministerial coordination in social policy making is the outcome of the existence of multiple principals (the PTE, the VPTE, and OBs) for multiple agents (the ministries and deputy ministries from the social area). The low stability and high rotation in office may have originated in the tensions between OBs and the political apex of the government over the orientation and pace of the social policy–making process. That interviewees identified OBs and the political apex of the government as principals of different nature and similar hierarchy indicates the existence of these tensions and disagreements; otherwise, social policy units would recognize only one of these actors as their principal.

Under these conditions, the social policy formulation process is weakly institutionalized. The primacy of vertical political coordination over horizontal technical coordination discourages the use of technical input and capacity in decision-making processes, and leads instead to prioritizing other types of interests and short-term horizons. This low connectedness, as well as the underutilization of functionally specialized units, complicates the production of adaptable policies in a public policy area with high uncertainty about both levels of service demand and benefit specificity. The network structures also complicate the development of technically coherent and coordinated policies.

These findings converge with some of the patterns previously identified in the literature on Bolivia. The SNAs presented here show, as do IDB (2005) and Zuvanic, Iacovello, and Rodríguez-Gusta (2010), the comparatively high rotation of officials at the central level of government in Bolivia and their comparatively low technical expertise. And, like Madrid (2011, 2012) and Van Cott (2008), the SNA carried out here establishes the central role of OBs in both the political and the policy formulation process. To these convergent tendencies, this SNA adds previously unavailable quantitative and qualitative evidence that documents with stronger empirical support the mechanisms by which these factors—rotation in office, level of technical expertise, and the role of OBs—shape the social policy formulation process.

Despite those similarities, the SNA findings here diverge from the previous literature in two important aspects. First, the patterns identified in the actual social policy networks at the central level of government in Bolivia show how the coordination problems emerging from the high rotation and low technical expertise of officials already identified in the literature may be counterbalanced, one way or another, by vertical coordination of the policy formulation process by the president. And, second, the SNAs show, contrary to the literature, how the governmental apex and OBs operate as competitive sources of authority and political power for the policy units.

Note

1. By then, the government led by Evo Morales of the Movement toward Socialism (MAS) was well into its first term in office. Since then, the MAS has increased its electoral control and dominance in the party system.

References

IDB (Inter-American Development Bank). 2005. *The Politics of Policies: Economic and Social Progress in Latin America and the Caribbean 2006 Report.* Washington, DC: Inter-American Development Bank.

Lewis, D. 2008. *The Politics of Presidential Appointments: Political Control and Bureaucratic Performance.* Princeton, NJ: Princeton University Press.

Madrid, R. 2011. "Bolivia: Origins and Policies of the Movimiento al Socialismo." In *The Resurgence of the Left in Latin America*, edited by S. Levitsky and K. M. Roberts, 239–59. Baltimore: The Johns Hopkins University Press.

Madrid, R. 2012. *The Rise of Ethnic Politics in Latin America.* New York: Cambridge University Press.

Moe, T. M. 1993. "Presidents, Institutions, and Theory." In *Researching the Presidency. Vital Questions, New Approaches*, edited by G. C. Edwards, J. H. Kessel, and B. A. Rockman, 337–86. Pittsburgh: University of Pittsburgh Press.

Van Cott, D. L. 2008. *Radical Democracy in the Andes.* Cambridge: Cambridge University Press.

Zuvanic, L., M. Iacovello, and A. L Rodríguez-Gusta. 2010. "The Weakest Link: The Bureaucracy and Civil Service Systems in Latin America." In *How Democracy Works: Political Institutions, Actors, and Arenas in Latin American Policymaking*, edited by C. Scartascini, E. Stein, and M. Tommasi, 147–76. Washington, DC: Inter-American Development Bank.

6

Social Policy Formulation in the Caribbean: The Cases of The Bahamas and Trinidad and Tobago

In January 2018, during the interviews for these case studies, the governments of both The Bahamas and Trinidad and Tobago consisted, at the political and the bureaucratic levels, of experienced policy makers. The incumbent parties in both countries were no strangers to office: the Free National Movement was leading the government in The Bahamas for the fourth time, and the People's National Movement of Trinidad and Tobago was entering its 45th year in office—in both cases after several turnovers resulting from competitive elections under their respective Westminster majoritarian electoral systems. The permanent bureaucracy in both countries was also remarkably experienced: members had over a decade of government service and averaged five years in their current positions, which they reached after rotating among several ministries, typically within the social policy area ministry—as is common practice under the Westminster model of bureaucracy.

This chapter addresses the question of who decides on social policy formulation in the Caribbean by investigating two similar cases: The Bahamas and Trinidad and Tobago. These cases share four characteristics critical for the political economy analysis of social policy making: both countries (1) have parliamentary democracies with Westminster-type electoral systems and institutional arrangements; (2) inherited from the colonial period and maintained a Whitehall-style civil service; (3) have a formal policy-making process marked by cabinet initiatives, interministerial committees for policy drafting, stakeholder consultations, and cabinet approval; and (4) have economies that depend mostly on revenues from a single source—tourism in The Bahamas and oil in Trinidad and Tobago. The countries differ in population size (Trinidad and Tobago has four times the population of The Bahamas), per capita income (gross national income per capita measured in purchasing power parity is over 45 percent higher in Trinidad and Tobago), and population density, which is significantly lower in The Bahamas. They also differ in the ethnic makeup of their populations: in The Bahamas, 85 percent of the population is of black African origin, 12 percent white, and 3 percent Asian and Latin American, whereas in Trinidad and Tobago Indians constitute 37.6 percent of the population, Africans 36.3 percent, mixed 24.2 percent, whites 0.6 percent, Chinese 0.3 percent, and Lebanese 0.1 percent (The Bahamas Government Census; Trinidad and Tobago Census 2011). Despite these differences, the similarities between the two countries suggest they would both have hierarchically structured social policy formulation processes with the cabinet as the main source of ideas and power, the finance ministry as the central actor for the distribution of resources, and social area ministries, nongovernmental organizations (NGOs), private sector actors, and multilateral institutions as secondary sources of ideas and information.

The social network analyses of social policy formulation processes in The Bahamas and Trinidad and Tobago, however, show somewhat different patterns. The networks through which ideas and information circulate are not hierarchically structured, and the cabinet is not the main source of ideas. The finance ministry does not dominate the network of resources; instead, that network relies heavily on the permanent secretaries at the social area ministries. And, although the cabinet and the prime minister are the main sources of power in both countries, their centrality differs across the countries, as does the participation of other governmental and nongovernmental actors in the power networks. This chapter looks into these cases by presenting, comparing, and discussing these patterns and their cross-country differences.

The Formal Structure of the Policy-Making Processes in The Bahamas and Trinidad and Tobago

The literature on the policy-making processes in The Bahamas and Trinidad and Tobago is virtually nonexistent. Despite some comparative work on civil services in the Caribbean (Draper 2001; Lodge, Stirton, and Moloney 2015; Mateo Díaz and Echebarría 2008; Rodríguez Gustá and Iacoviello 2008;) and a few pieces focused on ethnic recruitment and promotion in Trinidad and Tobago (Brown 1999; Premdas 2007) and the budgetary process in both countries (Abuelafia 2013a, 2013b), no systematic description or analysis of policy-making processes exists for either of the countries. Although such an analysis is beyond the scope of this chapter, sufficient information exists to describe the formal structure of policy-making processes in The Bahamas and Trinidad and Tobago, and to use that description as a benchmark to compare the effective social networks that actually carry out social policy formulation.

Two main colonial legacies—the Westminster-style parliamentary regime and the Whitehall-style civil service—characterize the institutional setting of policy-making processes in both countries. Both The Bahamas and Trinidad and Tobago are governed by prime ministers and cabinets selected from parliaments elected by the people in single-member districts under simple majority vote. Both countries have asymmetrical bicameral parliaments in which the first chamber (the House of Assembly in The Bahamas and the House of Representatives in Trinidad and Tobago) has procedural and power advantages over the second chamber (the Senate); both countries also employ heads of state (in the case of The Bahamas, the British sovereign represented by the governor-general; in Trinidad and Tobago, the president of the republic) with largely ceremonial functions (Constitution of the Commonwealth of The Bahamas 1973; Constitution of Trinidad and Tobago 1976). With these institutional arrangements, both countries have two-party systems and, after an initial dominance by the party that conducted the process of independence, have experienced turnover in government between the two main parties. In The Bahamas, which has cleavages based more on class, that turnover has occurred between the more populist and social liberal–oriented Progressive Liberal Party and the more conservative Free National Movement; in Trinidad and Tobago, with cleavages based more on ethnicity, turnover has occurred between the People's National Movement—which represents the Afro and Creole ethnicities—and the National Alliance for Reconstruction, and its successors the United National Congress and the People's Partnership, which represent the Indian and Asian ethnicities (Premdas 2007; Wells-Symonette 2002).

The executive branch of government in both countries is organized following the Whitehall model of civil service. Ministries are led by ministers, who are politically appointed cabinet members; but the ministries are run by permanent secretaries and staffed by deputy secretaries, directors, assistant directors, researchers, and clerks—all professional, politically neutral civil servants recruited through merit-based competitive examinations. Permanent secretaries have constitutional status in The Bahamas (Constitution of the Commonwealth of The Bahamas, article 88) and Trinidad and Tobago (Constitution of Trinidad and Tobago, article 85), and are appointed following similar procedures: by the governor-general on the recommendation of the Public Service Commission in The Bahamas, and by the Public Service Commission in Trinidad and Tobago, after consultation with the prime minister in both cases. Their role is the same in both countries: to act as "the vital link between the political directorate and the bureaucracy, with respect to the accurate interpretation of policy guidelines and the timely pursuance of government programmes" (Wells-Symonette 2002, 74). They perform this role by organizing the work of their ministry so it complies with the cabinet's policy directives, coordinating with the appropriate ministries in cases of multisectoral initiatives, and ensuring both that the necessary resources are allocated to fulfill policy directives and that "all aspects of various matters are fully examined at the official level—including the technical-professional level—before submission to the Minister" (Wells-Symonette 2002, 76). An additional, and crucial, similarity between The Bahamas and Trinidad and Tobago is that permanent secretaries are routinely reshuffled among ministries, so they can learn from and contribute their organizational expertise to different government agencies throughout their careers. These reshuffles typically either occur upon request or are triggered by resignations or retirements, not by political fiat. In both countries, the Public Service Commission appoints deputy secretaries, directors, assistant directors, and so forth, who are tasked with either formulating or implementing policies.

These two institutional legacies from the colonial period structure the main settings of the formal policy-making process in both The Bahamas and Trinidad and Tobago.[1] This process begins with a directive from the cabinet, initiated by the prime minister or by other ministers, which orders the development of a policy either to comply with the party manifesto under which the government was elected or to take up an emerging issue. This cabinet directive typically appoints a specific ministry to develop the policy on its own, or to chair an interministerial committee that would draft the intended policies. The minister appointed as the technical lead then asks the permanent secretary at the ministry to organize the process as required, that is, to task the appropriate units in the ministry with the drafting of a white paper, to set up meetings of the interministerial committee to develop or discuss policy drafts, or to do both. The permanent secretary then relays these instructions to undersecretaries and directors, who in turn order their staff to collect and analyze information, identify best practices, prepare budget estimates, and pour their data, analyses, and recommendations into a white paper. This white paper is reviewed by the Attorney General's Office (ATTG) in The Bahamas or the Ministry of Legal Affairs (MINLEG) in Trinidad and Tobago, as well as by the Ministry of Finance (MINFIN) in case the initiative includes budget requirements, and the Ministry of Public Service (MINPUBSERV) in case of human resource requirements. Subsequently, it is debated within the interministerial committee, provided such a committee has been specially appointed, or directly with stakeholders from outside the government in consultations run by senior staff from the lead ministry. After acknowledging or incorporating comments and suggestions from these consultations, the technical lead drafts the appropriate legal instruments—bills or subsidiary legislation—in consultation with the legal counsel and submits them, accompanied by a final version of the policy paper, for consideration by the minister in charge of the policy or chairing the interministerial committee. Once approved by the minister, the policy and its background paper are forwarded to the cabinet secretary, who then decides when and how to put them up for consideration by the cabinet. In turn, the cabinet may approve, reject, or demand amendments to the proposed policies and legal instruments—in which case the drafts are returned to the lead ministry and the legal counsel for reworking. Once the cabinet approves, it orders the appropriate ministries to initiate implementation in the case of subsidiary legislation or, in the case of a bill, orders the parliamentary secretary to table it in Parliament. Once both houses of Parliament give their approval, and the governor-general in The Bahamas or the president in Trinidad and Tobago grants consent, bills become laws and are referred back to the ministries for implementation. Figure 6.1 depicts the process.

This formal structure of the policy-making process leads to several expectations about its actual workings. First, it suggests that the main sources of policy ideas would be the prime minister and the cabinet, as authors and interpreters of the government party's manifesto and the emerging issues on the public agenda, whereas the ministries

FIGURE 6.1: **Formal Policy-Making Process, The Bahamas and Trinidad and Tobago**

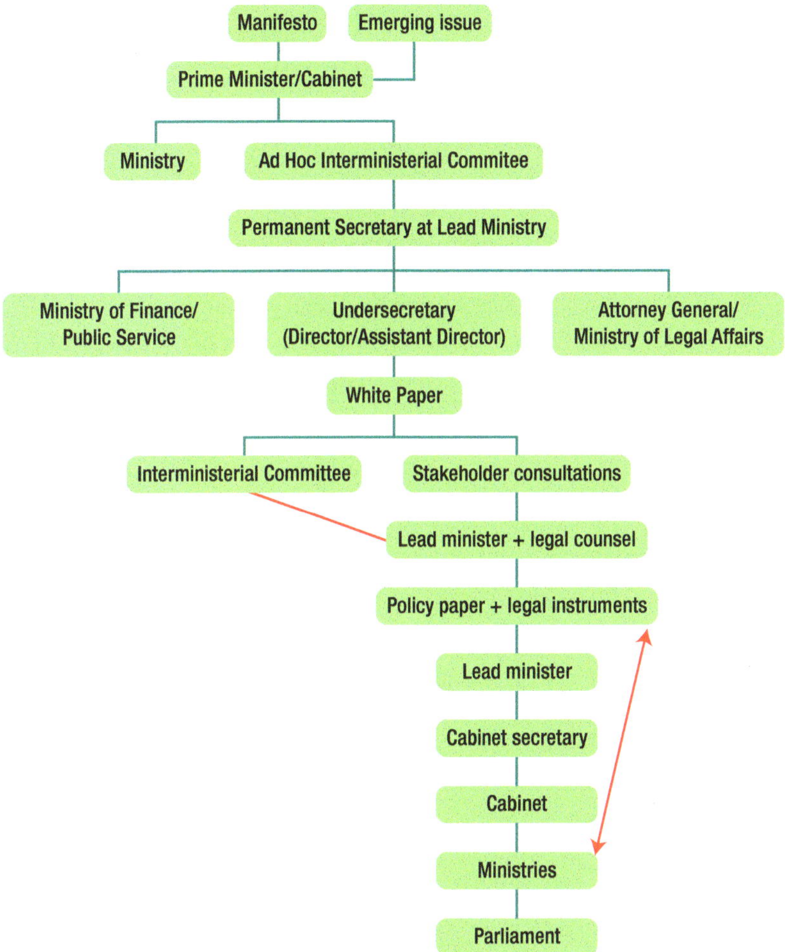

Sources: Constitution of the Commonwealth of The Bahamas; Constitution of Trinidad and Tobago; Manual of Cabinet and Ministry Procedure of the Government of The Bahamas; Civil Service Act of Trinidad and Tobago; Dolly et al. 2002; Wells-Symonette 2002.

would perform as consumers and executors of those ideas. Second, it suggests that the main sources of information for policy formulation would be the intraministerial units, the participating ministries in the interministerial committees, and the participating stakeholders in consultations, whereas the permanent secretaries, the legal counsel (the ATTG in The Bahamas and MINLEG in Trinidad and Tobago), and MINPUBSERV in The Bahamas would operate as recipients of information. The formal structure of the policy-making process also indicates that MINFIN and MINPUBSERV in The Bahamas would be the main providers of resources, whereas every other actor would be on the receiving end of the chain. Finally, this formal structure indicates that the cabinet would be the most powerful actor in the process, likely followed by the lead ministry and its permanent secretary as technical coordinators, the legal counsel offices as clearance units, and the cabinet secretary as agenda setter for Parliament. The ever-present possibility that the process may involve various ministries, with their corresponding permanent secretaries, directors, and so forth, makes it impossible to establish a precise, formally prescribed, number of participants. Should the process involve no interministerial committee and only one ministry, however, the minimum number of participants in the policy-making process would be 12, excluding the inherently indeterminate number of stakeholders taking part in consultations.

To investigate the extent to which the actual social policy formulation process corresponds to the formal structure of the policy-making process, we carried out social network analyses of social policy formulation in both The Bahamas and Trinidad and Tobago. Following the research design outlined in chapter 3, we employed snowball sampling to specify the network boundaries: during January 2018, we interviewed an initial sample of policy makers in each country—defined by selecting the top-tier officials in the social area ministries (that is, health, education, social development, labor, and planning)—using a questionnaire that contained (1) name-generator questions aimed at identifying the actors and administrative units with which the interviewees typically interact in the social policy formulation process and (2) name-interpreter questions to help identify the contents of their relations (see appendix B). We then used the same questionnaire to interview those actors absent from the initial sample who were mentioned by at least 75 percent of the initial interviewees, until no new actors were mentioned. The complete list of identified actors and their acronyms is included in appendix A.[2]

In Trinidad and Tobago, 42 percent of the initial sample was available for interview, and responses yielded a network size of 78 members. The average tenure of the interviewees was 5 years and 6 months, and all public officials interviewed except one had at least 10 years of experience in public service. In The Bahamas, 71 percent of the initial sample could be interviewed, and responses generated a network of 75 members. The average tenure of the Bahamian interviewees was 5 years and 9 months, and all the public officials interviewed had a minimum of 12 years in public service. These data on tenure and experience are consistent with both the theoretical expectations for Whitehall-style bureaucracies and the information available on these countries' civil services (Draper 2001; Mateo Díaz and Echebarría 2008; Rodríguez Gustá and Iacoviello 2008).

The network maps were then analyzed using the VisuaLyzer software to determine their density, cohesion, and centrality measures; establish their cores and peripheries; and identify their cliques and cutpoints. Using these measures, we compared the actual networks to the formal structure of the policy-making process, and the networks in The Bahamas to those in Trinidad and Tobago. The following sections present and discuss the network maps focusing on each specific relational content.

The Whole Network of Social Policy Formulation in The Bahamas and Trinidad and Tobago

This section presents and describes the maps for the whole network of actors that, according to the interviewees, participate in social policy formulation processes in The Bahamas and Trinidad and Tobago. These whole-network maps include all connections among all the actors named by the interviewees, regardless of the relational contents of their connections. The graphs are undirected so as not to depict any particular node (actor) as the source or the recipient of any particular relational contents. The size and color of the nodes are uniform, again, in order to avoid the depiction of any type of hierarchy among actors. Consequently, these maps constitute a neutral depiction of the networks of actors involved in social policy formulation. The only differentiating marks, the nodes inserted in red squares, identify the network's core; the nodes without red squares represent the periphery.

Figure 6.2 depicts the whole network of social policy formulation in The Bahamas. It is a connected network, with no isolate components; however, it is also a low-density network, with a 0.0951 value, indicating that only a few of the possible links among its nodes have actually emerged. Consistent with this low density, nodes and ties in this network have an average geodesic distance of 2.4, which indicates that, on average, any given actor must go through more than two other actors to contact any other given actor in the network. These traits suggest that some of the relational contents linking the actors in this network create either a hierarchical or a fragmented structure that prevents the emergence of other theoretically possible ties. This network structure may negatively affect the likelihood that the social policy–making process will generate adaptable, coherent, and coordinated policies.

The network of social policy formulation in The Bahamas displays two main features that differ from the formal structure of the policy-making process. The first is the number of participants: as argued previously, it is impossible to establish a formally prescribed number of participants, but the actual number of 75 vastly exceeds the minimum number involving only one ministry (12), and even the minimum theoretical number if all four social area ministries had their permanent secretaries, undersecretaries, directors, and assistant directors participate in an interministerial committee (24). The difference in the number of network members is explained by the presence of (1) stakeholders such as unions, business associations, and NGOs; (2) multilateral actors, such as the Inter-American Development Bank (IDB), International Labour Organization (ILO), Organization of American States (OAS), and United Nations (UN); and (3) other government agencies whose portfolios grant them access to information or resources that social area ministries require to formulate and implement their policies. Those government agencies include the Ministry of National Security (NATSEG) and the Ministry for the Environment (MINENV), with their respective permanent secretaries.

FIGURE 6.2: **Whole Network of Social Policy Formulation, The Bahamas**

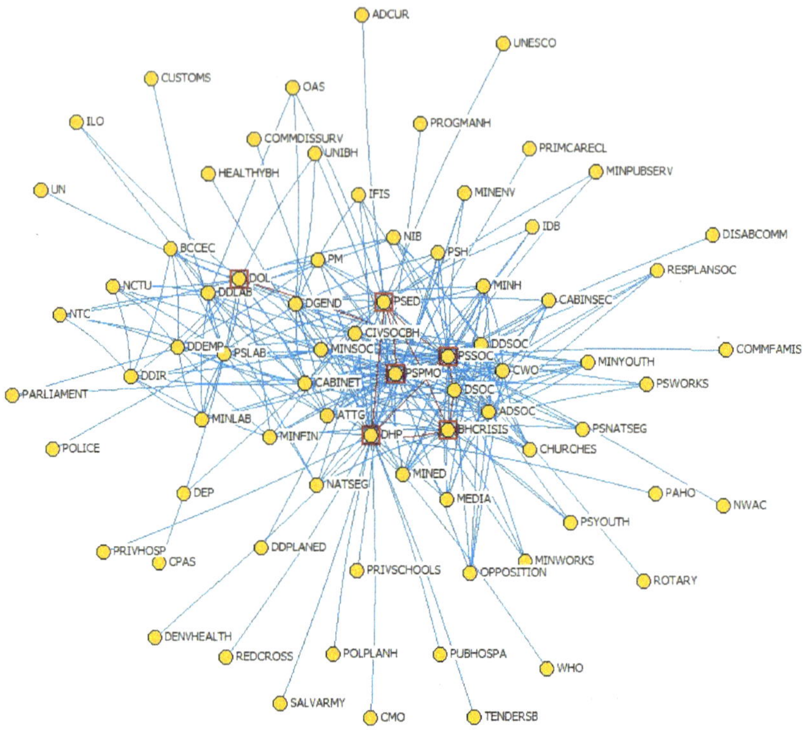

Source: Original figure for this publication.
Note: Nodes in red squares identify the network's core; other nodes represent the periphery. See appendix A for definitions of all abbreviations used in this figure.

The second difference is that the central and peripheral actors in the formal network switch places in the whole network. In the formal network, the cabinet, the legal counsel (the attorney general in The Bahamas), and the lead ministry were the core actors. In the whole network, however, the permanent secretaries at the Ministry of Education (PSED), Ministry of Social Services (PSSOC), and Office of the Prime Minister (PSPMO); the directors of Health Policy (DHP) and labor policy (DOL); and an NGO (The Bahamas Crisis Center [BHCRISIS])—all peripheral actors in the formal structure—now constitute the core of the social policy formulation network. In short, all the core actors in the formal network are peripheral actors in the actual network, and all the core actors in the actual network are peripheral actors in the formal network.

This network also presents two notable traits of its own. First, its cutpoints are all government actors: the PSED, the PSSOC, the permanent secretary at the Ministry of Labour (PSLAB), the DHP, and the director of Gender Policy (DGEND). Considering the formal structure of the policy-making process and the relatively low turnover of senior public officials, it seems unlikely that the social policy formulation network in The Bahamas would become disconnected by the severance of any one of its cut-points. Second, the network presents a high number of cliques: 103 in 264 reported ties. The prevalence of cliques means that 39 percent of nodes are highly connected in a cohesive way distinct from the rest of the network by virtue of their own relational contents. To understand how these distinct links affect the social policy formulation process, it is necessary to disaggregate the whole network according to the different relational contents reported by the actors.

Figure 6.3 depicts the whole network of social policy formulation in Trinidad and Tobago. This network is also connected, with no isolated components, and has low density. Its density, however, is considerably higher than that of The Bahamas network: 0.2118 compared to 0.0951. This higher density is the result of having established 636 links for 78 nodes, compared to 264 links for 75 nodes in The

FIGURE 6.3: **Whole Network of Social Policy Formulation, Trinidad and Tobago**

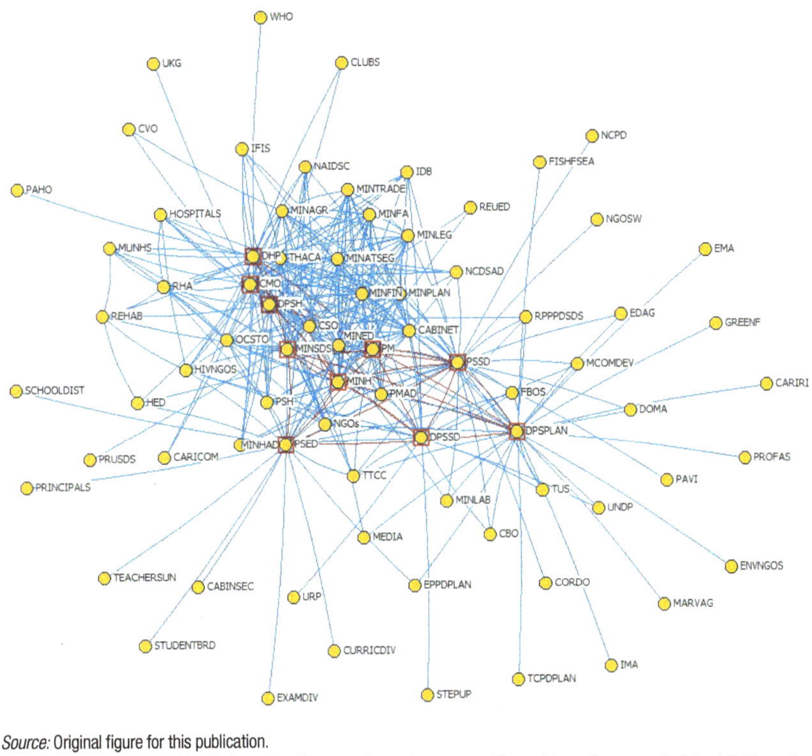

Source: Original figure for this publication.
Note: Nodes in red squares identify the network's core; other nodes represent the periphery. See appendix A for definitions of all abbreviations used in this figure.

Bahamas network. Consistently, the average geodesic distance between nodes is slightly lower than in The Bahamas: 2.36 compared to 2.4. Still, these network traits indicate that in Trinidad and Tobago, as in The Bahamas, some relational contents generate a hierarchical network structure that prevents the emergence of other, theoretically possible, ties. This network structure, like the one in The Bahamas, may also complicate the development of adaptable, coherent, and coordinated social policies.

The social policy formulation network of Trinidad and Tobago shares with The Bahamas network the same differential features relative to the formal structure of the policy-making process. The number of participants is higher than the minimum and higher than the theoretical number including all social area ministerial teams in an interministerial committee: 78 actors. As in The Bahamas, this network size is explained by the presence of stakeholders (such as unions, NGOs, and the Trinidad and Tobago Chamber of Commerce [TTCC]), multilateral actors (such as IDB and the Caribbean Common Market [CARICOM]), and other government agencies, such as NATSEG and the Ministry for Community Development (MCOMMDEV), with their respective permanent secretaries. Also as in the The Bahamas network, the central and peripheral actors in Trinidad and Tobago's formal network change places in the whole network of social policy formulation. The core actors in the actual network are the same type of actors as in The Bahamas: permanent secretaries (at the Ministry of Education [PSED] and the Ministry of Social Development Services [PSSD]), deputy permanent secretaries (at the Ministries of Planning [DPSPLAN], Health [DPSH], and Social Development Services [DPSSD]), and directors (at the Director of Health Policy [DPH]). In the Trinidad and Tobago network, unlike the one in the The Bahamas, the prime minister (PM), a central actor in the formal structure of the policy-making process, is at the core, together with the Ministry of Social Development and Family Services, whereas nongovernmental actors are all peripheral.

Again, just as in The Bahamas network, the Trinidad and Tobago network has only governmental actors as cutpoints: the PSED, the PSSD, the DPSPLAN, the DPSSD, the DHP, the chief medical officer (CMO), and the Central Statistics Office (CSO). The formal structure of the policy-making process and the relative stability of senior public officials suggest that the network has a low likelihood of breakup.

The Trinidad and Tobago network has a comparatively lower share of cliques than The Bahamas network: 123 for 636 reported ties, compared to 103 in 264 ties. Only 19.3 percent of the actors in the Trinidad and Tobago network are connected differently than the other network members by virtue of their relational contents. Still, the question of how, and to what extent, these cliques may affect the social policy formulation process remains to be answered. Doing so requires unpacking the different relational contents.

The Networks of Ideas in The Bahamas and Trinidad and Tobago

This section describes and compares the network maps for the circulation of ideas in the social policy formulation processes of The Bahamas and Trinidad and Tobago. The first map corresponds to The Bahamas network (figure 6.4). The green nodes indicate that the actors represented by them are net producers of ideas within the network. The red nodes, on the contrary, indicate that the actors are net recipients of ideas. The yellow node indicates that the actor in question provides and receives ideas from the same number of actors. The size of the nodes conveys the extent of their provision or reception of ideas: the higher the number of links that provide or receive ideas, the larger the node. The nodes in squares constitute the core of the network, whereas the remaining nodes constitute its periphery.

FIGURE 6.4: **Network of Ideas in the Social Policy Formulation Process, The Bahamas**

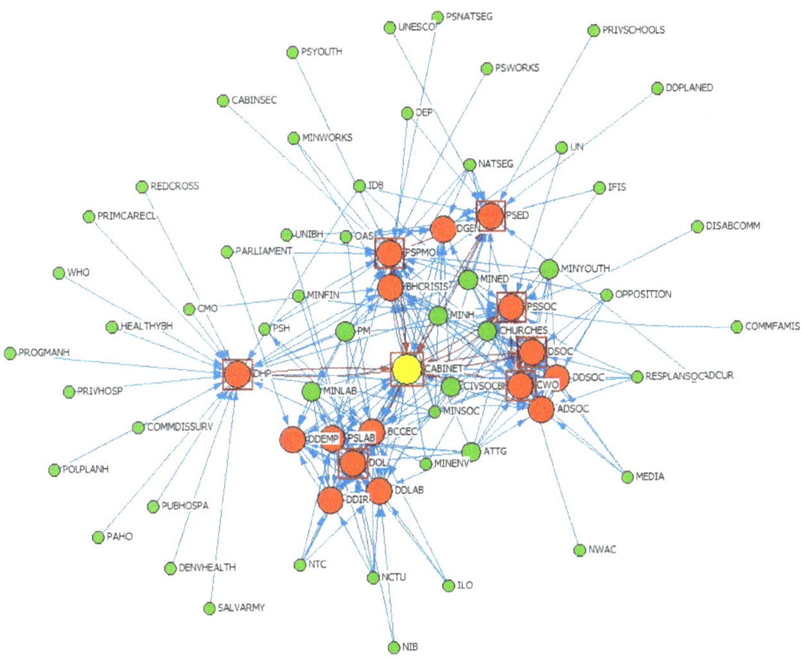

Source: Original figure for this publication.
Note: Green nodes are net producers of ideas within the network, red nodes are net recipients of ideas, and the yellow node indicates that the actor provides and receives ideas from the same number of actors. The size of the nodes conveys the extent of provision or reception of ideas. Nodes in squares constitute the core of the network; remaining nodes constitute its periphery. See appendix A for definitions of all abbreviations used in this figure.

The ideas network in The Bahamas is a connected, low-density network with a 0.1138 value and only 267 ties among 69 nodes. Consistent with the structure of the whole network, the average geodesic distance is 2.6219. Contrary to the expectations from both the formal structure of the policy-making process and the structure of the whole network, The Bahamas ideas network is not particularly hierarchical. This pattern can be explained by four factors.

First, the degree centrality scores, which measure the extent to which any given actor is connected to the other actors in the network, show that none of the actors in this network has more than 50 percent degree centrality. Thus, no actor is connected to a majority of the other actors in the network, so none occupies a clearly central position. The cabinet has the highest degree centrality, with a score of 47 percent, closely followed by the PSSOC with 45.58 percent. The third position in degree centrality corresponds to the PSPMO, with 38.2 percent, and the fourth position to the DHP, with 3.2 percent; all the other actors in the network have scores below 35 percent.

Second, eight actors at the core of the network have relatively low degree centrality scores. Apart from the aforementioned cabinet, PSSOC, PSPMO, and DHP, other actors include the PSED with 25 percent, the chief welfare officer (CWO) with 30.8 percent, the director of social services (DSOC) with 32.3 percent, and the DOL with 33.8 percent. These scores indicate that the large core, which takes up 11.5 percent of the network size, has no dominant actor.

Third, none of the actors at the core of the network is a net provider of social policy ideas. The cabinet is a recipient as much as a provider, and most of the permanent secretaries and policy directors of the social area ministries—with the exception of the permanent secretary at the Ministry of Health (PSH)—are net recipients of ideas. Although the PM and the Ministries of Education (MINED), Health (MINH), Labour (MINLAB), and Social Services (MINSOC) are net providers, their degree centrality scores are low: 11.7 percent, 14 percent, 16.1 percent, 11.7 percent, and 20.5 percent, respectively. These scores corroborate, as figure 6.4 clearly shows, the absence of a dominant provider of ideas in the network.

Fourth, of the 50 cliques identified in The Bahamas ideas network, only two are purely intraministerial (ADSOC-CWO-DDSOC-DSOC-MINSOC-PSSOC and ADSOC-CWO-DDSOC-DSOC-PSSOC-RESPLANSOC). All other cliques involve either other government agencies—both from within and beyond the social area—or nongovernmental actors. Thus, no actor or clique of actors either encapsulates or coordinates the circulation of ideas.

These patterns contrast with the expectations from the formal structure of the policy-making process. In the formal structure, the cabinet is the main source of ideas, followed by the social area ministries; however, in The Bahamas network the cabinet is not a net provider of ideas and the social area ministries compete for the provision of ideas with several other actors of similar centrality. In The Bahamas formal network, senior officers at the social area ministries are key providers of ideas, but in the actual network they are net recipients of ideas. The social policy formulation process in The Bahamas is thus dominantly triggered not by political directives from the cabinet on the basis of the governing party's manifesto but by a variety of influencers connected to the various layers of policy makers in the administrative machine.[3] The network structure lacks hierarchy but is not exactly fragmented: the prevalence of governmental actors among the membership and their connectedness prevents fragmentation.

The network of ideas in the social policy formulation process of Trinidad and Tobago presents similar patterns. It is also a connected, low-density network, with an even lower value than in The Bahamas (0.0664 compared to 0.1138) and only 165 ties among 71 nodes. It is also a nonhierarchical network, again contrary to the expectations from both the formal structure of the policy-making process and the structure of the overall Trinidad and Tobago network. The same four factors as in The Bahamas contribute to explain this pattern, albeit with minor variations.

First, the degree centrality scores, though somewhat higher than in The Bahamas, also indicate the lack of a clearly dominant actor in the Trinidad and Tobago network. Although the DPSPLAN has a score of 60 percent, followed by the PSSD (44.2 percent), and the CMO and PSED (both with 35.7 percent), all other actors in the network have scores below 30 percent.

Second, although the DPSPLAN, the only core actor in the network, is connected to a majority of the nodes, many other actors contest its centrality position (see figure 6.5). The closeness centrality scores, which measure the extent to which any given node is close to each of the other nodes in the network, indicate how close this competition is: although the DPSPLAN has a score of 0.009; the PSSD, Prime Minister's Advisors (PMAD), and Ministry of Planning (MINPLAN) have scores of 0.008; and 13 other actors—including the cabinet—have scores of 0.007. Again, as in The Bahamas, Trinidad and Tobago's network of ideas has no clearly dominant actor.

Third, none of the actors at the core of the network, or with higher degree centrality, is a net provider of ideas. The DPSPLAN, PSSD, CMO, PSED, DHP, DPSH, DPSD, Chief Administrator for the Tobago House of Assembly (THACA), and cabinet are all net recipients of ideas. And, again as in The Bahamas, although the MINH, MINPLAN, PM, PMAD, Ministry of Health Advisors (MINHAD), and TTCC are net providers, their degree centrality scores are comparatively low: 11.4 percent for MINPLAN and PMAD, and 8.5 percent for the rest. These scores corroborate, as the figure shows, the absence of a dominant provider of ideas in the Trinidad and Tobago network.

Fourth, of the 43 cliques identified in the Trinidad and Tobago ideas network, only two (CMO-DHP-DPSH-MINH and CMO-DHP-DPSH-MINHAD) are intraministerial. All other cliques involve other government agencies, private sector actors, or both. As in The Bahamas, the circulation of social policy ideas in Trinidad and Tobago is not encapsulated or coordinated from above.

FIGURE 6.5: **Network of Ideas in the Social Policy Formulation Process, Trinidad and Tobago**

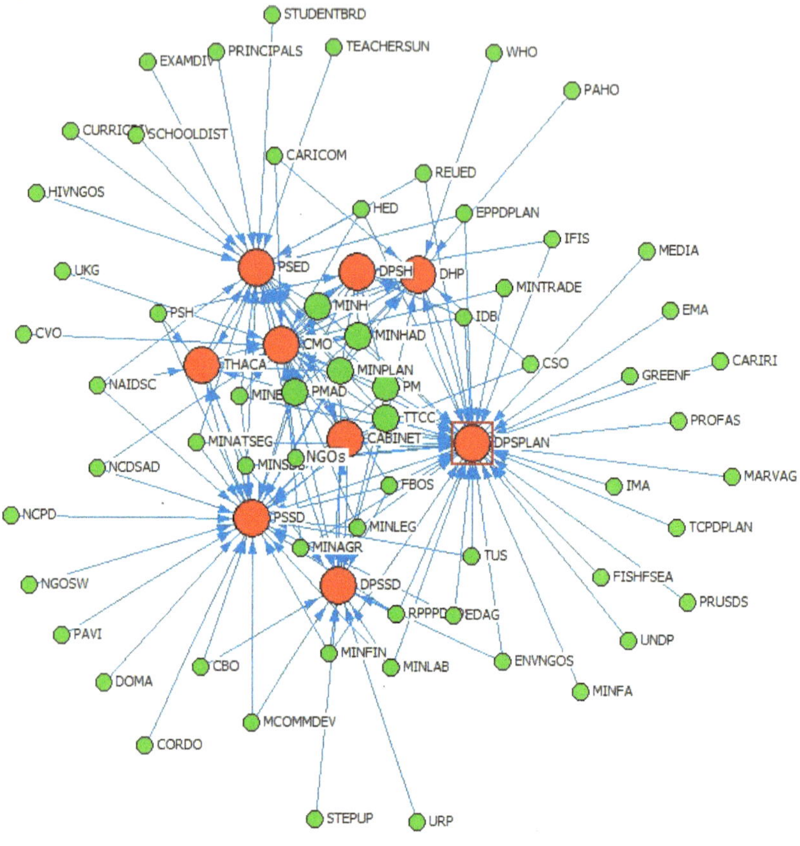

Source: Original figure for this publication.
Note: Green nodes are net producers of ideas within the network, and red nodes are net recipients of ideas. The size of the nodes conveys the extent of their provision or reception of ideas. Nodes in squares constitute the core of the network; remaining nodes constitute its periphery. See appendix A for definitions of all abbreviations used in this figure.

Consequently, the network of ideas in the social policy formulation process of Trinidad and Tobago contrasts with the expectation from the formal structure of the policy-making process. Again, the cabinet is not the main source, or even a net provider, of ideas. The senior officers at the social area ministries are also net recipients, rather than providers, of policy ideas. And the social policy formulation process is triggered not by cabinet or PM directives to comply with the election manifesto but rather by a series of inputs from a diverse set of actors, both public and private.[4] Because of the prevalence and connectedness of governmental actors in its membership, the network structure, as in The Bahamas, is neither hierarchical nor fragmented.

The Networks of Information in The Bahamas and Trinidad and Tobago

This section describes and compares the network cabinet for the circulation of information in the social policy formulation processes of The Bahamas and Trinidad and Tobago. The first map corresponds to The Bahamas network (figure 6.6). The green nodes indicate that the actors represented by them are net producers of information within the network. The red nodes, on the contrary, indicate that the actors are net recipients of information. The yellow node indicates that the actor in question provides information to and receives information from the same number of actors. The size of the nodes conveys the extent of their provision or reception of information: the higher the number of links that provide or receive information, the larger the node. The nodes in squares constitute the core of the network, and the remaining nodes constitute its periphery.

The information network in The Bahamas is a connected, low-density network with a 0.1096 value and only 288 ties among 73 nodes. Consistent with the structure of the whole network, the average geodesic distance is 2.4349. Like the ideas network, this network is not particularly hierarchical, and the positions of the actors are, to a significant extent, the reverse of those expected from the formal structure of the policy-making process.

The information network in The Bahamas is not particularly hierarchical because it has no dominant provider of information, its core consists exclusively of net recipients of information, and these net recipients are the actors with highest degree centrality scores. The network has no dominant provider of information insofar as 59 out of 73 network members are net providers, only one (MINSOC) has over 20 percent degree centrality, and only eight have more than a 10 percent score: the cabinet, PM, PSH, MINH, MINED, Deputy Director for Employment (DDEMP), denominational churches, and Civil Society of The Bahamas, an umbrella organization under which most Bahamian NGOs come together.

The core of the network, as shown in figure 6.6, consists entirely of net recipients of information: the DHP, PSED, PSPMO, PSSOC, and Deputy Director of Labour Policy (DDLAB). These core actors have the highest degree centrality scores: 66.6 percent (PSSOC), 43 percent (PSED), 40.2 percent (PSPMO), and 38.8 percent (DHP). Only the DDLAB has a relatively lower score of 31.9 percent, just below the 33.3 percent of the permanent secretary at MINLAB and The Bahamas Chamber of Commerce and Employers Confederation (BCCEC). A network consisting entirely of net recipients is, predictably, the other side of the coin of the dispersion in the field of information providers. Information in the social policy formulation process in The Bahamas flows from a large number of governmental and nongovernmental actors to a small set of government agencies.

FIGURE 6.6: **Network of Information in the Social Policy Formulation Process, The Bahamas**

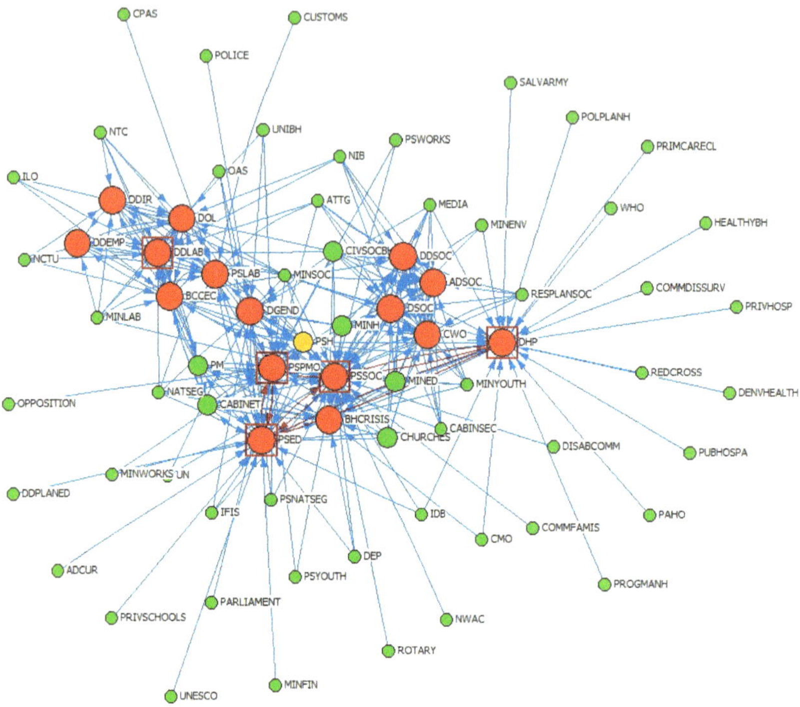

Source: Original figure for this publication.
Note: Green nodes are net producers of information, red nodes are net recipients of information, and the yellow node indicates that the actor provides information to and receives information from the same number of actors. The size of the nodes conveys the extent of their provision or reception of information. Nodes in squares constitute the core of the network; remaining nodes constitute its periphery. See appendix A for definitions of all abbreviations used in this figure.

These patterns are, to some extent, the reverse of those expected from the formal structure of the policy-making process. Whereas the formal structure suggests that the main sources of information are the intraministerial policy units, The Bahamas information network shows that those units are actually net recipients, not net providers, of information. According to the formal institutional design, the Attorney General's Office (ATTG), the Minister of Finance (MINFIN) and the Minister of Public Service (MINPUBSERV) operate as net recipients of information; however, they in fact perform as net providers.

Despite its divergence from the formal design, the actual network of information conforms with the expectations of that design in three ways. First, social area ministries and nongovernmental stakeholders act as net providers of information. Second, the permanent secretaries of the social area ministries act as net recipients, with the exception of the PSH, who is a provider as much as a recipient. Finally, no dominant entity encapsulates or coordinates information: only 2 of 76 cliques identified are purely intraministerial (ADSOC-CWO-DDSOC-DSCOC-MINSOC-PSSOC and ADSOC-CWO-DDSOC-DSCOC-PSSOC-RESPLANSOC); the rest involve other government agencies, nongovernmental actors, or both. The latter suggests, as was the case with the ideas network, that the network structure is neither hierarchical nor fragmented.

The network of information in the social policy formulation process of Trinidad and Tobago presents similar patterns. It is also a connected, low-density network, with an even lower value than in The Bahamas (0.0936 compared to 0.1096) and only 246 ties among 73 nodes. As in The Bahamas, the network in Trinidad and Tobago is nonhierarchical, and the positions of the actors are, to a significant extent, contrary to the expectations from the formal structure of the policy-making process. The same factors as in The Bahamas contribute to explain these patterns.

The information network in Trinidad and Tobago, as in The Bahamas, is not particularly hierarchical because it has no dominant provider of information, its core consists almost exclusively of net recipients of information, and these net recipients are the actors with highest degree centrality scores. No dominant provider of information exists because 63 of 73 actors in the network are net providers, none of those net providers has a degree centrality score higher than 14 percent, and only six actors have scores above 10 percent: NGOs have 13.8 percent, MINED has 12.5 percent, NGOs specialized in HIV issues (HIVNGOS) have 12.5 percent, and MINPLAN, PMAD, and the Ministry of Social Development and Family Services (MINSDS) have 11.1 percent.

Three actors constitute the core of this network, as marked by the squares on the nodes in figure 6.7. Two of those actors (the DPSPLAN and PSSD) are net recipients of information, whereas the CSO provides information to and receives it from the same number of actors. These three actors have the highest degree centrality scores: 97.2 percent for the CSO, 62.5 percent for the DPSPLAN, and 51.3 percent for the PSSD. As in The Bahamas, this centrality is the predictable complement to the dispersion in the field of information providers.

As in The Bahamas, these patterns are to some extent the reverse of those expected from the formal structure of the policy-making process. Contrary to expectations, the Trinidad and Tobago information network shows that intraministerial policy units are net recipients, rather than net providers, of information and that the Ministries of Finance and Legal Affairs operate as net providers of information, instead of as net recipients.

Still, again as in The Bahamas case, three aspects of the Trinidad and Tobago information network are consistent with the expectations from the formal design. First, the social area ministries and nongovernmental stakeholders act as net providers of information. Second, the permanent secretaries of the social area ministries are net recipients of information, with the exception of the PSH, which is a net provider. Finally, no dominant entity encapsulates or coordinates information: only 2 of 89 cliques identified were purely intraministerial (CMO-DHP-RHA, and DHP-DPSH-RHA);

FIGURE 6.7: **Network of Information in the Social Policy Formulation Process, Trinidad and Tobago**

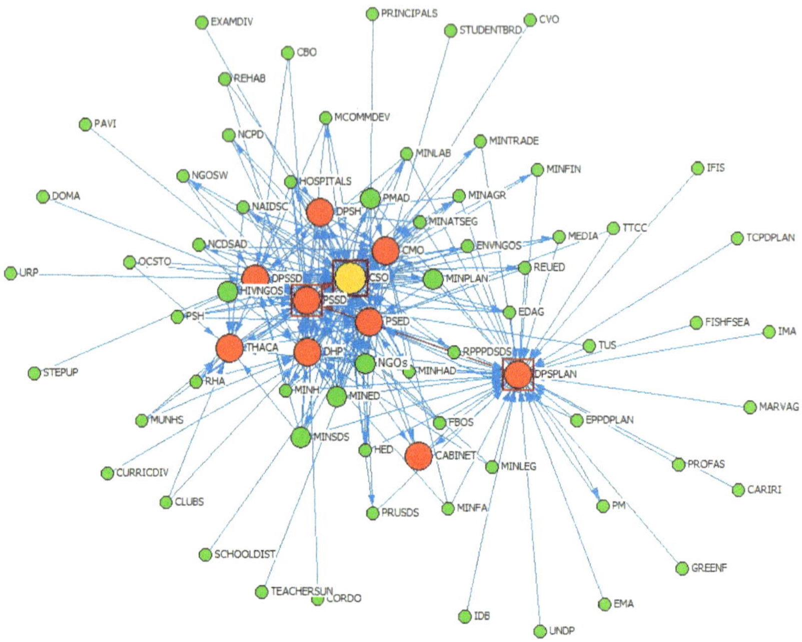

Source: Original figure for this publication.
Note: Green nodes are net producers of information, red nodes are net recipients of information, and the yellow node indicates that the actor provides information to and receives information from the same number of actors. The size of the nodes conveys the extent of their provision or reception of information. Nodes in squares constitute the core of the network; remaining nodes constitute its periphery. See appendix A for definitions of all abbreviations used in this figure.

the rest involved other government agencies, nongovernmental actors, or both. The latter suggests, as in The Bahamas, that the network structure's lack of hierarchy does not entail fragmentation: the prevalence and connectedness of governmental actors appear to prevent that outcome.

The Networks of Resources in The Bahamas and Trinidad and Tobago

This section describes and compares the network maps for the circulation of resources in the social policy formulation processes of The Bahamas and Trinidad and Tobago. The resources in question include not only monies but also logistical assistance (for example, mobilization of one agency's human and budgetary resources to identify target beneficiaries of a program run by another agency) and nonmonetary forms of aid (for example, food and clothing). The first map corresponds to The Bahamas network (figure 6.8). The green nodes indicate actors who are net providers of resources within the network. The red nodes, on the contrary, stand for actors who are net recipients of resources. The yellow nodes indicate that the actors provide to and receive resources from the same number of actors. The size of the nodes conveys the extent of their provision or reception of resources: the higher the number of links that provide or receive resources, the larger the node.[5] The nodes in squares constitute the core of the network, and the remaining nodes constitute its periphery.

FIGURE 6.8: **Network of Resources in the Social Policy Formulation Process, The Bahamas**

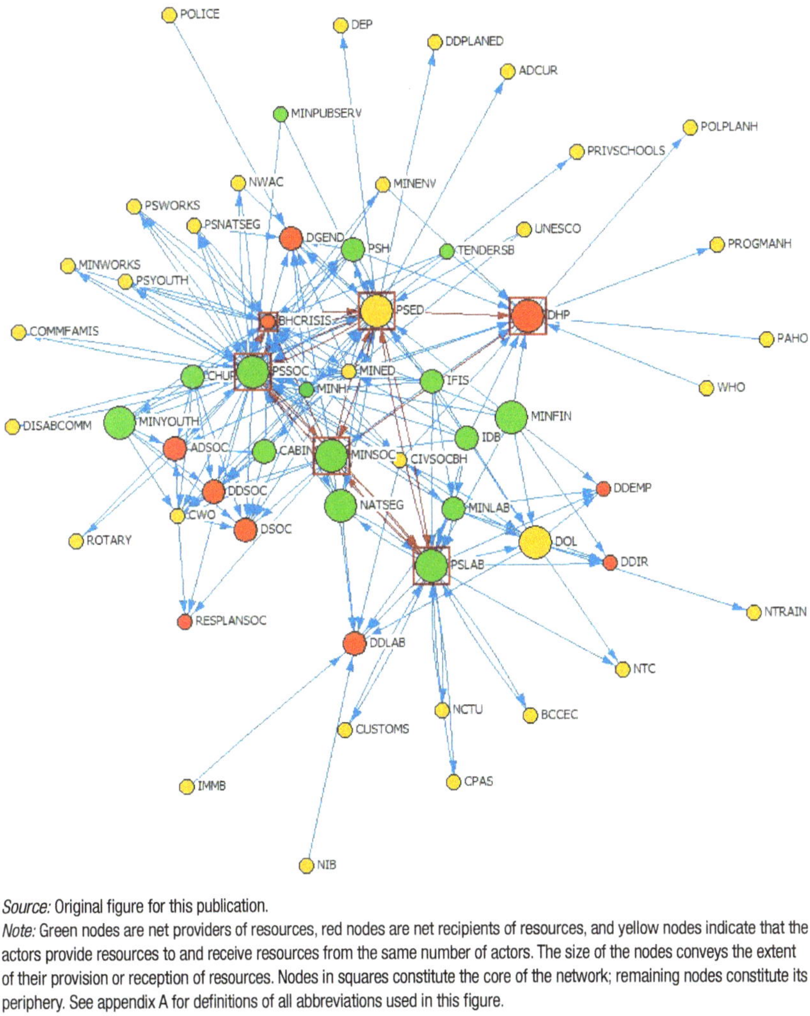

Source: Original figure for this publication.
Note: Green nodes are net providers of resources, red nodes are net recipients of resources, and yellow nodes indicate that the actors provide resources to and receive resources from the same number of actors. The size of the nodes conveys the extent of their provision or reception of resources. Nodes in squares constitute the core of the network; remaining nodes constitute its periphery. See appendix A for definitions of all abbreviations used in this figure.

The resources network in The Bahamas is a connected, low-density network, with a 0.1291 value and only 206 ties among 56 nodes. Consistent with the structure of the whole network, the average geodesic distance is 2.4192. Contrary to expectations from the formal structure of the policy-making process, this is not a hierarchical network, and MINFIN and MINPUBSERV are not central actors in it.

The resources network in The Bahamas is not hierarchical because it has no dominant provider. This finding is, to some extent, but not entirely, the consequence of including information about the circulation of logistics and nonmonetary assistance as types of resources. Although the most senior officials consistently mention MINFIN as both a provider of monetary resources and a veto actor in the process of obtaining such resources, other officials, as well as nongovernmental actors, mention different government actors as providers of funds. The more frequently named are the permanent secretaries, which explains their relatively high degree centrality scores: 94.6 percent for PSSOC, 57.1 percent for the PSED, and 48.4 percent for the PSLAB.

Despite their relatively high scores, the permanent secretaries are not dominant providers either. Although they constitute part of the core of this network, their out-degree centrality scores, which indicate the number of actors in the network to whom they provide resources, are either identical to or barely above their in-degree scores, which indicate the number of actors in the network from whom they receive resources. The differences in scores in the cases of the PSSOC and PSLAB are explained by only one and two ties, respectively; and the PSED is as much a provider as a recipient of resources.

Arguably, the relatively high degree centrality of these permanent secretaries simply reflects the fact that, according to the Constitution and the Manual of Cabinet and Ministry Procedure, these officials are in charge of both executing the budget within their ministries and procuring whatever other nonmonetary resources their ministries may need to carry out their tasks. But, as depicted in figure 6.8, some non-social area agencies also provide resources to social area units besides the permanent secretaries; these actors include MINFIN, NATSEG, the Ministry of Youth (MINYOUTH), the denominational churches (CHURCHES in the figure), and international financial institutions (IFIs). Despite admittedly lower degree centrality scores than those of the permanent secretaries, these actors are stronger net providers, insofar as their out-degree scores are consistently higher than their in-degree scores (that is, they provide resources to many more actors than they receive resources from).

The resources network in the social policy formulation process of The Bahamas is also not a hierarchical network because resources circulate among government agencies and nongovernmental actors without any agency or actor being able to significantly affect circulation by blocking the flow of resources. This aspect of the network structure is indicated by the nature of the cliques and the cutpoints. Of the 56 cliques in the network, 51 involve several ministries or nongovernmental actors, and all these interagency cliques involve more than one net provider of resources. Consequently, in all but five cliques, the circulation of resources could be blocked only by agreement among several providers. The only cutpoints that could affect the circulation of resources are the permanent secretaries in the social area, except for the PSH. Even if they decided to block resources, however, they would disconnect only between three and four actors from the network (that is, less than 10 percent of network members). All in all, then, the absence of dominant providers also implies the absence of central actors that could disrupt the flow of resources. This absence of hierarchy does not lead to a fragmented network structure, however, because the main net providers of resources are highly interconnected governmental actors.

Three notable traits must also be underscored in The Bahamas resources network. First, second-tier social area agency actors, such as the DOL and DHP, are either as much recipients as providers of resources or net recipients altogether, insofar as they receive monetary resources from MINFIN to fund their operations and nonmonetary resources from other agencies or nongovernmental actors to enable design and implemention of their operations. Second, nongovernmental actors typically exchange nonmonetary for monetary resources with social area units; thus, with the exceptions of the churches and BHCRISIS, they are as much providers as recipients. Finally, the cabinet secretary (CABINSEC in the figure) is a net provider of resources. This finding would seem to reflect this office's role as agenda setter for the cabinet and, therefore, as veto actor for decisions about resources; the CABINSEC does not directly provide any resource but, by setting the cabinet's agenda, enables other actors to operate as providers and recipients.

The network of resources in the social policy formulation process of Trinidad and Tobago presents patterns consistent with those identified in The Bahamas. It is also a connected, low-density network, with a slightly higher value than in The Bahamas (0.1357 compared to 0.1291) and only 187 ties among 53 nodes. Trinidad and Tobago, like The Bahamas, has a nonhierarchical network in which MINFIN, also contrary to expectations from the formal structure of policy making, is not a central actor.

The resources network in Trinidad and Tobago is not hierarchical because it has no dominant provider of resources, its six-actor core includes only one net provider of resources, and the other five actors—either net recipients or as much recipients as providers—have the highest degree centrality scores. No dominant provider of information exists for three reasons: (1) 19 of 53 actors in the network are net providers; (2) apart from the PSSD, none of those net providers has degree centrality scores higher than 26.4 percent; and (3) 10 actors have scores above 10 percent: MINFIN, MINH, MINPLAN, MINED, and the Ministry of National Security (MINATSEG); the cabinet; the PM, the PSH; IDB; and the IFIs.

The core of this network is constituted by the PSED, PSSD, DPSH, DPSSD, CMO, and Office of the Chief Secretary of Tobago (OCSTO). But only the PSSD is a net provider of resources, and it shares with the PSED the second-highest degree centrality score (65.3 percent), after the DPSSD by two points; the PSSD and PSED are, respectively, as much a provider as a recipient and a net recipient of resources.

As in The Bahamas, senior officials in Trinidad and Tobago also mention MINFIN as a net provider and veto actor for monetary resources, but they simultaneously report, as shown in figure 6.9, that ministries, permanent secretaries, deputy permanent secretaries, the cabinet, and nongovernmental actors such as TTCC are also net providers of resources. Moreover, again as in The Bahamas, Trinidad and Tobago's MINFIN is not a central actor compared to other government agencies that operate as net providers: its degree centrality score is 19.2 percent, compared to 26.9 percent for MINH and MINED, 15.3 percent for MINPLAN, and 11.5 percent for the cabinet and the Ministry of Agriculture (MINAGER) and MINATSEG; and it shares an out-degree centrality score of 19.2 percent with the MINED.

FIGURE 6.9: **Network of Resources in the Social Policy Formulation Process, Trinidad and Tobago**

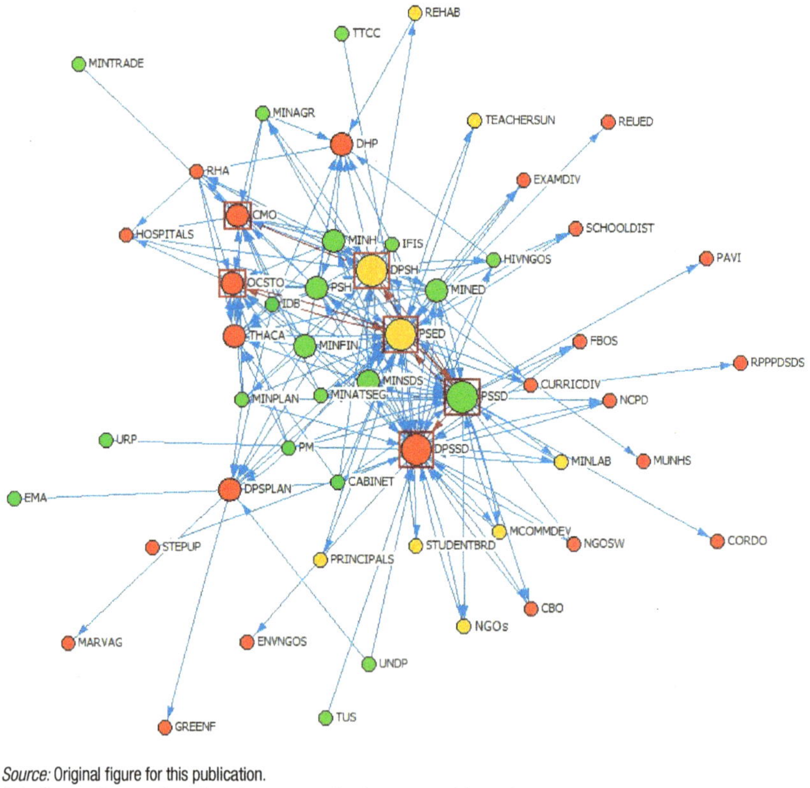

Source: Original figure for this publication.
Note: Green nodes are net providers of resources, red nodes are net recipients of resources, and yellow nodes indicate that the actors provide resources to and receive resources from the same number of actors. The size of the nodes conveys the extent of their provision or reception of resources. Nodes in squares constitute the core of the network; remaining nodes constitute its periphery. See appendix A for definitions of all abbreviations used in this figure.

As in The Bahamas, the resources network in the social policy formulation process in Trinidad and Tobago is not hierarchical also because no agency or actor can effectively block the flow of resources. The structure of the cliques and the nature of the cutpoints explain this pattern. Of the 59 cliques in the network, 51 involve several ministries, nongovernmental actors, or both; and 49 of these 51 interagency cliques involve more than one net provider of resources. Consequently, in only 10 cliques could the unilateral decision of a provider block the circulation of resources. The only cutpoints that could affect the circulation of resources are the PSSD, PSED, and DPSH. But, again as in The Bahamas, if these actors decided to block resources, they would disconnect only between one and five actors from the network (that is, less than 10 percent of network members). In Trinidad and Tobago as in The Bahamas, then, the absence of dominant providers also implies the absence of central actors that could disrupt the flow of resources, and the prevalence and connectedness of the governmental actors that operate as net providers prevent the absence of network hierarchy from resulting in a fragmented network structure.

Finally, the resources network in Trinidad and Tobago also presents the cabinet as a net provider, thereby confirming its position as veto actor for the distribution of resources; and it depicts second-tier social area agencies as net recipients. Still, the Trinidad and Tobago and The Bahamas networks differ in that the former presents nongovernmental actors as net recipients whereas in the latter those actors are as much providers as recipients.

The Networks of Power in The Bahamas and Trinidad and Tobago

This section describes and compares the network maps of power in the social policy formulation processes of The Bahamas and Trinidad and Tobago. The graphs are directed, so the origin of the arrows indicates the source of power; their destination points to the unit over which that power is exercised. The first map illustrates The Bahamas network (figure 6.10). The green nodes indicate that the actors represented by them are net sources of power. The red nodes, on the contrary, indicate that the actors are net subjects of power. The yellow nodes indicate that the actors recognize and are recognized as sources of power by the same number of actors. The size of the nodes conveys their centrality to the network of power: the higher the number of actors they are subject to or subjected by, the larger the node. The nodes in squares constitute the core of the network, and the remaining nodes constitute its periphery.

The power network in The Bahamas is a connected, low-density network with a value of 0.1842, only 292 ties among 57 nodes, and an average geodesic distance of 2.2870, also in line with the value of the whole network. Still, it is a relatively more hierarchical network whose structure is more aligned with the expectations from the formal structure of the policy-making process.

FIGURE 6.10: Network of Power in the Social Policy Formulation Process, The Bahamas

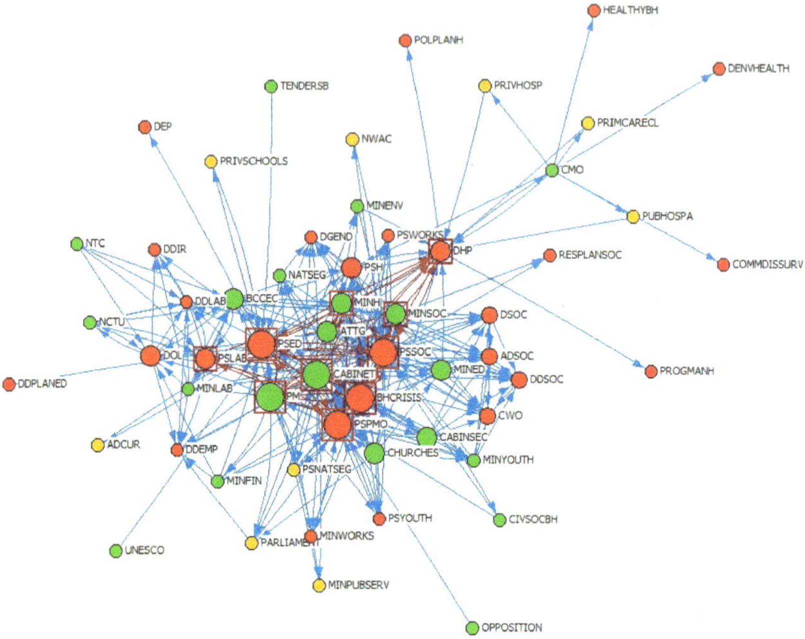

Source: Original figure for this publication.

Note: Green nodes are net sources of power, red nodes are net subjects of power, and yellow nodes recognize and are recognized as sources of power by the same number of actors. The size of the nodes conveys centrality to the network of power. Nodes in squares constitute the core of the network; remaining nodes constitute its periphery. See appendix A for definitions of all abbreviations used in this figure.

The power network in The Bahamas is more hierarchical and in line with the formal policy-making process for four reasons. First, the net sources of power with higher degree centrality scores located at the core of the network are the actors formally prescribed as net sources of power in the policy-making process: the cabinet and the PM. The cabinet has a degree centrality score of 67.8 percent, the second highest in the network, and also holds the highest closeness centrality score (68.2 percent) and third-highest betweenness centrality value (15.6 percent). Its position in the network, as figure 6.10 shows, is that of the most central net source of power. The PM, as leader of the cabinet, follows as the second most central actor at the core of the power network, with 53.5 percent degree centrality, 63.6 percent closeness centrality (the third-highest score), and 9.6 percent betweenness centrality (the sixth-highest score in the network). The data on the network's cliques corroborate these core positions. The cabinet is present in 49 of 69 cliques and the PM in 39 cliques. Thus, as expected, they operate as the political coordinators of social policy formulation.

Second, the actors at the core of the network with similar or higher degree centrality are, as expected from the formal structure of the policy-making process, the permanent secretaries of the social area ministries. The actor with highest degree centrality (73.2 percent) is the PSSOC, who also holds the second-highest closeness centrality score (65.1 percent) and the fourth-highest betweenness centrality score (14.3 percent). The PSED has the fourth-highest degree centrality (57.1 percent) and closeness centrality (60.8 percent) scores, and the second-highest betweenness centrality score (22.6 percent). The PSLAB and PSH, though not at the core of the network like the PSSOC and PSED, also have relatively high centrality scores: the PSLAB has the eighth-highest degree centrality score (35.7 percent), and the PSH holds the twelfth position with 26.7 percent; they have similar closeness centrality values (51.3 percent and 53.8 percent, respectively) and betweenness centrality scores (4.2 percent and 5.9 percent, respectively). Again, the data from the network's cliques are consistent with both the centrality scores and the expectations from the formal structure of the policy-making process: taken together, the permanent secretaries of social area ministries participate in 56 of 69 cliques. This finding is in line with the expectation that they operate as technical coordinators of the social policy formulation process.

Third, the social area ministries are all net sources of power and, with one exception, actors whose degree centrality scores are above average and relatively high for this particular network's structure. MINSOC and MINH are at the core of the network, with degree centrality scores of 32.1 percent and 28.5 percent, respectively. MINED, though not a core actor, has an above-average degree centrality value of 23.2 percent. Only MINLAB is at the periphery and has a below-average degree centrality score (17.8 percent).

Finally, two other government actors expected to be powerful on the basis of the formal structure of the policy-making process are also net sources of power and relatively central in the actual power network: the CABINSEC and the ATTG. Both have a degree centrality score of 21.4 percent. ATTG has a 50 percent closeness centrality value, and CABINSEC has a 47 percent value. Though not at the core of the network, both actors are, as figure 6.10 indicates, certainly close to it.

Despite the interpretation that the power network structure in the social policy formulation process in The Bahamas is relatively more aligned with the expectations of the formal structure of the policy-making process, one could argue that the cabinet, PM, and social area ministries are all net sources of political power and that the permanent secretaries are, on the contrary, net subjects of power. In that case, their positions within the network would not be consistent with expectations. Given their formal positions, however, as subordinate simultaneously to the cabinet, PM, ministers, and attorney general, and as sources of power only to the senior officers in their particular ministries, their actual position as net subjects of power would not be beyond expectations. Moreover, the actual network reveals that permanent secretaries recognize each other as sources of power. Although not explicitly borne out as an expectation from the formal structure of the policy-making process, this finding is, nevertheless, consistent with the prescriptions that permanent secretaries chair interministerial committees when their ministries are the technical lead and that they coordinate the collective work of the government under the supervision of the cabinet secretary. Their mutual recognition as sources of power among the permanent secretaries adds biunivocal ties that, added to their ties with other actors both higher and lower in the hierarchy, result in their position as net subjects of power.

Importantly, three nongovernmental actors hold central positions in the power network of the social policy formulation process in The Bahamas: BHCRISIS, BCCEC, and CHURCHES. BHCRISIS is at the core of the network, has the third-highest degree centrality score (58.9 percent), and holds closeness and betweenness centrality values above the network's average. This is also the case with BCCEC and CHURCHES: their degree centrality scores are 33.9 percent and 26.7 percent, respectively, and their closeness and betweenness centrality values are above average. Although their scores do not place them in the core with BHCRISIS, they indicate that business and religious actors are influential in social policy formulation.

The network of power in the social policy formulation process in Trinidad and Tobago presents similar, though not identical, patterns. The Trinidad and Tobago network is also low density, with an even smaller value than in The Bahamas (0.1763 compared to 0.1842); an almost equivalent average geodesic distance (2.2852 compared to 2.22870); and 243 ties among 53 nodes. Like that in The Bahamas, the power network in Trinidad and Tobago is relatively more hierarchical and has a structure consistent with the expectations from the formal structure of the policy-making process. It is not, however, as hierarchical and consistent with expectations as is the power network in The Bahamas.

The cabinet and the PM in the Trinidad and Tobago network are, as in The Bahamas network, net sources of power located at the core of the network; however, unlike in The Bahamas, they are not as central to it. The PM holds the fourth-highest degree centrality score (48 percent), followed by the cabinet with 43.3 percent. Each occupies the second and third positions in closeness centrality, with 64.1 percent and 62.6 percent, respectively, and the fourth and fifth positions, with above-average betweenness centrality scores. These relatively less-central positions compared to The Bahamas network are corroborated by the data on the Trinidad and Tobago network's cliques. The PM participates in 46 of 72 cliques—eight percentage points lower than the PM in The Bahamas. In turn, the cabinet participates in only 35 of 72 cliques—23 percentage points lower than in The Bahamas. These patterns indicate that, though core actors, the cabinet and the PM are not the main political coordinators of the social policy formulation process.

The permanent secretaries in the social area ministries of Trinidad and Tobago are also, as in The Bahamas, at the core of the network with similar degree centrality scores as the cabinet and PM; however, unlike in The Bahamas, not all of them are net subjects of power. The PSSD and PSED have 76.9 percent and 65.3 percent degree centrality scores, respectively, but the PSSD is a net subject of power and the PSED a net source. The PSH is a net source of power but is also a peripheral actor. The data from the Trinidad and Tobago network's cliques appear to corroborate this position: taken together, the permanent secretaries at the social area ministries participate in 52 of 72 cliques—nine percentage points lower than in The Bahamas network.

The CABINSEC is also a central actor in the Trinidad and Tobago network, but, unlike in The Bahamas, the Ministry of Legal Affairs (MINLEG) (the Trinidad and Tobago equivalent of the Bahamian ATTG) is not. Though not a core actor, the CABINSEC is a net source of power, and its degree centrality score (30.7 percent) and closeness centrality value (49.1 percent) are above average. In turn, as figure 6.11 indicates, MINLEG is as much a source as a subject of power, despite above-average centrality values.

FIGURE 6.11: Network of Power in the Social Policy Formulation Process, Trinidad and Tobago

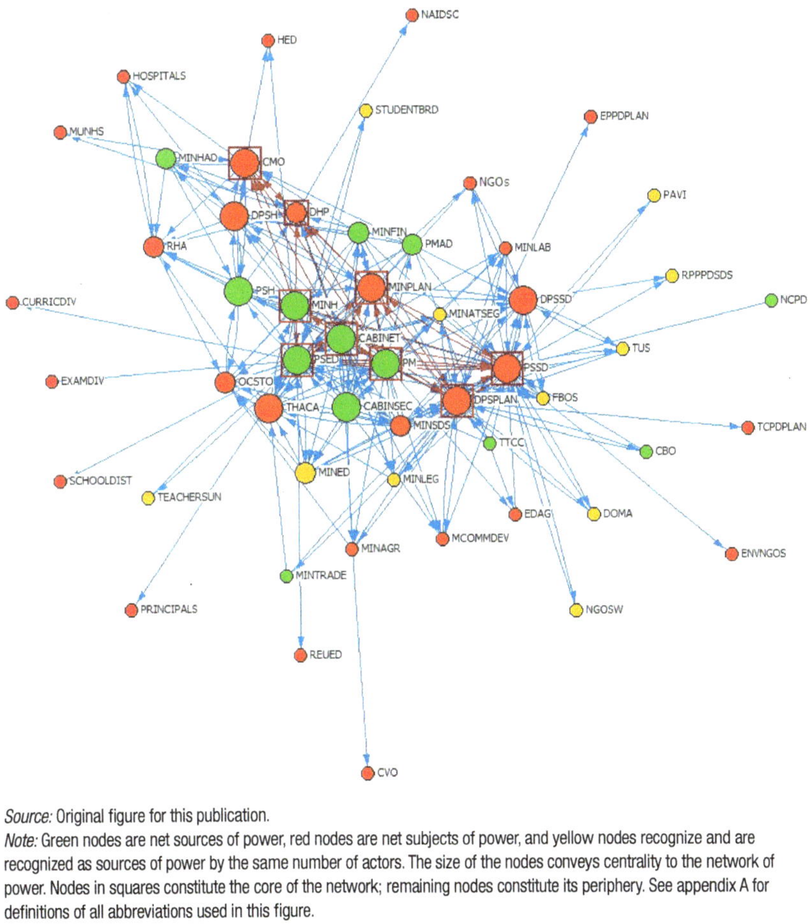

Source: Original figure for this publication.

Note: Green nodes are net sources of power, red nodes are net subjects of power, and yellow nodes recognize and are recognized as sources of power by the same number of actors. The size of the nodes conveys centrality to the network of power. Nodes in squares constitute the core of the network; remaining nodes constitute its periphery. See appendix A for definitions of all abbreviations used in this figure.

In contrast to The Bahamas case, only one social area ministry in Trinidad and Tobago's network is a net source of power: MINH, which is located at the core of the network with a degree centrality score of 32.6 percent. MINED and MINSDS are peripheral actors: the former is as much a source as a subject of power (with a degree centrality score of 19.2 percent, only slightly above the network's average of 17.6 percent) and the latter is a net subject of power, despite an above-average degree centrality value of 26.9 percent.

Also unlike The Bahamas, not a single nongovernmental actor is at the core of the power network of the social policy-making process in Trinidad and Tobago. Like its equivalent in The Bahamas, the main business association, TTCC, is a net source of power but is also a peripheral actor with a degree centrality score below the network's average. NGOs are peripheral and hold degree centrality values below average.

Summary and Conclusions

The social network analyses of the social policy formulation processes in The Bahamas and Trinidad and Tobago show that the actual networks differ significantly from the formal structure of the policy-making process. These differences center around the networks of ideas, information, and resources. Contrary to expectations, none of the three networks in either country is hierarchically structured. In contrast, the networks of power are more consistent with the formal hierarchical structure of policy-making processes. Consequently, the answer to the question of who decides on social policy formulation in The Bahamas and Trinidad and Tobago depends, essentially, on the matter to be decided. Although several actors decide on which ideas to adopt, which information to consider, and what and how resources are distributed, only the highest political and bureaucratic authorities decide on how to politically and technically coordinate social policy formulation.

Whereas the formal structure of the policy-making process in both countries indicates that the cabinet and PM are the main sources of ideas, followed by the social area ministries, the actual networks show no dominant provider of ideas. The core actors in these networks, the permanent secretaries and other senior officials from the social area ministries, are net recipients, rather than providers, of ideas. And the cabinet, PM, and social area ministries, although either net providers or as much providers as recipients of ideas, are peripheral and not central to the networks—and consequently unable to dominate them. Social policy ideas in these countries come from various sources, none of which is central enough to the networks for it to become the main influence.

The formal structure of the policy-making process indicates that the intraministerial policy units, the participating ministries in the interministerial committees, and the participating stakeholders in consultations are the main sources of information in both countries, but the actual networks of information show, again, no dominant provider of information. The core actors in these networks, the permanent secretaries and the senior policy officers at the social area ministries, are all net recipients of information, not providers. And, although the social area ministries and some nongovernmental stakeholders are net providers of information as expected, they are peripheral actors not central to the networks. Social policy information in these countries, therefore, comes from a variety of sources, none of which exerts a dominant influence on information flows.

The formal structure of the policy-making process indicates that the Ministry of Finance is the main provider of monetary resources and—at least in The Bahamas—the Ministry of Public Service is the main provider of nonmonetary resources, but the actual networks of resources in both countries show, once again, no dominant provider of resources. The core actors in these networks, the permanent secretaries at the social area ministries, either are barely net providers of resources—their out-degree ties are barely above their in-degree ones—or are net recipients. And, although the Ministry of Finance is a net provider in both networks, it is a peripheral actor and faces competition as provider from the cabinet secretary, the agenda setter for cabinet decisions. Resources for social policy formulation in these countries are, therefore, controlled by several actors, none of which is so central to the networks that it can cut the others off.

Where the formal and the actual networks meet is in the distribution of power. Both in The Bahamas and in Trinidad and Tobago, the cabinet and PM are, as expected, core actors in the power networks and are the main net sources of power. They are not alone, however: the social area ministries, permanent secretaries, and other senior administrative officials at those ministries are also core actors. Although interviewees perceive the ministries, together with the cabinet secretary, as net sources of power, the permanent secretaries are cast as net subjects of power, operating under the authority of their ministers and the government's political apex. Social policy formulation in these countries is, therefore, as expected, politically coordinated by the cabinet and PM, and technically coordinated by the social area ministries. The clear lines of authority for coordination that emerge from the structures of both power networks suggest they may have the potential to overcome the absence of hierarchies in the ideas, information, and resources networks, and thus manage social policy–making processes so they can generate adaptable, coherent, and coordinated policies.

The Bahamas and Trinidad and Tobago present highly similar networks in all the relational contents analyzed here, but with three differences of note. First, although nongovernmental actors have influence in the ideas and information networks of both countries, the actors that actually exercise influence differ in their sociological type across relational contents. In The Bahamas' networks, the employers—represented by BCCEC—play about as central a role as the longstanding NGO BHCRISIS, but they are also net recipients of ideas and information because of the number of links they have with various government agencies and other nongovernmental actors. In Trinidad and Tobago, by contrast, TTCC, though a peripheral actor, is both a net provider of ideas and information and a relatively more central node in the network than the other nongovernmental actors.

Second, although in both countries the core of the power network centers around the cabinet and PM, the status of the social area ministries and legal counsel offices differs. In The Bahamas, both the social area ministries and the ATTG are net sources of power that, though not core actors, are still central and influential above average. In Trinidad and Tobago, only MINH is deemed a net source of power.

The third difference concerns the participation of nongovernmental actors in the power network. In The Bahamas, both BCCEC and major NGOs like BHCRISIS and the Civil Society of The Bahamas are either at the core or are mostly central actors as well as net sources of power. In Trinidad and Tobago, however, only TTCC is a net source of power, but not one located at the core of the network.

These differences suggest that the level of institutionalization of links between governmental and nongovernmental actors varies across countries. Although both countries regularly carry out stakeholder consultations as part of the social policy formulation process, the more central position of nongovernmental actors in The Bahamas may reflect the existence of formal arenas of interaction, such as the National Tripartite Council (NTC), in which BCCEC and the National Congress of Trade Unions meet to discuss labor policy with, and under the supervision of, the DOL. Such formal arenas of interaction are absent in Trinidad and Tobago. This difference in the level of institutionalization of stakeholder participation in social policy making increases the likelihood that The Bahamas would generate more adaptable, coherent, and coordinated social policies than Trinidad and Tobago.

The patterns identified in the social network analyses of the social policy formulation processes in The Bahamas and Trinidad and Tobago point to at least three issues that merit comparative analysis. First is the influence of the type of civil service: the Whitehall type present in these Caribbean countries seems not only to provide the process with a relatively hierarchical, routinized, and orderly administrative machine but also to generate a social policy formulation process that, as the power networks in these two cases show, clearly and effectively maintains the differentiation of technical and political coordination roles. How does this influence compare to the dynamics that may be at work in Latin American countries where the civil service is not the Whitehall type? Do presidential regimes and proportional electoral systems affect the dynamics identified here? The preceding case studies of Argentina and Bolivia show that technical coordination tends to be absent and that political coordination is paramount, so more detailed comparative analysis is indeed required.

Second is the issue of the circulation of ideas and information: the regular recourse to interministerial committees and stakeholder consultations in these Caribbean countries seems to generate flows of ideas and information that are not encapsulated, as may be the case elsewhere, in cliques that link ministerial units only to those under their portfolio and to their private sector clients. How does this situation compare to the flow of information and ideas in other countries where interministerial committees and stakeholder consultations are not as frequent or mandated? Do any differences exist across social policy areas? The case studies of Argentina and Bolivia indicate contrasting patterns that warrant a closer comparative look.

Finally, the third issue involves the matter of the potential effects of the size and ethnic makeup of the population; despite the differences across countries in these two cases, neither of these factors appears to have any discernible effect on social policy formulation processes. Would the case be similar in larger, more and less ethnically diverse countries? How, if at all, would these variables interact with the types of political regime, electoral system, and civil service? The centrality of grassroots organizations in the Bolivian case and the absence of political parties as actors in the Argentine case suggest the need for comparative analysis.

Notes

1. This description of the formal policy-making process is a stylized version reconstructed on the basis of the Constitution of the Commonwealth of The Bahamas, the Constitution of Trinidad and Tobago, the Manual of Cabinet and Ministry Procedure of the Government of The Bahamas, the Civil Service Act of Trinidad and Tobago, and the depictions by Dolly et al. (2002) and Wells-Symonette (2002). It includes only the steps in which substantive decisions on policy content are informed or made, and only the actors with power to shape those decisions. It therefore excludes all steps and actors whose involvement in the process is merely procedural, rather than substantive.
2. The consistency of responses to the name-generator questions across interviewees from the same policy areas was, on average, 0.91 for The Bahamas and 0.94 for Trinidad and Tobago. Following standard procedure about intercoder reliability, the network boundaries were considered to have been adequately established.
3. Only three nongovernmental actors have above-average degree centrality scores: The Bahamas Chamber of Commerce with 33.8 percent; BHCRISIS with 26.4 percent, and the Civil Society of The Bahamas with 16.1 percent.
4. As in The Bahamas, no influencer dominates this network in Trinidad and Tobago. The only nongovernmental actor with above-average degree centrality is TTCC with 8.5 percent.
5. Note that interviewees report their connections with other actors, not the amounts of money or other forms of aid they provide to or receive from them.

References

Abuelafia, E. 2013a. *Budget Policymaking Process in The Bahamas.* Washington DC: Inter-American Development Bank, Caribbean Country Department.

Abuelafia, E. 2013b. *Trinidad and Tobago Budget Policymaking Process.* Washington DC: Inter-American Development Bank, Caribbean Country Department.

Brown, D. R. 1999. "Ethnic Politics and Public Sector Management in Trinidad and Tobago and Guyana." *Public Administration and Development* 19 (4): 367–79.

Dolly, C. H. et al. 2002. "Ministers and Permanent Secretaries: An Uncertain Environment." In *Governance in the Caribbean*, edited by S. Ryan and A. M. Bissessar. Kingston, Jamaica: Sir

Arthur Lewis Institute of Social and Economic Studies (SALISES), University of the West Indies.
Draper, G. 2001. "The Civil Service in Latin America and the Caribbean: Situation and Future Challenges: The Caribbean Perspective." Draft Working Paper.
Lodge, M., L. Stirton, and K. Moloney. 2015. "Whitehall in the Caribbean? The Legacy of Colonial Administration for Post-Colonial Democratic Development." *Commonwealth & Comparative Politics* 53 (1): 8–28.
Mateo Díaz, M., and K. Echebarría, eds. 2008. *Report on the Situation of the Civil Service in the Caribbean*. Washington DC: Inter-American Development Bank Regional Policy Dialogue, Public Policy Management and Transparency Network.
Premdas, R. 2007. *Trinidad and Tobago: Ethnic Conflict, Inequality, and Public Sector Governance*. London: Palgrave.
Rodríguez Gustá, A. L., and M. Iacoviello. 2008. "Comparing the Civil Service in Four English-Speaking Countries: A Quantitative and Qualitative Approach." In *Report on the Situation of the Civil Service in the Caribbean*, edited by M. Mateo Díaz and K. Echebarría, 169–204. Washington DC: Inter-American Development Bank Regional Policy Dialogue, Public Policy Management and Transparency Network.
Trinidad and Tobago. 2011. "Population and Housing Census." https://cso.gov.tt/census/2011-census-data/.
Wells-Symonette, L. 2002. *Understanding Government: with a Bahamian Perspective*. Orlando, FL: Rivercross Publishers.

7

Comparing Social Policy Formulation Networks in Latin America and the Caribbean

This chapter compares the main results from the social network analyses of Argentina, The Bahamas, Bolivia, and Trinidad and Tobago, and attempts to explain the emergent similarities and differences by looking into several macro- and microinstitutional factors. The first section compares the results for all networks and relational contents analyzed in the country studies. The second section focuses on macroinstitutional explanations by looking into the effects of political regime types, federalism and decentralization, and party system types. The third section focuses on two microinstitutional factors: bureaucratic systems and governance structures. The concluding section recaps the main points and proposes further research. As mentioned throughout the book, some of the case studies display patterns that may reflect governance and management styles of particular administrations and time periods. That these patterns appear relevant in Argentina and Bolivia but not so much in The Bahamas and Trinidad and Tobago is telling of some of the differences this chapter intends to highlight.

The Networks of Social Policy Formulation across Countries

The findings from the social network analyses of social policy formulation processes in Argentina, The Bahamas, Bolivia, and Trinidad and Tobago indicate the existence of some important structural similarities and differences across countries—for the whole networks as well as for the networks of specific relational contents. Table 7.1 summarizes some of the patterns discussed in the following paragraphs.

One of the most notable similarities is the gap between the expected and the actual size of the whole networks of social policy formulation. In all four cases, the

This chapter is coauthored with Mariano Tommasi.

TABLE 7.1: **Comparative Characteristics of Social Policy Formulation Networks, Selected Countries in Latin America and the Caribbean**

<table>
<tr><th></th><th>Argentina</th><th>Bolivia</th><th>The Bahamas</th><th>Trinidad and Tobago</th></tr>
<tr><td rowspan="2">Central actors in whole network</td><td colspan="2">Extragovernmental actors</td><td colspan="2" rowspan="2">Government actors</td></tr>
<tr><td>Various</td><td>Grassroots organizations</td></tr>
<tr><td>Network of ideas</td><td colspan="4">Social area officials are typically net recipients</td></tr>
<tr><td>Net providers</td><td>Various</td><td>Grassroots organizations</td><td colspan="2">Various (more governmental than extragovernmental)</td></tr>
<tr><td rowspan="2">Cliques</td><td colspan="4">All have encapsulated cliques</td></tr>
<tr><td>Disconnected</td><td>Connected at top</td><td colspan="2">Interministerial</td></tr>
<tr><td>Network of information</td><td>Fragmented (two clusters)</td><td>Fragmented</td><td colspan="2">Connected</td></tr>
<tr><td>Coordination</td><td>Uncoordinated</td><td>President and grassroots organizations</td><td colspan="2">Interministerial</td></tr>
<tr><td rowspan="2">Social policy units</td><td colspan="2">Net recipients</td><td colspan="2" rowspan="2">Net providers</td></tr>
<tr><td>From various sources</td><td>From grassroots organizations</td></tr>
<tr><td>Network of resources</td><td colspan="4">Finance ministry central but not dominant</td></tr>
<tr><td>Other providers</td><td>Various</td><td>International finance institutions, nongovernmental organizations</td><td colspan="2">Social area ministries</td></tr>
<tr><td>Network of power</td><td colspan="4">Highest political authority is central but faces competition</td></tr>
<tr><td>Other important actors</td><td>Provincial governments</td><td>Grassroots organizations</td><td>Social area ministries and others</td><td>Social area ministries</td></tr>
<tr><td>Features of social policies</td><td>Unstable, nonadaptable, incoherent, and uncoordinated</td><td>More stable, adaptable, coherent, and coordinated because of political coordination</td><td>Stable, adaptable, coherent, and coordinated</td><td>Slightly less stable, adaptable, coherent, and coordinated</td></tr>
</table>

Source: Original table for this publication.

actual size of the networks was larger than the size expected from the institutional analysis of the formal social policy-making process. In Bolivia, The Bahamas, and Trinidad and Tobago, the actual networks roughly tripled the expected size: from 24 actors to 65, 75, and 78, respectively. In Argentina, the expected size varied between 8 and 91 actors, but the actual size was 130. The same factor—the number of extra-governmental actors that interviewees reported as participants in social policy formulation processes—largely explains these gaps. And the gaps are not surprising; the informal functioning of an institution typically involves a larger number of actors than does its formal functioning. Governments typically interact, at least to some degree, with societal stakeholders in the process of policy making.

The centrality of these extragovernmental actors differs, however, across countries. In Bolivia, grassroots organizations are among the most central actors in the network, and in Argentina the Catholic Church, the media, some trade unions, and professional associations also enjoy relatively high network centrality scores. By contrast, in The Bahamas and Trinidad and Tobago, extragovernmental actors are located in the network's periphery. This difference insinuates another: the relatively higher centrality of governmental actors in the networks of the Caribbean countries. These patterns, as discussed in this chapter, may have diverse explanations.

Another remarkable similarity across countries is found in their networks of ideas. Senior social area officials are typically net recipients, rather than providers, of ideas and are thus less central to the networks than expected from the formal policy-making structure. This situation is, to some extent, a direct effect of the participation of extragovernmental actors. International financial institutions are among the net providers that regularly feature in the ideas networks across countries, as are unions and business associations.

Two relevant differences exist, however, between Bolivia and the other cases. First, whereas in Bolivia the most important net providers of ideas are grassroots organizations, the other countries have a wider variety of influencers, none of which dominates the network. Bolivian grassroots organizations are the main actors in the ideas network as measured by all centrality scores. In contrast, no extragovernmental actor appears as a net provider of ideas with significant network centrality in Argentina, The Bahamas, or Trinidad and Tobago. Several unions, business, and professional associations provide social policy ideas in Argentina, but none has above-average centrality scores. Governmental actors, despite low centrality scores, are the main providers of ideas in both The Bahamas and Trinidad and Tobago; and extragovernmental net providers are marginal to the networks.

Second, although both Argentina and Bolivia have policy area cliques that encapsulate ideas, in Bolivia these cliques are coordinated from above by political authorities, and no actor clearly emerges as coordinator in the other cases. In the Bolivian case, most cliques connect units from each of the social policy areas to the apex of the government—that is, the president, the vice president, or the political coordination ministry and vice ministries—which suggests that these authorities organize the flow of ideas. In contrast, the network of ideas in Argentina has no core, and its eight cutpoints typically connect extragovernmental actors within dyadic links; therefore, no single actor either dominates or coordinates the flow of ideas. In The Bahamas and Trinidad and Tobago, cliques are typically interministerial, so they do not encapsulate ideas. Because no actor—either governmental or extragovernmental—is central enough in either of those networks, however, the circulation of ideas is not coordinated.

The structure of the information networks differs markedly across countries along three dimensions: their fragmentation, the relative positions of social policy units, and their coordination. The networks in Argentina and Bolivia are fragmented both within and across policy areas whereas the networks in the Caribbean cases are mostly connected within and across policy areas. The Argentina network has two clusters: one grouping the actors connected to the labor policy area and the other linking participants in the health, education, and social assistance areas. Each of these clusters is itself fragmented into several dyadic links that account for almost two-thirds of the network's ties. The Bolivia network is fragmented across policy areas; no clique involves more than one social area ministry or connects deputy ministries, cabinet chief offices, or general directorates from different ministries. The networks in The Bahamas and Trinidad and Tobago are structured as a set of interministerial cliques that typically include both top managerial and intermediate technical officials from each policy area. These patterns suggest that information flows both within and across areas in the Caribbean cases but only within areas in the South American cases.

The relative positions of social policy units also contrast across regions. In Argentina and Bolivia these units are net recipients of information, but they operate as net providers in The Bahamas and Trinidad and Tobago. Again, the Bolivian case differs from the rest because its network has dominant providers of information whereas the other networks lack any such actor. This pattern is consistent with the cross-country differences in the coordination dimension. The Bolivian network is coordinated by its two most central actors, which are also the dominant providers of information: the grassroots organizations and the president. In contrast, the most central actors in the networks in Argentina, The Bahamas, and Trinidad and Tobago are net recipients of information; and no net provider is central enough to operate as a coordinator.

The networks of resources are similarly structured across countries. None of the cases has a dominant provider of resources, contrary to expectations based on the formal rules of policy-making processes. Although each country's finance ministry has a relatively high centrality score, all four ministries typically face competition for network centrality from international financial institutions and nongovernmental organizations, as well as from other governmental units. Still, notable differences exist in the relative positions of the competing providers. In Argentina, the formally expected dominant providers are the most important net providers, even though their centrality scores are too low to afford them a dominant position in the network, and the competing providers have even lower scores. In Bolivia, the Ministry of Economy and Public Finance faces close competition from nongovernmental organizations and the World Bank, as well as from top management positions in each social area ministry. In contrast, in both The Bahamas and Trinidad and Tobago, the permanent secretaries at the social area ministries are more central than the finance ministries. The centrality of the social area ministries points, again, to a structural difference between the Caribbean and the South American countries: governmental actors appear to be more central to the networks in both The Bahamas and Trinidad and Tobago than in Argentina and Bolivia.

The networks of power share two important features across countries: (1) the highest political authorities are the most central sources of power, but (2) those authorities compete with many other sources. This competition occurs in Argentina with the president and the cabinet chief; in Bolivia with the president and the Ministry for the Presidency; and, in The Bahamas and Trinidad and Tobago, with the cabinet and the prime minister. These central positions are consistent with the expectations from the formal policy-making structure, although in Argentina, unlike the other countries, the net subjects of power are more central to the network than the net sources.

That these formal authorities face competition for power is, of course, not surprising: both intra- and extragovernmental actors typically seek to shape policies in any policy-making process. The notable traits of these networks are the differences in the nature and position of the most important competing sources of power. Again, the Bolivian case is the exception: in Bolivia the most central competing net sources of power are grassroots organizations whereas in the other countries governmental units are more central competitors than societal actors. In Argentina, the competing net sources of power with higher centrality scores are the provincial governments, whereas other intragovernmental units (such as social area secretaries) or extragovernmental actors (such as unions and business associations) have significantly lower centrality scores and are typically connected to the network only by dyadic links. In The Bahamas, the competing net sources of power are the social area ministries, the cabinet secretary, the attorney general, and, somewhat more peripherally, The Bahamas Chamber of Commerce. In Trinidad and Tobago, the cabinet secretary is also a competing net source of power, but among the social area units only the Ministry of Health and Ministry of Social Development and Family Services and the permanent secretary at the Ministry of Health are central competitors; no extragovernmental actor is a net source of power.

These structural characteristics of the networks of social policy making suggest contrasting expectations about the features of social policies across countries. In Argentina, the fragmentation of networks, the relative disconnection across social area units, and the absence of cores and coordination within networks suggest a low likelihood for social policy–making processes to generate stable, adaptable, coherent, and coordinated social policies. In Bolivia, the fragmentation of networks, the disconnection among social area units, and the encapsulation of ideas and information would suggest similar outcomes; however, the political coordination of networks by the president and the grassroots organizations would somewhat offset those tendencies and increase the potential for adaptability, coherence, and coordination of social policies. In The Bahamas and Trinidad and Tobago, the higher centrality of governmental actors, the prevalence of interministerial links across relational contents, and the importance of social area units in the resources and power networks suggest a higher likelihood for social policy–making processes to generate stable, adaptable, coherent, and coordinated policies. This likelihood, though, would be slightly higher in The Bahamas than in Trinidad and Tobago because the former has highly institutionalized stakeholder consultation mechanisms that the latter seems to lack.

Macroinstitutional Factors

Three macroinstitutional factors emerge as potential explanations for the patterns identified in the cross-country comparisons in the previous section: the type of political regime, the party systems, and the nature of federalism or decentralization.

The sample of countries analyzed in this book includes two cases of presidentialism (Argentina and Bolivia) and two cases of parliamentarism (The Bahamas and Trinidad and Tobago). Following Tsebelis (2002) and subsequent literature, the main structural difference between these types of political regimes relevant for policy-making processes is the number of institutional (veto) players, which would be higher in presidential than parliamentary regimes because presidential systems divide the executive from the legislative branch of government and simultaneously make the branches share legislative power (Gehlbach and Malesky 2010; Haggard and McCubbins 2001; Tommasi, Scartascini, and Stein 2014). This difference should affect the social policy formulation networks in at least three ways: their size, the centrality of political authorities within them, and their potential for coordination. In terms of size, networks are expected to be larger in presidential than parliamentary countries because the larger number of relevant institutional players should create opportunities for the participation of more actors, both intra- and extragovernmental. In terms of centrality, political authorities (that is, chief executives and ministers) should be more central to the networks in parliamentary than in presidential regimes. In parliamentary regimes, unification of the executive and legislative branches of government should increase the interactions between those authorities and the rest of network, whereas the division of power in presidential regimes should result in more fragmented interactions across branches. In terms of potential for coordination, networks are expected to facilitate coordination more in parliamentary than in presidential regimes, because separation-of-powers systems such as the latter typically increase the number of participants in the policy-making process, and with them the obstacles for coordination.

Interestingly, the type of political regime does not seem to affect the size of the networks as expected in these cases. The whole network of social policy formulation is larger in Argentina than in the Caribbean countries, but the Caribbean networks are larger than Bolivia's.[1] In addition, the data show that the difference in network sizes across countries is due not to the presence or absence of the legislature but to the number of intra- and extragovernmental actors mentioned by the interviewees. Congress and Parliament appear in all these networks. The number of societal actors is higher in the Argentine and Bolivian networks than in the Caribbean countries, and the number of governmental actors is higher in the Caribbean and Bolivia than in Argentina.

The type of political regime does, however, seem to explain the differences in the centrality of political authorities and the potential for coordination across cases. The cabinets and prime ministers of The Bahamas and Trinidad and Tobago are more central to the networks of power than the presidents of Argentina and Bolivia. The same finding holds for the social area ministers when considered as net sources of power or as net providers of information and ideas. Political authorities in the Caribbean countries interact more with both governmental units and extragovernmental actors than do those authorities in Argentina and, to a lesser extent, Bolivia, as observable in their centrality scores and their participation in interministerial cliques. The potential for coordination appears to be higher in the Caribbean parliamentary countries than the South American presidential democracies because of the higher centrality and connectedness of governmental actors in The Bahamas and Trinidad and Tobago.

This higher potential for coordination is consistent with the expectations for parliamentary compared to presidential regimes: the fusion of the executive and the legislature leads politicians who occupy (prime) ministerial positions to develop more links within and outside government than do presidents or ministers in presidential regimes, who can delegate some of those links to legislators. Taken together, the networks of ideas, information, and power corroborate these expectations by depicting the political authorities in The Bahamas and Trinidad and Tobago as systematically more linked than their counterparts in Argentina and Bolivia—not only to the technical bureaucracies in the social area ministries and the relevant societal actors but also among themselves.

Regime types can only go so far as explanatory variables here. The fact remains that the presence of civil society in the Argentine and Bolivian networks is, albeit for diverse reasons, weightier than in the cases of The Bahamas and Trinidad and Tobago. This situation undoubtedly finds its roots, to some extent, in the economic structure of each country; the South American economies are larger and more complex than the Caribbean ones. Still, the effects of those economic structures on policy making are not direct or even straightforward; they are processed through institutions and practices—such as political parties and party systems—that are beyond constitutional rules.

The party system variable has the highest variation across cases in this sample. The Argentine party system has become increasingly fragmented since 2005, when the division of the Peronist party (Partido Justicialista [PJ]) between a more left-wing populist and clientelistic faction led by Cristina and Nestor Kirchner and a more centrist but still clientelistic faction led alternatively by Eduardo Duhalde and Sergio Massa became more stable. At the same time, the non-Peronist parties oscillated between competition among the Radical Civic Union (UCR), Republican Proposition (PRO), and Civic Coalition, and, lately, their convergence in the Cambiemos coalition led by Mauricio Macri. The Bolivian party system has been structured around the hegemony of a social movement–based party, the Movimiento al Socialismo (MAS), in which various ethnic- and rural-based grassroots organizations converge, together with the country's main peasant and industrial unions (Madrid 2012; Van Cott 2008). The Bahamian party system is structured around the competition between the left-wing populist Progressive Liberal Party, which purports to represent the poor and lower-middle-income voters, and the conservative market-oriented Free National Movement, which courts lower-middle- to upper-income voters (Wells-Symonette 2002). The party system in Trinidad and Tobago is structured around ethnic cleavages: the People's National Movement, backed by most of the population of African descent; the Democratic Labour Party, supported mostly by the East Indian segment; and the People's Partnership coalition, formed lately by several multiethnic small parties (Bissessar 2017).

These party systems should have different effects on the size and structure of social policy formulation networks in Bolivia and Trinidad and Tobago compared to Argentina and The Bahamas. The ethnic components of party bases and competition in the former two countries should lead to larger networks in order to accommodate diverse ethnic groups, to a higher centrality of ethnic grassroots organizations regardless of the relational contents of links, and to positions for those organizations as net providers of ideas and net sources of power. The more ideologically oriented political competition pattern in The Bahamas should lead to the opposite: smaller networks, with societal actors in peripheral positions. The fragmented nature of the Argentine party system, in turn, should lead to larger networks as a consequence of a higher number of partisan veto players and to a proliferation of societal actors seeking to circumvent the potentially weak parties and influence social policy making by providing ideas and information as well as by exercising power in their respective areas of interest.

These theoretical expectations hold only in the case of Bolivia. It has the smallest networks in the sample, but its grassroots organizations (paired only with the president) are the most central actors—as well as the main net providers of ideas and sources of power among extragovernmental actors—which explains the growth in network size beyond the formal design of the policy making process. Argentina has the largest networks in the sample, although not because of partisan veto players, which are thoroughly absent, but because of societal actors. Those societal actors, as expected, proliferate in the ideas, information, and power networks, albeit in dyadic links that result in low centrality scores. This finding for Argentina is consistent with the description of the workings of institutions and the policy-making process in previous literature (for instance, Spiller and Tommasi 2007), which emphasizes the weakness of Congress and the porosity of the administration to various special interests. The Caribbean countries do not conform to any expectations: The Bahamian networks are not the smallest, and they feature civil society actors in central positions in the ideas, information, and power networks; the Trinidadian and Tobagonian networks are not the largest, nor do they feature ethnic-based parties or grassroots organizations in any central position.

The fact that the party system effect seems to be present only in Bolivia begs the question of whether the proliferation of societal actors in Argentina, their relative absence in Trinidad and Tobago, and their limited presence in The Bahamas can be explained by another macroinstitutional factor such as the structure of the state. In this respect, the federalism and decentralization variable also presents distinct patterns across cases. Argentina is one of the most decentralized federations in the world, and the importance of subnational political authorities in national level policy making is well studied (Ardanaz, Leiras, and Tommasi 2014). Bolivia is well-known for its vigorous decentralization program, which took place in the 1990s and left an important imprint on the country (Faguet 2012). The Bahamas is a unitary state that has only very recently started decentralization initiatives. Trinidad and Tobago has been experimenting with decentralization in health and education since the mid-1990s while retaining the major policy-making roles at the central level of government.

As would be expected, subnational authorities are more central in the federal and more experienced decentralized countries (Argentina and Bolivia) than in the recently and less decentralized unitary cases (The Bahamas and Trinidad and Tobago). The data also show that subnational authorities are more central in decentralized policy areas, typically health and education. Despite that centrality, subnational authorities are not more connected to societal actors than to national authorities in any of the networks in these four countries, not even in Argentina and Bolivia where the proliferation of such actors would potentially invite those links. This finding may result from a sampling bias caused by the fact that the snowballing procedures employed for the case studies began with national officials, but the societal and subnational actors interviewed typically reported more connections with national actors than with subnational or societal actors, respectively.

Microinstitutional Factors

The preceding discussion suggests that some microinstitutional factors—such as the type of bureaucratic system and the type of governance and coordination structures—may account for the patterns that macroinstitutional factors seem unable to explain.

The countries analyzed in this book present two different types of bureaucratic systems. On the one hand, The Bahamas and Trinidad and Tobago have meritocratic bureaucracies composed of permanent civil servants recruited on the basis of merit and incorporated into the bureaucracy as professional bureaucrats (IDB 2005). These bureaucracies explicitly follow Whitehall-type arrangements and decision-making procedures: each ministry has permanent secretaries tasked with coordinating both the internal workings of their ministries and the relations with other ministries; ad hoc interministerial committees regularly formulate and discuss policies that have cross-jurisdictional aspects; white papers are regularly developed and published; policy changes require stakeholder consultations; and bureaucrats regularly interact with political appointees and ministers, after which the cabinet and Parliament make final decisions (Civil Service Act of Trinidad and Tobago; Manual of Cabinet and Ministry Procedure of the Commonwealth of The Bahamas; Dolly et al. 2002; Draper, n.d.; Rodríguez Gustá and Iacoviello 2008; Wells-Symonette 2002). This type of bureaucracy should result in (1) relatively higher centrality scores for technical (that is, subministerial) social policy units, (2) relatively higher involvement in interministerial cliques, (3) positions as net providers of ideas and information, and (4) relatively higher potential for coordination.

On the other hand, Argentina and Bolivia combine three types of bureaucracies: administrative, clientelistic, and —albeit marginally—meritocratic. The administrative type, which typically applies to low and intermediate tiers of officials, formally includes recruitment and assessment by merit. Such merit-based practices carry some job security but are rarely applied in practice, replaced instead by political criteria. The clientelistic type is purely political and typically applies to top and managerial positions (IDB 2005). Each country presents, in the social policy area, one enclave of meritocratic bureaucracy: the National Social Security Administration in Argentina and the Unit for Social and Economic Policy Analysis in Bolivia. Most positions, however, are either administrative or clientelistic. The combination of these types of bureaucracies should result in (1) relatively lower centrality scores for technical social policy units, (2) relatively lower involvement in interministerial cliques, (3) positions as net recipients of ideas and information, and (4) relatively lower potential for coordination.

The results of the social network analyses conform to these expectations. Technical social policy units are more central to the networks in The Bahamas and Trinidad and Tobago, significantly more involved in interministerial cliques than their equivalents in Argentina and Bolivia, positioned as net providers of ideas and information instead of net recipients, and more likely to coordinate than in the South American cases. Thus, the type of bureaucratic system would seem not only to explain the relative positions of technical social policy units and the structure of ideas and information networks but also to account for the absence of party system effects in the Caribbean countries, which could arguably be contained by meritocratic bureaucracies.

Neither the macroinstitutional factors discussed in the previous section nor the types of bureaucratic systems appear to explain the different patterns of coordination displayed by the power networks. Specifically, whereas in Bolivia, The Bahamas, and Trinidad and Tobago the political authorities are both the most central actors and the most important net sources of power, in Argentina those authorities are the main net sources of power but are not the most central actors in the network. Differences in governance and coordination structures within executive offices may account for this pattern.

In this respect, Argentina's formal structure of decision making is notably more of an incomplete contract. Bolivia and the Caribbean countries, as revealed in the country studies, have formal rules that prescribe in precise detail how ordinary policy-making processes work and the ways chief executives may intervene within them. These rules prescribe that policy making in The Bahamas and Trinidad and Tobago must be coordinated by the prime minister, the cabinet, and the permanent secretaries. In Bolivia, all policies must be collectively debated in the cabinet and, in the case of social policies, previously discussed in the specialized cabinet committee called the National Council of Economic and Social Policies before the president makes a final decision. In contrast, Argentina has no established procedures for cabinet or presidential decision making beyond the general stipulations in the Law of Administrative Procedure that legal counsel must review any decision before its publication and that ministerial stakeholders must be consulted beforehand.

Consequently, the political authorities in The Bahamas, Bolivia, and Trinidad and Tobago are more constrained than the Argentine authorities in their ability to introduce and modify governance and coordination structures.

Theories of governance and coordination in the executive branch have proposed several typologies aimed at capturing different ways in which chief executives may organize and manage their staff (Ponder 2000; Porter 1980; Walcott and Hult 1995). These typologies build upon Johnson's (1974) basic scheme, according to which chief executives may use three patterns: (1) competitive, in which they stand at the center of decision-making processes by overlapping jurisdictions, duplicating assignments, and developing rivalries among their collaborators; (2) hierarchical, in which they delegate authority to top advisers who run a hierarchical organization with clearly specified functions and sift the information and policy alternatives that reach the apex; and (3) collegial, in which presidents operate as the hub of a wheel in which the spokes consist of a group of advisers who collectively discuss and propose alternatives. Walcott and Hult (1995) combine different traits of these basic categories to elaborate further distinctions and add one category of their own: market arrangements, by which presidents adopt a laissez-faire approach that leads to a situation in which ministers and advisers develop policies separately and compete for attention and ultimate favor. Hierarchical and competitive structures should result in chief executives' enjoying both the most central and the highest net source position in the network of power, whereas collegial and market structures should confer more centrality to ministers and secretaries and, therefore, diminish the scores for chief executives.

The data from each country's power networks are generally consistent with the formal governance and coordination structures in Bolivia and the Caribbean countries. The Bolivian president and the prime ministers, cabinets, and permanent secretaries of The Bahamas and Trinidad and Tobago are the most central actors and the main net sources of power in those country's networks. The Argentine network—in which the president, the cabinet chief, and the provincial governments are the most important net sources of power, but the most central actors are social area units positioned as net subjects of power—does not correspond either to a collegial governance structure such as that prevailing in the Caribbean countries or to a more hierarchical structure such as the one in Bolivia.

The combination of the indeterminacy of the formal rules and the relatively weak hierarchy of the power network's structure suggests that the political authorities in Argentina appear to rely on informal hierarchical or laissez-faire arrangements that confine their intervention to problem solving of turf and budgetary conflicts. Unlike in Bolivia and the Caribbean countries, in Argentina the president and cabinet chief have relatively few links within government beyond the ministers and some top secretaries, and virtually none with extragovernmental actors. Because the Argentine social policy units also present relatively few interministerial links not only in the power network but also in the ideas, information, and resources networks, the political authorities would seem to encourage social area ministries to develop policy on their own within their respective areas and to intervene only in order to solve budgetary conflicts or make final policy decisions. In a policy environment marked by incomplete rules, the adoption of such governance and coordination structures would not be an automatic result of the indeterminacy of formal rules but a contingent outcome of that very indeterminacy.

These microinstitutional factors also account for the cross-country differences in the features of social policies more consistently than macroinstitutional factors. The higher centrality and connectedness of technical and political authorities typical of the Whitehall type of bureaucracy and the more collegial coordination structures typical of parliamentary governance as present in the Caribbean countries facilitate the generation of more stable, adaptable, coherent, and coordinated social policies. In contrast, the higher centrality of societal actors and political authorities and the lower stability and connectedness of technical authorities typical of the clientelistic type of bureaucracy and the more hierarchical coordination structures present in Argentina and Bolivia complicate the development of social policies endowed with such features.

Conclusion

This chapter reviewed and compared the evidence that emerged on social policy formulation networks in the four country cases. The Bahamas and Trinidad and Tobago display features consistent with their parliamentary type of political regime and their Whitehall type of bureaucracy, including a strong role for interministerial interactions and centrality of governmental actors. Bolivian social policy making is characterized by the centrality of grassroots organizations across all relational contents (ideas, information, resources, and power) and the coordination role of the president. Argentine social policy making is marked by fragmentation. Microinstitutional factors—such as bureaucratic systems and coordination structures—seem to account for these features more than macroinstitutional variables, but party systems and state structures appear to have consistent effects on the size and structure of networks.

The comparative analysis provided here could be extended in a number of directions. First, a natural extension would be to include other countries with a wider set of institutional characteristics, such as variations in the nature of welfare regimes as well as in the design of their main social policy programs. Another potential extension would be to compare social policy networks over time. Such comparison would help distinguish deep structural characteristics of policy making from possible conjunctural factors associated with one particular administration or transition, and would simultaneously allow for a better understanding of the power this type of network analysis may have to identify deep causal factors.

Note

1. These results may partly be due to the methodology's sensitivity to the personal social networks of the interviewees: given that networks emerge from the responses of the actors, if any actor's network is smaller than that of its functional equivalent in another country, the ensuing network would also be smaller, and personal network sizes are random.

References

Ardanaz, M., M. Leiras, and M. Tommasi. 2014. "The Politics of Federalism in Argentina and its Implications for Governance and Accountability." *World Development* 53 (C): 26-45.

Bissessar, A. M. 2017. *Ethnic Conflict in Developing Societies. Trinidad and Tobago, Guyana, Fiji, and Suriname*. London: Palgrave Macmillan.

Dolly, C. H. 2002. "Ministers and Permanent Secretaries: An Uncertain Environment." In *Governance in the Caribbean*, edited by S. Ryan and A. M. Bissessar. Kingston, Jamaica: Sir Arthur Lewis Institute of Social and Economic Studies (SALISES), University of the West Indies.

Draper, G. n.d. "The Civil Service in Latin America and the Caribbean: Situation and Future Challenges: The Caribbean Perspective." Draft Working Paper.

Faguet, J. P. 2012. *Decentralization and Popular Democracy: Governance from Below in Bolivia*. Ann Arbor: Michigan University Press.

Gehlbach, S., and E. J. Malesky. 2010. "The Contribution of Veto Players to Economic Reform." *Journal of Politics* 72 (4): 957–75.

Haggard, S., and M.D. McCubbins. 2001. *Presidents, Parliaments, and Policy*. Cambridge: Cambridge University Press.

IDB (Inter-American Development Bank). 2005. *The Politics of Policies: Economic and Social Progress in Latin America and the Caribbean 2006 Report*. Washington, DC: Inter-American Development Bank.

Johnson, R. T. 1974. *Managing the White House*. New York: Harper & Row.

Madrid, R. 2012. *The Rise of Ethnic Politics in Latin America*. New York: Cambridge University Press.

Ponder, D. E. 2000. *Good Advice: Information & Policy Making in the White House*. College Station, TX: Texas A&M University Press.

Porter, R. B. 1980. *Presidential Decision Making: The Economic Policy Board*. Cambridge: Cambridge University Press.

Rodríguez Gustá, A. L., and M. Iacoviello. 2008. "Comparing the Civil Service in Four English-Speaking Countries: A Quantitative and Qualitative Approach." In *Report on the Situation of the Civil Service in the Caribbean*, edited by M. Mateo Díaz and K. Echebarría, 169–204. Washington, DC: Inter-American Development Bank Regional Policy Dialogue, Public Policy Management and Transparency Network.

Spiller, P., and M. Tommasi. 2007. *The Institutional Foundations of Public Policy: A Transactions Cost Approach*. Cambridge: Cambridge University Press.

Tommasi, M., C. Scartascini, and E.H. Stein. 2014. "Veto Players and Policy Adaptability: An Intertemporal Perspective." *Journal of Theoretical Politics* 26 (2): 222–48.

Tsebelis, G. 2002. *Veto Players. How Political Institutions Work*. Princeton, NJ: Princeton University Press.

Van Cott, D. L. 2008. *Radical Democracy in the Andes*. Cambridge: Cambridge University Press.

Walcott, C. E., and K. M. Hult. 1995. *Governing the White House from Hoover to LBJ*. Lawrence, KS: University Press of Kansas.

Wells-Symonette, L. 2002. *Understanding Government with a Bahamian Perspective*. Orlando, FL: Rivercross Publishing.

8

Social Networks and the Political Economy of Social Policy Making

Countries in Latin America and the Caribbean have faced a rocky end of decade. The ways some of them have dealt with massive popular protests and their aftermaths provide illustrative examples that not all countries are cut from the same cloth. In some cases, differences arise from the countries' contrasting levels of economic development and basic sociodemographic characteristics. Responses have also been shaped, however, by the networks of decision making within governments.

The chapters in this volume have briefly introduced a theoretical approach to the study of the political economy of social policy based on the methodology devised by Spiller, Tommasi, and other authors on the policy-making process (among the many relevant papers and books, see for example Spiller and Tommasi 2007), and have added a methodological approach to the study of the social networks that operate in social policy making. The previous chapters also offered empirical evidence that illustrates the structure and functioning of the social networks operating in the formulation and implementation of social policy in Argentina, The Bahamas, Bolivia, and Trinidad and Tobago. This concluding chapter aims to look at the empirical regularities emergent from the case studies through the lens of the political economy approach to the policy-making process, provide some concluding remarks, and propose a research agenda that combines political economy and social network analysis (SNA).

Social Networks and Social Policy–Making Processes

The political framework within which countries design and implement policies is very different from the formal framework in which, for example, ministers make decisions according to technocratic recommendations, and those in charge of implementation follow the recommendations and plans as designed. In contrast, the actors formally empowered by the organizational chart do not necessarily make actual policy decisions: the technocracy has little influence, plans change, and program designs generally do not take into account the characteristics of the networks of actors in charge of implementation. Likewise, restrictions on human capital, funding, and planning cause implementation to differ in both time and form from original plans. Earlier studies on policy formulation and implementation processes (IDB 2005) uncovered the role of actors' incentives in the implementation of policies that were stable, adaptable, efficient, coherent, and focused on the public good. This book takes a step further than those studies, using SNA to identify specific actors that take part in the decision-making process. This exercise helps to explain why some programs work or are put into practice whereas others are left behind, as well as to determine which network members must be involved in order to achieve certain goals.

The SNAs performed for the case studies presented in this book made it possible to identify the central actors in the networks for the formulation and implementation of different types of social programs at different government levels in Argentina, The Bahamas, Bolivia, and Trinidad and Tobago. In turn, this identification made it possible to determine the nature of the resources with which every actor maintains its centrality in networks. Comparing information derived from network analysis with the description of formal structures of the programs and decision-making processes of social policy then made it possible to tentatively characterize the nature of the transaction costs and decision-making processes of the programs under analysis.

In general, the social policies formulated by these actors encompass all social sectors: education, employment, and contributive and noncontributive social protection. As a consequence, the policies are characterized by a considerable uncertainty about the demand for services, a high degree of specificity, marked complexity and restrictions on the exchange with beneficiaries, and a sector-contingent frequency of interaction, albeit high in the aggregate. Social policy formulation, therefore, has transaction costs and requires—according to the political economy framework provided in chapter 2—a decision-making process that is strongly institutionalized, led by officials with long-term horizons, and organized in stable information exchange networks, within which policies are effectively coordinated. SNA shows that such characteristics do not always exist.

Argentina

The SNA of Argentine social policy making provides evidence of a fragmented and unstable policy-making process. First, the networks are low in density and highly fragmented. These conditions make it more difficult to coordinate public policies across areas and ministries. Second, the low relevance of the bureaucratic system can be appreciated in the scant mention, and correspondingly low centrality scores, of second- and third-line government agencies (and their secretaries and undersecretaries, let alone directors). The absence of a strong bureaucracy allows nongovernment actors to enter the policy-making arena and achieve important positions within the policy-making networks. This situation fragments decision making even more and generates additional layers of instability if these actors or their access to policy makers change over time. The process is further complicated for those policies affected by the influence of subnational actors. Third, in contrast to expectations from the formal structure of the policy-making process but consistent with previous literature, Congress's position in the networks of ideas, information, and power is always peripheral. Also echoing the previous literature and their characterization as clientelistic, personalistic, or both, Argentine political parties are completely absent from these networks.

These patterns suggest that social policies would tend to be of low quality. In particular, policies would tend to be unstable (that is, they would change frequently with shifts in political winds) and have relatively low levels of coordination, efficiency, and enforcement. Whereas the political economy approach helps identify the institutional sources of instability, inefficiency, and low coordination and enforcement, SNA can pinpoint the organizational sources and procedural mechanisms that help reproduce those features of social policies. The relationship between labor and education policy units illustrates this point. The political economy approach may explain their disconnection and lack of coordination by the fact that education policy is decentralized to provincial governments whereas labor policy is a centralized responsibility of the federal government. SNA shows that these areas barely interact beyond the ministerial level: labor policy units typically cluster around unions and business associations, as if the contents of, for example, training programs do not merit technical input and coordination with the education area. These findings suggest that fragmentation and disconnection characterize policy areas with both high and low specificity of transactions, thus corroborating how these networks help reproduce inefficiency in social policy making.

Bolivia

In the social policy formulation network at the central government level in Bolivia, the main actors are the president and the grassroots organizations. Both actors maintain their centrality in the network by producing ideas, accessing information, and exercising political power over administrative units and officials in the social sector. Evidence collected in the case study suggests a weakly institutionalized decision-making process, because it lacks connections between social policy units—regardless of the relational content under study—and those units are influenced by actors who are formally or informally recognized as hierarchically superior.

The aggregation technologies that allow policy units to act jointly and function effectively consist not of the legal or administrative responsibilities and competencies specified by regulations but rather of the vertical coordination exercised by the Presidency and the grassroots organizations. In turn, this coordination rests on other actors' recognition of the authority of the president and the grassroots organizations as well as on the mutual political influence exerted between these two actors. In short, the aggregation technology that makes it possible to weather the high transaction costs inherent in social policy formulation seems to be not the technical capacity of the units specialized in social policy but rather the high capacity for political articulation by the grassroots organizations and the apex of the central government. Although not a solution to the weak institutionalization of the decision-making process, this articulation does allow that process to operate effectively (that is, to produce minimally stable policies of limited efficiency).

The political economy approach to policy making in Bolivia had already shed light on the sociological links between government and grassroots organizations, and on the institutional sources—namely, the pervasiveness of instability and clientelism—of the central government bureaucracy's low levels of meritocratic recruitment and technical competence. SNA helps illuminate the organizational workings of the grassroots-based Movimiento al Socialismo (MAS) government by pinpointing the links between the president, the grassroots organizations, and specific technical units below the ministerial level, and showing their disconnect with other social area units beyond their ministerial jurisdictions. These findings not only reveal the mechanisms by which the government operates but also explain that any coordination achieved and sustained in social policy making is more likely to be political than technical in nature. Thus, social policies in Bolivia may be coordinated and more efficiently executed by political means but would be only as stable and adaptable as the political coordinators that deliver them. Certain policy areas—such as health and education—that involve highly specific and frequent transactions are more likely to require political coordination efforts, whereas other areas—like labor—with less complex transactions may be less coordinated.

The Bahamas and Trinidad and Tobago

No comprehensive studies have addressed policy making in the Caribbean countries. Although this lack of information provided an additional incentive to pursue these country case studies, it also makes the comparability of the results in this book more difficult. One characteristic that emerges from the comparative data in Franco Chuaire and Scartascini (2014) is that Caribbean countries have more stable policies and on average have satisfactory scores on issues of coordination and implementation. These results are in line with the existence of a more stable and professionalized civil service. Interestingly, the SNAs show that, because of the participation in both cases of nongovernmental actors, civil servants are not as central to the production of ideas and information as expected.

Consequently, although the political economy approach sheds light on the regime and bureaucracy type rules that make the civil service a highly institutionalized set of actors, the organizational workings revealed through SNA show that government officials do not wield all the power. This finding could partly be explained as a matter of design, because both The Bahamas and Trinidad and Tobago use stakeholder consultation as a formal mechanism of policy making. Still, the circulation of ideas and information is not encapsulated, which shows the institutional strength of another Whitehall-type policy-making rule: the recourse to interministerial committees for policy development.

In all, these patterns suggest that policies are more stable and coordinated, although not necessarily better enforced or adaptable to changing circumstances. The higher centrality and connectedness of government actors across relational contents, plus the centrality of political authorities in the power network, facilitate coordination and, in general, the reduction of transaction costs. This seems to be the case regardless of the nature and frequency of transactions typical of each social policy area.

Social Networks in the Political Economy of Social Policy Making

The comparative evidence from the case studies also suggests some general lessons about the political economy of social policy making in Latin America and the Caribbean. The first lesson is that social policy–making processes operate with essentially the same logic as public policy–making processes in general. This idea may be somewhat unexpected considering the significant expansion of social policy and social policy–making structures in recent decades, but it is not surprising considering the factors that typically explain the features of policy-making processes: the institutional rules of the policy-making game, the bureaucratic structures that help design and implement policies, and the societal stakeholders who strive to influence policy contents.

The case studies indicate that no institutionally distinct policy-making process exists for social policy. In Argentina, social policy at the federal level of government is formulated by political appointees who receive ideas and information primarily from extragovernmental stakeholders with which they interact in their respective ministerial jurisdictions. These political appointees obtain resources from various governmental and extragovernmental actors, and are politically coordinated by the president or the cabinet chief's office, with little technical coordination and interministerial links and no significant involvement from Congress. Even when decentralized social policy functions (that is, education and health) are concerned, interviewees do not report the respective federal councils as central actors in the policy-making process. These patterns are consistent with the general rules of the Argentine policy-making game, in which policies are essentially made by the political group that controls the federal executive branch and the parallel bureaucracy that each government hires, in direct contact with societal stakeholders, and contingently negotiated directly with subnational governments and the marginal participation of Congress.

In Bolivia, social policy is also developed by political appointees on the basis of ideas and information emergent from the apex of the government and the grassroots organizations, which constitute the political base of the government party. The process falls under the political coordination of these same actors, with resources provided by various intra- and extragovernmental actors, under the technical supervision of the Unit for Social and Economic Policy Analysis (UDAPE), with little interministerial technical coordination and marginal involvement from Congress. Again, these patterns correspond to the rules of the Bolivian policy-making game, in which policies are made by the president and the political group that controls the cabinet, with technical assistance from a few areas of career civil servants and no participation of Congress.

In both The Bahamas and Trinidad and Tobago, social policy is developed by permanent career civil servants within interministerial committees on the basis of ideas and information from several governmental and extragovernmental sources, including consultations with stakeholders, under the political coordination of the cabinet and the prime minister. These patterns also conform to the rules of the policy-making game in the two countries, in which Whitehall-type bureaucracies develop policies originating from ideas from various sources, with information essentially produced and circulated by government actors within interministerial committees and stakeholder consultations, under the political coordination of the government.

The case studies also show that the bureaucracies in charge of formulating social policy do not differ from those in charge of developing other public policies. In Argentina and Bolivia, the public officials who formulate social policies are political appointees with short tenures and little previous experience in office. This description is consistent with the general description of these countries' bureaucracies in the literature (IDB 2005; Spiller and Tommasi 2007). The public officials who develop social policies in The Bahamas and Trinidad and Tobago are career civil servants, with longer tenures and previous experience in office, as is the case in general for all public policy areas (Rodríguez Gustá and Iacoviello 2008).

The second general lesson from the case studies is that the sociological structure of the social networks of social policy formulation is similar across countries. This finding, again, comes as no surprise: theoretically, each social area ministry would interact frequently with the societal stakeholders in its jurisdiction, and each social area unit would develop cohesive networks with those stakeholders. Still, it is noteworthy to observe that—regardless of the differences in size, wealth, and organizational density of the civil society across countries—the network structures in each social area incorporate the same types of actors.

Thus, the networks in health policy include professional medical associations, unions, hospitals, specialized nongovernmental organizations (NGOs), and local community groups. The networks in education policy are made up of public and private schools, universities, teachers' unions, and specialized NGOs. The networks in social assistance policy comprise grassroots social movements, NGOs, and subnational governments. The networks in labor policy encompass unions and workers' confederations, social movements representing the unemployed, and business associations. In all networks, international financial institutions participate as providers of ideas or resources.

The third general lesson is that societal actors contribute to social policy making mainly by providing ideas and information. This finding holds for the whole range of societal stakeholders in Argentina, The Bahamas, and Trinidad and Tobago. The analysis shows an important difference in Bolivia, where grassroots organizations not only provide ideas and information but also operate as political coordinators of social policy formulation. Interviewees in all countries also mentioned societal actors in regard to resources and power, but they did so less frequently than in regard to ideas and information, indicating that societal actors are significantly less central to the resources and power networks. In addition, the structures of the ideas and information networks across countries show that societal actors typically participate in those networks by way of dyadic ties to area-specific policy units. With the exceptions of unions in Argentina—participating in the health, education, and labor policy networks—and NGOs across all four cases, societal stakeholders connect only to the public officials of their specialized jurisdiction.

These three patterns suggest two general conclusions about the political economy of social policy making in Latin America and the Caribbean. One conclusion is that social policy-making processes do not appear to have a corporatist nature. Societal actors may propose ideas and provide information to policy makers—either through informal bilateral links, as in Argentina and Bolivia, or through formal consultation processes, as in The Bahamas and Trinidad and Tobago—but they typically do not set policy jointly with governments. The evidence for this conclusion is that, despite the presence of some formal corporatist arrangements such as the Council for the Minimum Wage in Argentina and the National Tripartite Council in The Bahamas, interviewees do not mention them or the societal actors that would theoretically be equal partners in these corporatist structures as central nodes in the networks of resources and power. On the contrary, the data from these two types of networks seem to suggest that social policies are ultimately decided mainly by the apex of government. The interaction of the apex with societal actors may be more direct, as in Bolivia, or indirect, as in the other cases, but except for the case of Bolivia interviewees do not depict that interaction as a link in which governments are subjected to the political power of societal stakeholders.

This finding leads to the second conclusion: that the coordination challenges emerging from the dyadic links between societal actors and social policy units have a basis in the social policy-making structure and, therefore, pose difficult institutional trade-offs. On the one hand, governments could improve informational efficiency and reduce transaction costs of social policy making by setting up formal deliberation arenas in which societal actors participate via encompassing organizations that aggregate the currently dyadic interactions. But these arrangements would reduce the adaptability, and perhaps also the legitimacy, of social policies in two ways. First, such arrangements could potentially dilute the specific viewpoints of currently autonomous actors within those encompassing organizations. Second, they could confer on these organizations veto power over policies hitherto decided upon by democratically elected officials.

On the other hand, the alternative arrangement of mandatory stakeholder consultations, such as the ones institutionalized in the Caribbean countries, would accrue informational gains and increase the legitimacy of policy decisions. It would do so, however, at the expense of higher transaction costs, particularly in countries such as Argentina and Bolivia, with denser and more intensely mobilized civil societies.

To navigate these trade-offs would require more detailed studies on the actual contributions of each societal actor to the policy-making process of each social policy area. The evidence collected so far has been insufficient to identify any of these actors, except for Bolivian grassroots organizations, as cutpoints in the networks. Rigorously identifying the cutpoints by pinpointing the exact relational contents exchanged with social policy units would help determine which type of institutional arrangement could improve the technical and political coordination of social policy making.

International financial institutions and multilateral development banks have been vilified many times in Latin America and the Caribbean because of their unrestricted and total access to policy makers and their influence over policy contents. As our analysis has suggested, their role tends to be less important than most people would presume; it is particularly telling that such institutions are mentioned in the text very few times. In order to be influential, these institutions need to understand the social network of decision making. They risk greatly diminished influence if, because of bureaucratic or historical reasons, they maintain most of their dialogue with actors who are not central to the decision-making process. This book has the additional value of identifying their role and suggesting to them ways in which their advice could be more effective.

Social Network Analysis, Political Institutions, and Economic Development

As mentioned in the introduction and throughout the book, the selection of country cases was not random. It was important to have both presidential and parliamentary countries, as well as different levels of economic development. The effect of these dimensions was not as relevant as originally thought, and it is difficult to isolate them from other confounding differences across these countries.

The type of political regime does not seem to affect the size of the networks as expected in these cases. The whole network of social policy formulation is larger in Argentina than in the Caribbean countries, but the networks in the

Caribbean are larger than that in Bolivia. In addition, the data show that the explanation for the difference in network sizes across countries is not the presence or absence of the legislature, which appears in all these networks, but rather the number of intra- and extragovernmental actors mentioned by the interviewees. The Argentine and Bolivian networks have higher numbers of societal actors than the networks in the Caribbean countries, but networks in the Caribbean countries and Bolivia have higher numbers of government actors than does Argentina's network. The type of political regime does seem to explain, however, the differences in the centrality of political authorities across cases. The cabinets and prime ministers of The Bahamas and Trinidad and Tobago are more central to the networks of power than are the presidents of Argentina and Bolivia. This finding also holds for the social area ministers when considered as net sources of power or net providers of information and ideas. Political authorities in the Caribbean countries reportedly have more interaction with both governmental units and extragovernmental actors than those in Argentina and, to a lesser extent, in Bolivia, as observable in their centrality scores and their participation in interministerial cliques.

Economic development, at least measured in terms of gross domestic product per capita, does not seem to be a relevant factor in either the structure of the social networks or the outcomes. In every case, actors external to the formal process exercise influence over the actual process, particularly the flow of ideas. In both the relatively rich Caribbean countries and Bolivia, international agencies play a relevant role in decision making and producing public policies. This role is much less marked in Argentina. As such, the overall size of the economy may matter. Importantly, colonial heritage, although not explicitly considered, seems to have an effect on network structures. Without a doubt, the more recent colonial heritage in the Caribbean has marked the configuration of government structures and the stability of the permanent secretaries in the bureaucracy.

Social Network Analysis: Scope, Limitations, and Research Agenda

The evidence collected from the SNAs and compiled in this volume generally corroborates the theoretical assumptions about the importance of networks for the political economy of social policy. The structure of these networks, the nature of the connections among actors, and the consistency or inconsistency between actual social networks and formal institutional design make it possible to identify (1) the types of networks and actors that can contribute to or hinder the operation of social programs, (2) the key actors whose cooperation or exclusion is needed to produce certain types of outcomes in social programs, and (3) the institutional designs that may be suitable for encouraging or discouraging certain interactions and behaviors. SNA therefore complements studies of the political economy of social policy by providing empirical evidence of the actors that configure such political economy, their links, and the effects those links have on the dynamics and results of decision-making processes.

On the basis of such empirical evidence, SNA can shed light on the organizational and sociological sources, and the procedural routines and mechanisms by which the institutional factors identified by the political economy approach to policy making may shape policy processes and outcomes. The type of evidence produced by SNA makes it possible to establish the actors, relational contents, and structural links that facilitate or hinder the flow of information, ideas, resources, and power—and thus their ability to coordinate, introduce and maintain coherence, and help adapt and stabilize policies within social policy-making processes.

Although its importance is acknowledged by those responsible for public policy formulation and implementation, political economy is often not fully or systematically taken into account. As a result, policy makers generally do not adequately factor the restrictions and opportunities stemming from such analysis into operational policy design and thus fail to prevent the inefficiencies and transaction costs that may arise. SNA can help widen the analytical scope because it considers both the formulation and implementation of public policies, can be applied to different administrative levels of the public sector or society in general, and can be adjusted to actor networks of different sizes and complexities. In this respect, SNA is useful for studying more limited networks of beneficiaries or of those officials responsible for decision making in certain locations. It can also be used to analyze networks existing among high authorities in the central government, or even for the study of wider actor networks across several sectors or different policy areas and government levels.

SNA does have three important limitations, two of which are methodological. First, SNA is subject to bias from the sources of network data. In the country cases compiled in this book, the bias comes from the interviewees: their replies to the name-generator questions to identify network members and to the name-interpreter questions to specify relational contents may have been biased by either the size of their personal networks or the nature of the policy initiatives pursued at the time of the interview. Not all interviewees, not even those with the same rank or even within the same policy unit, interact with the same (number of) actors. The reported size and structure of the networks may therefore vary significantly from one interviewee to the next. Intercoder reliability, although acceptable in these case studies, does not fully shield responses from this kind of bias. This limitation is particularly the case because interviewees may sometimes respond to the questionnaire by referring to examples from specific policy initiatives, namely those they were developing at the time of the interview, and the network for developing those particular initiatives may have differed in size and structure from the network involved in other initiatives. To minimize this potential source of bias, the questionnaire was formulated in a general way, making reference to routine tasks and not specific initiatives, but respondents sometimes resorted to examples and could not be confined to general answers.

Second, SNA faces challenges in terms of comparability. Although the country studies in this book were designed as polls, using the same questionnaire across cases in order to make the responses and the ensuing network maps comparable, the data sometimes lacked intracase benchmarks for comparison. Although some literature on the policy-making process in Argentina is robust enough to allow for comparisons, and some aggregate data on Bolivia allow them as well, virtually no benchmark exists for the Caribbean cases. The solution chosen for this research, to compare the networks against the formal rules of the policy-making game, could certainly be criticized as naïve: no institution operates as formally designed. In the absence of empirically grounded benchmarks, however, comparing the social networks with those theoretically consistent with the formal rules proved useful to describe the lay of the land.

Finally, SNA faces a practical limitation for the study of policy-making networks: it requires the active participation of high-level authorities and societal actors, as well as data collection on extensive networks of a large number of actors. SNA carries the risk that ministers, deputy ministers, cabinet chiefs, and other senior staff may reject visualization and participative methods, such as the elaboration of network maps through focus groups—or even in the context of an individual interview—as unknown and time-consuming methodologies. In such circumstances, the semistructured interview, its subsequent visualization by the researcher, and data triangulation by means of other information sources prove more efficient and viable for the practice of research. In addition, there are possible political limitations against stimulating the interest and desire of the authorities to become involved with this type of research into political economy aspects, which may be sensitive and require the anonymity of both informants and collected data.

As for the analysis of extensive networks of actors, the scope of SNA can be limited because it relies on visualization techniques and computer programs to develop actor maps that require, as an input, double-entry tables for each identified node. This requirement may hinder the use and interpretation of SNA in the case of networks with large numbers of actors. In these cases, it would be advisable to consider a more limited research question that narrows the analysis to a specific network with fewer actors or to break down the analysis into different networks.

Even with these practical restrictions, applying SNA to social programs can contribute substantially to illuminate the political economy of social policy and to design strategies that deal with both the opportunities for and the obstacles to effective policies imposed by that very same political economy. Improving the effectiveness of these contributions would require working on a research agenda made up of at least the following three components.

1. *Describe the actual social networks underlying the formulation and implementation of social programs in different social policy areas, each with different levels of benefits.* The theory of the political economy of social policy

recognizes differences in the structure and importance of social networks for the organization and functioning of programs contingent on the policy area, and in the extent to which each of these programs involves actions in different social policy areas. The case studies compiled in this volume have provided evidence of one program in the health area and another of conditional cash transfers that combines health, education, and social protection benefits. A pending task would be to perform analyses, using this approach, on education and employment programs and to increase the number of cases of programs providing different types of benefits. The studies have also revealed the importance of distinguishing social networks operating at the formulation stage of programs from those operating at the implementation stage, as well as distinguishing social networks at central government levels from those at subnational levels. Future research could explore the relevance of these distinctions in other cases. Research carried out in these directions would help determine on a broader empirical basis whether substantial differences exist among the actual social program networks of different areas and complexity levels, and to what extent those networks resemble or not the formal structures planned in the institutional designs for each program.

2. *Combine information about network structure with information about the substantial content of the relations among actors.* The theory of the political economy of social policy holds that the different actors involved in the social policy-making process (political leaders, parties, national and subnational technical officials, unions, business associations, and so on) differ in their interests, preferences, and resources when it comes to taking part in this process. The research gathered in this book has accounted for those differences by focusing on the different relational contents of the links that tie the various actors in the analyzed networks. A pending task is to produce information about these contents for new cases of social programs of different areas, degrees of benefit complexity, and administrative organization across government levels. Adding this information would help determine which actors are key to carrying out specific activities—producing ideas or information, providing economic resources, coordinating programs, and influencing their operations—in certain social policy areas, types of programs, and levels of government.

3. *Systematically use this information about social network structure, actor type, the nature of their relations, and the resources supporting them in order to investigate the effective dynamics of the social policy-making process.* The theory of the political economy of social policy argues that the differences in each of those factors—networks, actors, relational contents, and resources—produce differences in the dynamics of the policy-making process and thus in their characteristics and results. The evidence presented in the empirical chapters

of this volume supports this argument. The main challenge in applying SNA to the study of political economy consists of putting the rich and wide array of information SNA generates at the service of research. Such information, by focusing on social policy-making processes, can show the advantages and disadvantages of the institutional design of social programs, their administrative organization, their actual functioning, and, more generally but no less important, the public policy-making process through which social policies are formulated and implemented.

As the case studies reflect, SNA can play a major role as a policy-making tool. First, it can help government actors better understand the complexity of the organization they work with and propose institutional changes that may improve decision-making processes. Second, it can help international organizations and donors identify the key nodes in the networks that would help bring about policies that have proven successful in other countries. It could also help those organizations and donors identify ways to be more effective in terms of both advice and financing. Finally, SNA can help policy makers better understand why some policies work and others do not, which may be independent of the quality of the policy itself. The efficiency and effectiveness of policies depend on the quality of both the policy and the network in which the policy is implemented.

What Social Network Analysis Adds to the Process

Social policy in Latin America and the Caribbean has experienced a radical change in recent decades, particularly with regard to the resources allocated for social programs. Some of the funded programs have been successful—mainly the conditional cash transfer programs—as evidenced by impact evaluations. Not all programs, however, have had the same impact, the same efficiency, or the necessary resources allocated to them. As pointed out in chapter 1, in the education area, for example, the region has an alarming deficit.

The lack of investment, of sufficient investment, or of effective investment in some sectors or programs is not something that can be explained by ignorance of successful formulas. Rather, it responds to the fact that decision making in public policy design and implementation is the result of a political process in which many agents—each with its own interests and incentives within a given institutional framework—participate. Thus, the potential of public policies to produce positive results depends to a large extent on the quality of the process through which policies are defined, approved, and implemented, and on how institutional and social actors behave and interact.

In order to understand public policy decisions, therefore, it is essential to carry out a political economy analysis that identifies these actors, their interests, and the way they relate to each other. SNA allows for delving more deeply into the identification of network members, determining the nature of the relations that bind them, and analyzing the function and importance of each actor, as well as the network structures and their effects on their own functioning. In doing so, this type of analysis can reveal the possibilities, restrictions, and nature of the transaction costs networks generate to the process of formulation and implementation of public policies. On that basis, SNA can provide the foundations to introduce changes in the processes or, at least, to consider these possibilities and restrictions in the design, implementation, and improvement of such policies.

The present volume is an attempt to fill the existing void in research by providing the necessary tools to carry out this type of analysis and by illustrating its productivity through several case studies. It may thus serve as a fundamental tool for both researchers and those in charge of designing and implementing public policies in the region. Better understanding of who the actors in charge of policy making are, their interests, and how ideas, information, and resources flow makes it easier to understand why countries design policies in the way they do; why some can respond better to unrest, social crises, or pandemics; and how multilateral organizations and donors can help countries improve their policy-making processes and outcomes.

References

Franco Chuaire, M., and C. Scartascini. 2014. "La política de las políticas públicas: Re-examinando la calidad de las políticas públicas y las capacidades del Estado en América Latina y el Caribe." Policy Brief No. 220, Inter-American Development Bank, Washington, DC.

IDB (Inter-American Development Bank). 2005. *The Politics of Policies: Economic and Social Progress in Latin America and the Caribbean 2006 Report.* Washington, DC: Inter-American Development Bank.

Rodríguez Gustá, A. L., and M. Iacoviello. 2008. "Comparing the Civil Service in Four English-Speaking Countries: A Quantitative and Qualitative Approach." In *Report on the Situation of the Civil Service in the Caribbean*, edited by M. Mateo Díaz and K. Echebarría, 169–204. Washington, DC: Inter-American Development Bank Regional Policy Dialogue, Public Policy Management and Transparency Network.

Spiller, P., and M. Tommasi. 2007. *The Institutional Foundations of Public Policy: A Transactions Cost Approach.* Cambridge: Cambridge University Press.

APPENDIX A

Whole Networks of Social Policy Formulation for Country Case Studies

Whole Network of Social Policy Formulation in Argentina

Acronym	Name
62ORG	62 Peronist organizations
ADIMRA	Association of Metal Industries of the Argentine Republic
AFIP	Federal Revenue Administration
AMA	Argentine Medical Association
AMET	Association of Technical School Teachers
AMIA	Association of Argentine Israelite Mutual Organizations
ANSES	National Social Security Administration
ASCIM	Adviser to the Secretary for Interministerial Coordination
ASHOKA	Ashoka Foundation
BCRA	Central Bank of the Argentine Republic
BDP	Barrio de Pie Social Movement
BNA	Argentine National Bank
CACOM	Argentine Chamber of Commerce
CACONST	Argentine Chamber of Construction
CAMEMP	Business associations
CAMION	Truck Drivers Union
CARITAS	Caritas Argentina
CCC	Class Combatant Current
CEDES	Center for the Study of the State and Society

CEMIC	Centre for Medical Research and Clinical Education
CENTSAL	Health centers
CFED	Federal Education Council
CFPROF	Professional development centers
CGT	General Confederation of Workers
CIMIENTOS	Cimientos Foundation
CIPPEC	Center for Public Policy Implementation
CNCPS	National Council for Social Policy Coordination
COFENAF	Federal Council for Childhood, Adolescence, and Family
COFESA	Federal Health Council
COLEGIOS	Schools
COMRA	Medical Confederation of the Argentine Republic
CONAETYP	National Council for Education, Labour and Production
CONGRESS	National Congress
CONSEJ	Counseling centers
CREA	CREA Foundation
CSMMV	Council for the Minimum Wage
CTA	Argentine Workers Central
CTEP	Confederation of Popular Economy Workers
CTERA	Confederation of Education Workers of the Argentine Republic
DIRESCRUR	Headmasters of rural schools
DLEGANSES	Director of Legal Affairs at the National Social Security Administration
DPLANSES	Executive Director for Administration at the National Social Security Administration
ENSEÑAR	Enseñar Foundation
EPIDINST	Institute for Epidemiology
EUSOFT	Eusoft Limited
FIERRO	Martín Fierro Social Movement
FPENSAR	Pensar Foundation
FUEROSOCSEG	Social Security Judiciary Circuit
GAM	GAM Foundation
GLOBCOMP	Global Compact
GMUN	Municipal governments
GPCIAS	Provincial governments
HEALTHINDS	Health industries
IDB	Inter-American Development Bank
IDEA	Instituto de Desarrollo Empresario Argentino
IFIS	International financial institutions
IGLECAT	Catholic Church
INDEC	National Institute of Statistics and Census
INET	National Institute for Technical Education

ISALUD	ISALUD University
JGM	Cabinet Chief
LAZARTE	Lazarte Institute
LUMINIS	Luminis Foundation
MDS	Social Development Ministry
MEDEOS	MEDEOS Group
MEDIA	Mass media
MEVITA	Movimiento Evita
MINED	Education Ministry
MINERG	Energy Ministry
MINH	Treasury Ministry
MININTERIOR	Interior Ministry
MINJUS	Ministry of Justice
MINMOD	Modernization Ministry
MINPROD	Production Ministry
MINSAL	Health Ministry
MINTRAB	Labour Ministry
MINTRANS	Ministry of Transport
MOVSOCS	Social movements
NATMEDAC	National Academy of Medicine
NAVIOL	Navarro Viola Foundation
NGOs	Nongovernmental organizations
OBSUCA	Social Observatory of the Argentine Catholic University
OFICEMP	Employment offices
PAMI	Integral Medical Attention Program
PECOM	Pérez Companc Company
PJN	National Judiciary Branch
PLBELGRANO	Belgrano Plan
POLOB	Workers' Pole
PTE	President
REDESPAD	Parents' networks
SACPS	Secretary for Social Assistance and Protection
SADOP	Union of Private Teachers
SARPS	Secretary for Social Policy and Articulation
SCIM	Secretary for Interministerial Coordination
SCPP	Secretary for Public Policy Coordination
SCRSAL	Secretary for Health
SECGRANSES	Secretary General at the National Social Security Administration
SECOS	Secretary for the Social Economy
SEED	Secretary for Evaluation in Education
SEMP	Secretary for Employment
SGED	Secretary for Education Management

SICE	Secretary for Innovation and Quality in Education
SIEMPRO	Social Programs Evaluation System
SISU	Secretary for Socio-Urban Integration
SNAF	Secretary for Childhood, Adolescence, and Family
SPROMSAL	Secretary for the Promotion of Health
SPU	Secretary for University Policy
SRA	Argentine Rural Society
SRGSAN	Secretary for Health Regulation and Management
SSS	Secretary for Social Security
TUPAC	Tupac Amaru Social Movement
UATRE	Argentine Union of Rural Workers
UBA	University of Buenos Aires
UIA	Argentine Industrial Union
UIPBA	Industrial Union of the Buenos Aires Province
UN	United Nations
UNESCO	United Nations Education Commission
UNHORGS	Union-run health care organizations
UNICEF	United Nations Children's Fund
UNIONS	Unions
UNIVS	Universities
UNPOPF	United Nations Population Fund
UOCRA	Construction Workers' Union of the Argentine Republic
UOM	Union of Metal Workers
UPCN	National Union of Civil Workers
USAL	University of the Savior
UTA	Transport Workers Union
UTDT	Torcuato Di Tella University
UTHGRA	Union of Hotel and Restaurant Workers of the Argentine Republic
WHO	World Health Organization

Whole Network of Social Policy Formulation at the Central Level of Government in Bolivia

Acronym	Name
ADS	Departmental Health Assemblies
APMSD	Parliamentary Affairs Area at the Ministry of Health
BID	IDB (Inter-American Development Bank)
BM	WB (World Bank)
CAF	Andean Development Corporation
CAMEMP	Business associations

CEPO	Educational Councils of Aboriginal Peoples
CEUB	Executive Committee of Bolivian University
COLSAL	Professional health colleges
CONALCAM	National Coordination for Change
CONAN	National Council for Food and Nutrition
CONAPES	National Council of Economic and Social Policies
DGC	General Directorate for Cooperative Units at the Ministry of Labour Employment and Social Security
DGE	General Directorate for Employment at the Ministry of Labour, Employment and Social Security
DGPPS	General Directorate of Social Security Policy at the Ministry of Labour, Employment and Social Security
DGPT	General Directorate of Territorial Planning at the Ministry for Development Planning
DGSC	General Directorate for Oversight and Coordination at the Ministry for Development Planning
DGSPI	General Directorate for the Integral Planning System at the Ministry for Development Planning
DGSS	General Directorate for Health Services at the Ministry of Health and Sports
GAD	Autonomous Departmental Governments
GAM	Autonomous Municipal Governments
IDB	Inter-American Development Bank
JGME	Cabinet Chief at the Ministry of Education
JGMP	Cabinet Chief at the Ministry for the Presidency
JGMSD	Cabinet Chief at the Ministry of Health and Sports
JGMTEPS	Cabinet Chief at the Ministry of Labour, Employment and Social Security
JPFs	Parents' boards
MA	Ministry for Autonomous Governments
MAI	Ministry of Foreign Affairs
MAS	Movement toward Socialism (Movimiento al Socialismo)
MD	Ministry of Defence
MDPyEP	Ministry of Productive Development and Plural Economies
MDRyT	Ministry of Rural Development and Land
ME	Ministry of Education
MEFP	Ministry of Economy and Public Finance
MG	Ministry of Government
MMAyA	Ministry for the Environment and Water
MMIM	Ministry of Minning and Metallurgy
MOPSV	Ministry of Public Works, Services and Housing
MP	Ministry for the Presidency

MPD	Ministry of Development Planning
MSD	Ministry of Health and Sports
MTEPS	Ministry of Labour, Employment and Social Security
NGOs	Nongovernmental organizations
OBs	Grassroots organizations
PTE	President
SEDUCAS	Departmental Education Services
SINDIC	Unions
SINED	Teachers' unions
ST	Technical secretary
UAGSMP	Social Management Support Unit at the Ministry for the Presidency
UCPP	Programs and Projects Coordination Unit at the Ministry of Economy and Public Finance
UDAPE	Unit for Social and Economic Policy Analysis
UNICEF	United Nations Children's Fund
VCGGT	Deputy Ministry for Coordination of Government and Territorial Management
VCM	Deputy Ministry for Mining Cooperative Units
VCMSSC	Deputy Ministry for Coordination with Social Movements and Civil Society
VCyT	Vice Ministry of Science and Technology
VD	Vice Ministry for Sports
VDPMM	Deputy Ministry for Productive, Mining, and Metallurgic Development
VDRA	Deputy Ministry for Rural and Agricultural Development
VEAyE	Deputy Ministry for Alternative and Special Education
VER	Vice Ministry for Regular Education
VESCC	Deputy Ministry for Employment, Civil Service and Cooperative Units
VESFP	Deputy Ministry for Higher Education and Professional Training
VIO	Deputy Ministry of Equal Opportunity
VIPFE	Deputy Ministry for Public Investment and Finance
VMPE	Deputy Ministry for Micro and Small Enterprises
VMTI	Vice Ministry for Traditional Medicine and Intercultural Relations
VPC	Deputy Ministry for Planning and Coordination
VPCF	Deputy Ministry for Budgeting and Fiscal Accounting
VPEP	Deputy Ministry for Strategic Pluriannual Planning
VPIMGE	Deputy Ministry for Medium- and Large-Scale Production

VPMG	Vice-Ministry for Medium and Large Scale Industrial Production
VPTE	Vice President
VSP	Deputy Ministry of Health and Promotion
VT	Deputy Ministry for Land
VTCP	Deputy Ministry of Treasury and Public Credit
VTPS	Deputy Ministry of Labour and Social Security
WB	World Bank

Whole Network of Social Policy Formulation in The Bahamas

Acronym	Name
ADCUR	Assistant Director for Curriculum Ministry of Education
ADSOC	Assistant Director of Social Services
ATTG	Attorney General's Office
BCCEC	Bahamas Chamber of Commerce
BHCRISIS	Bahamas Crisis Center
CABINET	Cabinet
CABINSEC	Cabinet secretary
CHURCHES	Churches (Catholic, Anglican, Presbyterian)
CIVSOCBH	Civil Society of The Bahamas (umbrella group)
COMMFAMIS	Committee for Family Islands
CMO	Chief medical officer
COMMDISSURV	Communicable Diseases Surveillance Unit
CPAS	Consumer Protection Agencies
CSO	Central Statistics Office
CUSTOMS	Customs Agency
CWO	Chief welfare officer
DDEMP	Deputy Director for Employment
DDIR	Deputy Director for Industrial Relations
DDLAB	Deputy Director Department of Labour
DDPLANED	Deputy Director of Planning Ministry of Education
DDSOC	Deputy Director of Social Services
DENVHEALTH	Department of Environmental Health
DEP	Director of Education Policy
DGEND	Director of Gender Policy
DHP	Director of Health Policy
DISABCOMM	Disabilities Commission
DOL	Director of the Department of Labour
DSOC	Director of Social Services
HEALTHYBH	Healthy Bahamas Coalition

IDB	Inter-American Development Bank
IFIS	International financial institutions
ILO	International Labour Organization
IMMB	Immigration Board
MEDIA	News and social media
MINED	Ministry of Education
MINENV	Ministry for the Environment
MINFIN	Ministry of Finance
MINH	Ministry of Health
MINLAB	Minister of Labour
MINPUBSERV	Ministry of Public Service
MINSOC	Ministry of Social Services
MINWORKS	Ministry of Public Works
MINYOUTH	Ministry of Youth
NATSEG	Ministry of National Security
NCTU	National Congress of Trade Unions
NIB	National Insurance Board
NTC	National Tripartite Council
NTRAIN	National Training Association
NWAC	National Women's Advisory Council
OAS	Organization of the American States
OPPOSITION	Opposition
PAHO	Pan-American Health Organization
PARLIAMENT	Parliament
PM	Prime Minister's Office
POLICE	Bahamas Police Force
POLPLANH	Policy and Planning Unit Ministry of Health
PRIMCARECL	Primary care clinics
PRIVHOSP	Private hospitals
PRIVSCHOOLS	Private Schools
PROGMANH	Program Managers Ministry of Health
PSED	Permanent Secretary Ministry of Education
PSH	Permanent Secretary Ministry of Health
PSLAB	Permanent Secretary Ministry of Labour
PSNATSEG	Permanent Secretary Ministry of National Security
PSPMO	Permanent Secretary Office of the Prime Minister
PSSOC	Permanent Secretary Ministry of Social Services
PSWORKS	Permanent Secretary Ministry of Works
PSYOUTH	Permanent Secretary Ministry of Youth
PUBHOSPA	Public Hospitals Authority
REDCROSS	Red Cross
RESPLANSOC	Research and Planning Unit Ministry of Social Services

ROTARY	Rotary Club
SALVARMY	Salvation Army
TENDERSB	Tenders Board
UN	United Nations
UNESCO	United Nations Commission for Education
UNIBH	University of The Bahamas
WHO	World Health Organization

Whole Network of Social Policy Formulation in Trinidad and Tobago

Acronym	Name
CABINET	Cabinet
CABINSEC	Cabinet secretary
CARICOM	CARICOM Governments
CARIRI	Caribbean Industrial Research Institute
CBO	Community-based organizations
CLUBS	Local clubs
CMO	Chief medical officer
CORDO	NGO specialized in disabilities
CSO	Central Statistics Office
CURRICDIV	Curriculum Division Ministry of Education
CVO	Chief veterinary officer
DHP	Director of Health Policy
DOMA	Downtown Organization of Business Owners
DPSH	Deputy Permanent Secretary Ministry of Health
DPSPLAN	Deputy Permanent Secretary Ministry of Planning
DPSSD	Deputy Permanent Secretary Ministry of Social Development Services
EDAG	Economic Development Advisory Group
EMA	Evironmental Management Authority
ENVNGOS	Environmental NGOs
EPPDPLAN	Economic Policy Planning Division at the Ministry of Planning
EXAMDIV	Examinations Division Ministry of Education
FBOS	Faith-based organizations
FISHFSEA	Fishermen and Friends of the Sea
GREENF	Green Fund
HED	Health and Education Division Ministry of Health
HIVNGOS	AIDS-specialized NGOs
HOSPITALS	Hospitals
IDB	Inter-American Development Bank

IFIS	International financial institutions
IMA	Institute for Maritime Affairs
MARVAG	Maracas Valley Authority Group
MCOMMDEV	Ministry for Community Development
MEDIA	News and social media
MINAGR	Ministry of Agriculture
MINATSEG	Ministry of National Security
MINED	Ministry of Education
MINFA	Ministry of Foreign Affairs
MINFIN	Ministry of Finance
MINH	Minister of Health
MINHAD	Advisers to the Minister of Health
MINLAB	Ministry of Labour
MINLEG	Ministry of Legal Affairs
MINPLAN	Ministry of Planning
MINSDS	Ministry of Social Development and Family Services
MINTRADE	Ministry of Trade
MUNHS	Municipal Health Services
NAIDSC	National AIDS Commission
NCDSAD	Non-Communicable Diseases Adviser
NCPD	National Committee for People with Disabilities
NGOS	Nongovernmental organizations
NGOSW	NGOs for women
OCSTO	Office of the Chief Secretary of Tobago
PAHO	Pan-American Health Organization
PAVI	NGO specialized in blindness
PM	Prime Minister
PMAD	Advisers to the Prime Minister
PRINCIPALS	Principals' association
PROFAS	Professional associations (engineers, architects)
PRUSDS	Poverty Reduction Unit at the Ministry of Social Development Services
PSED	Permanent Secretary Ministry of Education
PSH	Permanent Secretary Ministry of Health
PSSD	Permanent Secretary Ministry of Social Development Services
REHAB	Rehabilitation Centers
REUDU	Research and Evaluation Unit at the Ministry of Education
RHA	Regional health authorities
RPPPDSDS	Research Policy and Program Planning Division at the Ministry of Social Development Services
SCHOOLDIST	School district supervisors
STATS	Statistical Office

STEPUP	STEP UP Program
STUDENTBRD	Student Board Services
TCPDPLAN	Town and Country Planning Division at the Ministry of Planning
TEACHERSUN	Teachers' association
THACA	Tobago House of Assembly Chief Administrator
TTCC	Trinidad and Tobago Chamber of Commerce
TUS	Trade unions
UKG	United Kingdom Government
UNDP	United Nations Program for Development
URP	Unemployment Relief Program
WHO	World Health Organization

APPENDIX B

Interview Guide

Date: ____

Name:____

Position: ____

Time in office: _______________________________________

Organization: ____

Introduction: Good day. We are carrying out a research project for the Inter-American Development Bank about the formulation of social policy at the national level. Since you represent an important actor in social policy making, we would like to learn from your opinions. We are conducting several interviews at the central government level, and in this context we would like to ask you some questions:

How would you describe the process of formulation of (educational, health, labor, planning) policies? Please describe the steps that are regularly followed in this process.

Apart from the actors you have just mentioned, what other actors participate in the process of formulating (educational, health, labor, planning) policies?

If you have to rank all the actors you have mentioned as participants in the process of policy formulation from the most powerful to the least powerful, how would you rank them? (At each ranking, ask why the actor is located in that position).

(If the interviewee has not mentioned any actor from beyond their ministry) With what other actors within the central level of government must your ministry liaise in order to complete the formulation of (education, health, labor, planning) policy?

(If the interviewee has not mentioned any actor from beyond their ministry) With what other actors beyond the government must your ministry liaise in order to complete the formulation of (education, health, labor, planning) policy? (Ask specifically about grassroots or aboriginal organizations, nongovernmental organizations, international multilateral agencies, and municipal government, if they are not mentioned).

Does your ministry directly consult with these actors beyond the ministry or the government, or does it go through other central government units?

What does each of these actors beyond your ministry contribute to the development of (educational, health, labor, planning) policy?

If you had to rank all the actors from beyond your ministry you have mentioned as participants in the process of policy formulation from the most powerful to the least powerful, how would you rank them? (At each ranking, ask why the actor is located in that position).

How do you decide if a(n) (educational, health, labor, planning) policy must be integrated into a multisectoral program or strategy? (Ask specifically about Zero Malnutrition if the answer is vague).

When a(n) (educational, health, labor, planning) policy is integrated into a multisectoral program or strategy, what actors organize interministerial coordination? (Ask specifically about interministerial councils if they are not mentioned).

What problems emerge or have typically emerged in interministerial relations in the process of formulating multisectoral programs or strategies? (Ask specifically about Zero Malnutrition if the answer is vague).

What actors have contributed to solving those problems? (At each mention of an actor, ask why it was important for problem-solving).

ECO-AUDIT

Environmental Benefits Statement

The World Bank Group is committed to reducing its environmental footprint. In support of this commitment, we leverage electronic publishing options and print-on-demand technology, which is located in regional hubs worldwide. Together, these initiatives enable print runs to be lowered and shipping distances decreased, resulting in reduced paper consumption, chemical use, greenhouse gas emissions, and waste.

We follow the recommended standards for paper use set by the Green Press Initiative. The majority of our books are printed on Forest Stewardship Council (FSC)–certified paper, with nearly all containing 50–100 percent recycled content. The recycled fiber in our book paper is either unbleached or bleached using totally chlorine-free (TCF), processed chlorine–free (PCF), or enhanced elemental chlorine–free (EECF) processes.

More information about the Bank's environmental philosophy can be found at http://www.worldbank.org/corporateresponsibility.

green press INITIATIVE